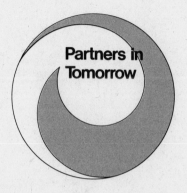

Partners in
Tomorrow

To Jan Tinbergen
on the occasion of his
seventy-fifth birthday

"What impresses me
and gives me hope is
the growth of the mind
and the spirit of man,
and not his being used as
an agent to convey a message".

Nehru, The Discovery of India

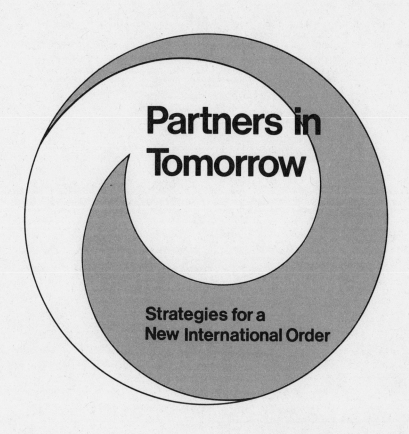

Partners in Tomorrow

Strategies for a New International Order

Edited by **Antony J. Dolman**
Jan van Ettinger

A Sunrise Book · **E.P. Dutton** · **New York**

For information contact: E.P. Dutton, 2 Park Avenue,
New York, N.Y. 10016

Library of Congress Catalog Card Number: 78-52977
ISBN: 0-87690-294-8 (cloth)
      0-87690-296-4 (paper)

Published simultaneously in Canada by Clarke, Irwin & Company
Limited, Toronto and Vancouver

10 9 8 7 6 5 4 3 2 1

First Edition

Printed on Recycled Paper

*321
Dol*

Preface

This collection of essays is not only an hommage to one of the
leading thinkers of our time. It is also a contribution to the
analysis and understanding of the problematique of our societies,
in some of the major aspects to which his work and life have
been dedicated. It brings together, in one volume, the reflections of individuals from many walks of life, different ideological allegiances and conceptions of social processes, sharing
in a common quest, made more urgent today by the unprecedented
onrush of events. All of them have been at one time inspired and
enlightened by Professor Jan Tinbergen.

Indeed , none of those, who during the last 25 years, directed
their actions and thoughts to the problems of world development
could fail to be aware of his contribution - so aptly recognized
by the first jury of the Nobel Prize in Economics - to the emergence of a new instrument of economic analysis, a major innovation
of growing importance to the understanding of economic mechanisms
and the process of decision-making.

No serious scholar would contend that the econometric discipline,
in spite of rapid progress, has become sufficiently reliable to
provide policy-makers with the ready-made answers which they so
often long for when confronted with difficult choices in complex
situations and the need to reconcile a variety of conflicting
objectives. And one must deplore the unfortunate tendency so
often conspicuous in those who directly or indirectly influence
public opinion to accept indiscriminately the results which spill
from a computer print-out. The same applies to the temptations of
professionals to get so absorbed in the complexities - and perhaps
the delights - of their discipline that they somehow lose sight
of its applicability to real situations, being above all preoccu-
pied with the coherence and elegance of their models.

No such danger ever threatened Jan Tinbergen, a man of science
constantly involved in the political struggle both at the national
and international levels. His most rigourous work has always been
informed, and if I may say, controlled by the nature of his ideals
and the strength of his commitment to them. The relevance of his
work to the advancement of practical solutions was always determi-
nant both in his choice of topics and in the method of handling
them.

His ideals, perhaps more than with any other person of the profession, are those which are central to the action of the United Nations. They endure through rapidly changing circumstances, but need to be constantly vitalized. Jan Tinbergen was, from his formative years, imbued with the humanistic, socialistic European tradition whose intellectual and spiritual message still has, in a world of many cultures, a seminal role to play. It is significant that at this very moment when this special tribute is being offered to Jan Tinbergen, a critical reappraisal of the content of development cooperation, as preached and practised during the last two decades, is under way within the United Nations as well as the wider circle of development economists and practitioners.

New analyses and new prescriptions are once again stressing the pre-eminence of social progress as an objective *per se* in the transformation of societies rather than an inevitable by-product of economic growth. This imperative was very much in the minds of the founders of the United Nations, labouring under the impact of the miseries experienced in the thirties. The search today is for development paths which will achieve a minimum of social progress *for all* within a reasonable time, whether in the context of high or of low rates of economic growth. It is also more and more realized that social justice must be promoted on a world-wide basis, that is, between nations as well as within nations; a context of too sharp inequalities is not conducive to a productive negotiation, or to the emergence of a world order.

The younger generation may not remember that the humanistic, socialistic tradition of Europe at its origin combined with its social aspirations the strongest possible element of internationalism. Indeed, cooperation across national borderlines was viewed by the under-privileged as the natural road to the advancement of their cause. This element tended to fade away after World War II, with the rapid and widespread introduction in capitalist societies of comprehensive welfare policies. The mechanisms required for the implementation of these policies implied a high degree of state intervention which could only be deployed within the limits of national boundaries and for the benefit of national constituencies.

Often, and in an increasing manner, welfare policies came in conflict with the rules of international conduct which had gradually emerged in the fields of international trade and money, and which could not be allowed to prevail over the aspirations of the masses. Tensions between the requirements of a social policy and the rules of the international economic system are perhaps today more acute than ever. Hence a disquieting tendency evident in so many quarters to de-emphasize or even deprecate the value of international links, sometimes including the benefits of a new type of relationship largely brought into existence through the instrumentality of the United Nations system.

The enduring conjunction in the person of Jan Tinbergen of a
devotion to social advancement and the belief in the practi-
cality of internationalism, is the very foundation on which
the international community must now build a new phase of
development cooperation. During the last years of the 1960s,
serving as Chairman, and, if I may say, as pilot of the Committee for Development Planning of ECOSOC, one of the most valuable organs of the United Nations system, Jan Tinbergen perceived the approach of a new decade as a unique opportunity to introduce, in the economic affairs of the world, an incipient
measure of international planning and collective management.

It was for him a privileged moment, one for which he had been
waiting, a kind of vindication of all his efforts, from the time
when he served the League of Nations under the darkest of circumstances to the optimistic - perhaps over-optimistic -days of
the 1960s, when he was so closely associated with the United
Nations. The International Development Strategy for the 1970s,
like all plans in this world of so many uncertainties and perhaps more rapidly than most, must be adjusted and even renewed.
The contribution of Jan Tinbergen is, in this phase, more necessary than ever.

When so many doubts are every day expressed in regard to the
capacity of our international institutions to cope efficiently
with growing problems, the unfailing faith in the United Nations
of a man of so great distinction is an incomparable asset. I am
confident that the essays prepared for this book, under the
inspiration of his message, will help to promote the conceptual
revival which is now called for, and with it the determination
to advance on the road of social progress and international
cooperation which he has so often charted for us.

Philippe de Seynes
New York
3 February 1978

Table of Contents

Part II: The New International Order: Special Problems

Contributors

Ibrahim Helmi Abdel Rahman (Egypt): Advisor to the President; formerly Executive Director of UNIDO.

Sartaj Aziz (Pakistan): Deputy Executive Director, World Food Council.

Henk C. Bos (Netherlands): Professor of Development Planning, Erasmus University; Member U.N. Committee for Development Planning.

Silviu Brucan (Romania): Professor of Political Science, University of Bucharest.

Sukhamoy Chakravarty (India): formerly Member Indian Planning Commission.

Harlan Cleveland (U.S.A.): Director, International Affairs Program, Aspen Institute for Humanistic Studies.

Louis Emmerij (Netherlands): Rector, Institute of Social Studies, The Hague; formerly Director, World Employment Programme.

James P. Grant (U.S.A.): President, Overseas Development Council, Washington, D.C.

Mahbub ul Haq (Pakistan): Director, Policy Planning and Program Review Department, World Bank.

Fereydoun Hoveyda (Iran): Permanent Representative at the United Nations, New York.

Idriss Jazairy (Algeria): Deputy Secretary-General for International Cooperation, Ministry of Foreign Affairs.

Johan Kaufmann (Netherlands): Ambassador to Japan; formerly Permanent Representative at the United Nations, New York.

Alexander King (U.K.): Chairman, International Federation of Institutes for Advanced Study, Solna, Sweden.

Elisabeth Mann Borgese (U.S.A.): Writer; Chairman, Planning Council, International Ocean Institute, Malta.

Don Mills (Jamaica): Permanent Representative at the United Nations, New York.

Marc Nerfin (Switzerland): President, International Foundation for Development Alternatives, Nyon.

Saburo Okita (Japan): Chairman, Japan Economic Research Center; Special Advisor, International Development Center of Japan.

Manuel Pérez Guerrero (Venezuela): Minister of State for International Economic Affairs.

Jan Pronk (Netherlands): Member of Parliament; formerly Minister for Development Cooperation.

Shridath S. Ramphal (Guyana): Secretary-General, Commonwealth Secretariat, London.

Justinian F. Rweyemamu (Tanzania): Professor of Economics, University of Dar-es-Salaam; Economic Advisor to the President.

Philippe de Seynes (France): Senior Special Fellow, United Nations Institute for Training and Research.

Juan Somavía (Chile): Director, Instituto Latinoamericano de Estudios Transnacionales, Mexico.

Inga Thorsson (Sweden): Under Secretary of State for Disarmament; Member of Parliament.

Robert Triffin (U.S.A.): Professor of Economics, Yale University, New Haven, Conn.

Barbara Ward (U.K.): President, International Institute for Environment and Development, London.

Maurice J. Williams (U.S.A.): Chairman, Development Assistance Committee, Organisation for Economic Cooperation and Development.

Introduction

Probably no one, with the exception of Jan Tinbergen himself, would question the legitimacy of publishing a collection of essays on the occasion of his seventy-fifth birthday. And, given the role he has played in the efforts made by the international community to reduce global inequities and to extend equality of opportunity, few could disagree that such a collection should focus on the subject of the New International Order (NIO). Contributors to this volume were thus asked to present their views on the process required to bring about a more equitable international social and economic order.

Given the fact that the North-South dialogue had, after the promise of progress suggested by the consensus reached at the Seventh Special Session, produced very little in the way of concrete results and that negotiation prospects in mid 1977 were undeniably bleak, contributors were requested to address one of two important questions. The first was "where do we stand?"; papers thus focusing on a review of the most significant recent developments and an assessment of the present state of the North-South dialogue. The second was "what next?"; papers thus focusing on an appraisal of NIO prospects and an identification of the areas in which North-South negotiations could and should concentrate. It was hoped that a volume which set out to address such crucial questions could be instrumental in promoting discussion of the NIO and, more particularly, of the various obstacles which jeopardize its implementation.

In total, 27 persons from 18 countries responded to the invitation to prepare an essay. Each did so in a personal and not in an official capacity; the function and country of each contributor are given in the preceeding pages for information purposes only. In reviewing their contributions, it became apparent that the suggested distinction between appraisals of the past and of the future was, as we perhaps should have expected, less than watertight. Contributors who focused their attention on critically reviewing past trends and events inevitably felt the need to make suggestions concerning ways in which the stranded North-South dialogue might be reactivated. Similarly, those who set out to appraise future NIO prospects frequently found it necessary to preface their views with a brief analysis of past developments.

For this reason we have chosen another form of presentation than
the one suggested by the questions posed to the contributors. The
essays have been divided into two parts. Part I contains general
appraisals of the NIO and, especially, of the process which has
been, or should be, established for its negotiation and implementation. Part II deals with a range of special problems at both the
international and national levels. These include such matters as
disarmament, ocean management, information and monetary reforms,
national development strategies. The division into two main parts
is recognized as being far from perfect; it is, however, sufficient to facilitate reading and is preferred to forcing contributions under an array of arbitrary headings.

We believe that this volume can indeed be instrumental in promoting discussion of the NIO; its publication comes at an appropriate time. The call for a more equitable international order cannot
remain unanswered. Both the solution of the problems which now
cripple the industrialized countries as well as those which have
long disfigured the countries of the Third World are dependent
upon the restructuring of the institutions and mechanisms which
govern the relationships between nations. It is in recognition of
the historical importance of the challenge presented by the NIO
and of the need to shape a new international development strategy
which provides for its implementation in the coming decades that
a number of important new initiatives at both intergovernmental
and extragovernmental levels have been, or soon will be, launched.

These initiatives are all designed to generate a "second round" of
debate on the process required to bring about a more equitable international order, to systematically monitor the progress of the
debate, and to give concrete shape - politically, conceptually as
well as empirically - to the required international development
strategy. At the intergovernmental level such new initiatives include the establishment within the United Nations of a Committee
of the Whole which will act as a focal point in overseeing and
monitoring the implementation of decisions and agreements reached
in the negotiations on the establishment of the new international
order in the appropriate bodies of the United Nations system.

Important initiatives at the extragovernmental level include the
setting up of the Brandt Commission, the organization of the
"North-South Roundtable" discussions by the Society for International Development, the cooperative efforts of the International
Foundation for Development Alternatives and those of the International Ocean Institute and the Foundation Reshaping the International Order. This plurality of initiatives at different levels
must be considered a positive sign. It calls, however, for much
higher levels of interaction than has so far been the case. It is
hoped that this collection of essays will contribute to providing
these new initiatives with both direction and substance.

The essays presented will be found to contain a wealth of ideas
and insights. We have made no effort to inventorize or categorize
them. Such distillation and interpretation was made impossible
by time constraints. Furthermore, we considered this inappropriate
since we felt that the reader - with his own frame of reference,
priorities and interests - should self be the judge of the contributions and determine in which ways their contents can be geared
to a "second round" of initiatives. The collection, however, is
united both by its recognition of the opportunity afforded by the
NIO to come to terms with a growing list of increasingly pressing
problems and of the need to overcome the present stalemate in
North-South negotiations. True, this volume contains neither a
formula for righting the world's wrongs nor an esoteric secret for
overcoming the inertia of political systems. The suggestions made
will, however, be found to be as interesting and relevant as they
are wide-ranging.

To the contributors who made this volume possible we extend our
grateful thanks; for their assistance in addition to their essay
thanks are especially due to Mahbub ul Haq and Philippe de Seynes.
We must also acknowledge the efforts of a small group of people
who labored hard to produce this collection of essays at very
short notice: to Dick Leurdijk for his ideas and assistance, to
Wim Brekelmans for his typographical suggestions, to Peet Gerritsma
and Lummy Koster for their resilience in typing the manuscript, and
to Carolien Bos for last minute help. We also gratefully acknowledge the assistance of Bouwcentrum, in terms of both people and
infrastructure, without which it would have been impossible to meet
the publishing deadline. While we are thus indebted to the many
persons who contributed to the preparation of this volume, we alone
are responsible for any shortcomings it may have.

Antony J. Dolman
Jan van Ettinger
Rotterdam
10 February 1978

Part I: The New International Order: General Appraisals

"... the ideas of economists and political
philosophers, both when they are right and
when they are wrong, are more powerful than
is commonly understood. Indeed the world is
ruled by little else. Practical men, who
believe themselves to be quite exempt from
any intellectual influences, are usually
the slaves of some defunct economist.
Madmen in authority, who hear voices in the
air, are distilling their frenzy from some
academic scribbler of a few years back. I am
sure that the power of vested interests is
vastly exaggerated compared with the gradual
encroachment of ideas".

John Maynard Keynes

The Most Basic Need: The Will to Develop Rationally

Ibrahim Helmi Abdel Rahman

Increasing Timidity

The future of the poor countries has previously been considered a
marginal problem for the industrialized countries. Less than one
per cent aid and some trade and financing measures seemed at one
time to be all that was needed from the rich countries. If these
were not sufficient, then it was only the developing countries
that would be blamed and suffer.

This opinion is no more accepted, at least as far as pronouncements and declarations go. Rather, it is generally considered that
the peace and prosperity of the advanced countries can only be
secured on the basis of a certain improvement in the economic and
social situations of the poor countries; and to realize this
objective, basic structural and policy changes will have to be
introduced in the development of the rich and the poor countries
as well as in international relations.

Hence the call for a new set of management policies and
strategies which in their totality may be called "the new order"
towards which all countries should work. There are still considerable differences of opinion and concepts about the future of the
world in 20 to 25 years from now, but no one seriously doubts
that certain basic questions are emerging, and that their answer
calls for new policies and sets of relations both between and
within the rich and poor countries. The basic questions include
the availability and allocation of food, energy, raw materials,
security and peace, population control, the provision of employment, the international division of labour and the environment,
to name just some of the most prominent world problems which have
been recognized and much discussed.

If we set aside the lack of agreement and precision with respect
to the proposed elements of the new order - which in any event
will continue to exist - we may be dissatisfied with the actions
which have so far been taken concerning their implementation.
Hence the need to raise the question of whether the world of the
poor and of the rich possesses the will to develop along the
lines of the proposals submitted. In other words, there seems to
be a certain reluctance, incapacity or timidity to take actions
now which seem necessary to secure peace, justice and development in the future. Many countries - rich and poor - take part in
the discussions, dialogues, resolutions and declarations about
the future, but fall short of even starting the initial steps
towards the realization of the objectives set. This general, rather
sweeping, statement should not be taken as a negative judgement on
the considerable efforts in many directions which are currently
being pursued, and which indeed should be continued and inten-

sified and amplified in the coming years. What is implied is that the declarations and pronouncements seem to be very far removed from what is actually going on; indeed, it is so far removed that one can justifiably doubt whether the necessary "will" to develop in fact exists.

The enquiry should proceed to examine the causes en propose solutions as may be necessary according to the findings. It may be that the centres of decision, which were supposed to act, are not honestly convinced of the substance of the proposed actions, which are derived from an estimation about the future situation, to which they do not agree. If decision-makers and public opinion in the advanced countries are not convinced that an energy gap in oil-supply will develop between 1985 and 1990 without immediate changes in current energy policy, then they will not consider seriously any proposal for new energy policies. It becomes a question of lack of conviction which inhibits implementation of the measures prescribed in the pronouncements. There may be another situation in which there is conviction but the inability to introduce the necessary measures due to the existence of strong opposing vested interests, or the absence of the instruments required to implement the measures. The situation in this second case is one of ineffectiveness of the decision-making machinery, due to its own shortcomings or to the strength of the opposition to it, or to both.

It is argued here that a third situation is most likely to be the one pertaining now.

It goes as follows: there is a considerable degree of acceptance, even conviction, about the reality, nature and magnitude of the forthcoming difficulties and hence of the need for basic new thinking and action. At the same time, there are strong opposing forces which, while not usually opposed to the objectives of change, are resistant to the procedure required for organizing it. Everybody wants to go to heaven but no one wants to die. This attitude gives the opponents of change not only the satisfaction of sharing in the thinking and declarations, which are virtues, but also of refusing actions for one pretext or another. One common and frequently quoted pretext is that "public opinion" under the present circumstances will not support the required actions. In other words, the political machinery, while convinced, is unable, because of the voting system and/or the pressure of current problems, to act. They will say, please do something to convince the voters, then we will go along. A variation of this situation, more common in the developing countries, is that the political machinery in power prefers traditional short term solutions which reduces its vulnerability to the radical solutions which are essential in the long run. In all of these cases, there is "timidity" and coolness about turning objectives into programmes of action.

Timidity by the political machinery of decision-making - national-

ly and internationally - can be camouflaged by more acceptable
slogans. The most common is that current problems should receive
priority and urgent attention, though it is known that these
problems in most cases have been created by previous in-action
and that their solution will in any case require periods of time
extending far beyond the coming election. In this way, the current
problems of inflation, stagnation, unemployment, monetary
instability, environmental degradation and others in the
industrialized countries, which no doubt require all attention,
are given as excuses for the failure to start serious action about
future - and possibly even more serious - problems. In the same
way, the developing countries are, in general, at present facing
problems of balance of payments, mounting debts, shortages of food
and energy, internal unrest, increasing unemployment, fluctuating
export proceeds and lack of capital and technology for development. How can decision-makers, faced with these immense and urgent
problems, spare the time, attention, and resources, to look far
ahead and to initiate new actions and possibly face political
risks in the process? The question, however, is whether they can
afford not to do so. The answer is political timidity or the
lack of will for rational development. The same phenomenon has
also been described as a "lack of governance".

Continuation of Intellectual Effort
The intellectual effort of studies, projections, models, discussions and proposals should in any case continue and for three
reasons. First, this is required; many studies and careful
examinations are still needed at the national, regional and
global levels for specific sectors and aspects. The analysis of
the past performance in development in the advanced and the
developing countries is not yet complete. Varying opinions and
projections will have to be reviewed and further scrutinized.

Second, this intellectual effort should be extended to include the
problems which are referred to above, namely, the incapacity of
the decision-makers to act and how to overcome their reluctance
or hesitation to face forthcoming events in good time so as to
avert more serious difficulties and, in so doing, to realize a
better future for all. In this analysis, one accepts the existing
system of decision-making represented by nation-states, together
with emerging regional and international groupings which may in
future increase in power. One also notes the business decision-
makers, including the financing and monetary centers and the
major transnational companies.

Third, the continued intellectual effort will provide material
for those decision-makers who either now or in the future, will
come forward to lead the construction of the new order. There are
already many of these centers, among governments, intergovernmental, non-governmental and business organizations, and they
have to be supported and stimulated.

In the following lines some problems which could serve as the subject of further study are outlined, not as a coherent or complete programme, but rather as observations and remarks about current activities or, rather, inactivities.

The timidity of the energy importing industrialized countries has been mentioned as an example. The most glaring examples of this attitude, however, are current armament policies and the increasing wastage of resources on non-essential luxury consumption. The developing countries, which may have more acceptable excuses because of their lack of experience, are increasing their public expenditures in non-priority areas far beyond their resources; in spite of population increases, they are neglecting economic growth in favour of superficial modernization, especially in the services sector. The advanced countries, however, have the longer experience, the better developed institutions, the greatest share of economic, military, and technological capacity, and hence the greater responsibility.

The advanced countries here include both the capitalist and the socialist groups since the period of the cold war and of sharply opposed ideologies has been followed by co-existence, then detente, and now stabilization and increasing cooperation. Although we do not yet have one system for the advanced countries and basic differences within this group still exist, the ideological dividing lines are less sharp. The same is even more true with respect to the developing countries. Some, such as the oil exporting countries, have surplus financial resources but remain undeveloped; others are at different stages of development. It is believed that the previous general - and rather sweeping - remarks nevertheless apply fairly to the development situation as a whole.

Development Interdependencies
The timidity of action, which can also be called a lack of effective leadership, will not by itself prevent the forces of change active within societies from exerting their pressures and thus leading to a continued series of events. The forces of change are in the minds of the people, as attitudes or value-systems and aspirations. They exist in the economic and business communities, where self-interest and livelihood are expressed in production, consumption, wealth, profit and income. It exists in the social classes and groupings, with their dynamics of conflict, compassion and compulsion within themselves and towards others. It exists in the structure of the nation-states and in multi-state organizations. And, finally, in the sense of insecurity and the desire to have hope for the future and satisfaction for the present.

At one time, not so very long ago, development was essentially seen as economic growth. Later, social and human development became equally important as an instrument of growth and also as a final objective in the application of a welfare concept. Economic

and social development within the welfare concept - however
defined - was subsequently recognized as being in need of a set
of international relations and rules beyond the one-state, in the
form of security and peace, trade and finance, technology
transfer, mobility of labour, and finally in the framework of the
world-problematique which has evolved in the last ten years,
culminating in a total concept which is being designated "the new
world order".

Across this spectrum of changing concepts, economic and social
development theories and practices have evolved in parallel.
Simple models of capital-output ratios, followed by national
planning techniques, development strategies and, to mention the
most recent additions, cooperation between developing countries,
self-reliance, collective self-reliance, North-South dialogue,
the concept of basic human needs, and the direct attack on
poverty.

If it is now considered that the development of Third World countries forms an integral part of future world development, rather
than simply comprising a marginal problem, and that the future is
defined by the policies and actions of the industrialized countries, then theories, and hence the practice, of development in
the poor countries must be directly linked to developments within
the advanced countries, and vice-versa. This leads to forms of
interdependence and hence modulation of national autonomy which,
if left to act within the existing power structure, will most
likely lead to the domination of the poor by the rich and to new
forms of colonialism and competing spheres of influence. This may
be the core of the affirmation that the future peace and prosperity of the industrialized countries is dependent upon an improvement in the quality of life and hopes for the future in the poor
countries. Therefore, it is in the self-interest of the advanced
countries to cooperate in the development of the poor countries.
The advanced countries, however, are seeking security not through
development but, unsuccessfully, through increasing armaments. No
wonder then, that they afford such low priority to problems of
development.

What can the developing countries do under these circumstances?
They now realize that they themselves, with their own resources
and policies, are primarily responsible for their own development. They may have come to believe in this concept, but they have
not yet put it fully to practice. But because of it, they look to
aid and assistance from the developed countries as a supplement to
their own efforts. In general, they realize that their pattern of
development will have to be different from that of the industrialized countries. They search and experiment with different
strategies with varying degrees of success. The measure of
success and failure is derived from a set of goals and objectives.
Here, the developing countries, implicitly and even explicitly,
adopt the present criteria of the industrialized countries as

their target - namely, modernization and "catching up" with the
rich. They pay the price - a dual society and wide income
disparities - then frustration and instability. They carefully
guard their recently acquired political independence and national
identity, but find under the pressure of events that they have the
political power of recognized independence, but within the framework of policies of development and international and regional
cooperation which reflect an increasing world interdependence in
which they are the weaker partner, and hence the fear of domination
- not only politically and economically - but even culturally.

Complementary Solutions

After amplifying these two sketchy scenarios, it may dawn on the
investigator that neither the advanced nor the developing countries will be very successful should they seek to solve their
major problems by themselves. And that if the two sets of problems
are put together, then the chances of reaching acceptable solutions
will be larger. In other words, there may be complimentarity of
solutions to the two integrated sets of problems. The integration
here would be between the rich and the poor and also in looking
into the major problems as multisided - economic, social,
political, technological and cultural - at the same time.

One may find useful examples to illustrate such a hypothesis.
Chancellor Kreisky of Austria has been advocating a Marshall-
like plan for infrastructure development in Africa, which will
stimulate production in heavy industry and hence employment and
recovery in Europe, and eventually pay its costs through better
utilization of African resources. A similar wider scheme has
recently been proposed within the European Community. An intensive
and determined approach to the problem of appropriate technology
for the developing countries would cost in money and human skills
a small fraction of the technological capacity in the advanced
countries but would lead, through cooperation with the poor
countries, to real and immediate savings in current development
budgets and result in an expert body of research and development
which is so far not really available to the developing countries.
The U.S. government has recently taken a symbolic step in this
direction by establishing a fund for appropriate technology. The
developing countries may well be advised to invert the priorities
in their development, giving much higher priority to R & D with
the support of the advanced countries. Many studies have already
shown that problems of energy, food, environment, employment and
others cannot be solved in the advanced countries except within a
wider framework which includes the poor countries.

A certain degree of self-sufficiency in food production in the
developing countries is required, since the transport and
distribution of bulky grains beyond certain limits across
continents and oceans will become impossible. Similarly, a certain
supply of manufactured goods should be made available in different
communities for local demand. Hence the need for a dualistic

approach in technology for the developing countries - or some of them at least - which will be a transitional stage towards a later, more equitable, international division of labour with its fairer share of industrialization and technological development for the developing countries. There will certainly be many other and better examples of "real" and "just" partnership between the developed and developing countries in solving what may in the first instance appear as separate problems for separate and very diverse communities.

Present Realities

We should not be transported very far, however, by hopes alone; we must return to the realities of the present, from which one would, in any event, have to start. At present, the industrialized countries are encountering strong opposition and extreme difficulties in their efforts to introduce a very limited set of adjustment policies designed to shift production and labour away from certain labour-intensive, non-competitive industries to other employment and to open, to a limited extent, their markets to low-cost manufactures from the developing countries. The opposition understandably comes from labour, supported emotionally by the public. No one notes that the same process of market development has been going on in the developing countries for decades through high-cost imports, mostly in the form of consumption goods, for a high income and corrupt minority. This has been going on to such an extent that many developing countries find it impossible to embark upon serious development without isolating themselves from the inflow of goods and ideas from the industrialized countries. Protectionism among the advanced countries is on the way as short term - and certainly wrong - policy of managing current difficulties. In this atmosphere, the talk about much larger adjustments that would eventually have to take place in the economic, social and political and international relations in the advanced countries seems to be completely irrealistic. On further reflection, however, it may be found to be part of a much more acceptable general solution in the interest of all parties concerned.

This leads to the conclusion that, in proposing general strategies of development for the future, it is necessary to map schematically the series of steps, starting from the present, that would lead eventually to the desired situations and avoiding the more serious problems which will develop if no such action is taken. Strategies may or may not be acceptable, but they will be implemented through a number of successive steps. Some, but not many, of them may for tactical reasons be diversionary and dispersionary.

This is of course the well known approach of the carrot and the stick. The stick is the dangers confronting communities and nations should the set of major world problems, including development, not be tackled rationally, collectively and in good time. The carrot is that if one bears for a while with the short term problems,

diffusing their most critical manifestation, while at the same
time gradually and systematically implementing a rational set of
global policies, then the present problems will be solved and the
feared problems of the future will be avoided. A rather sweet
carrot. Unfortunately, the political decision-makers in many
advanced and developing countries have their own approach to the
carrot and the stick. The carrot in this case is short term
solutions and further benefits at the cost of increasing inflation
and maintaining stagnation and, because of this, "please vote us
back into power and maintain political stability". The stick,
however, is even more macabre. If things go bad - as they certainly frequently do - then attacks should be mounted against one
class, group, or idea. Free trade may be the victim. The developing countries may be the villain. If all these fail, then it is
national honour that will be in danger and the call for war is
sounded. The stick will be death and destruction.

Cooperation and Understanding
Reference has already been made to the cold war between East and
West which, fortunately, has given way through fairly peaceful
means - but not without conflict or strain - to greater cooperation. There is no possibility of direct military confrontation
between the North and South. The large number of small wars that
took place and are taking place all over the developing world
- usually with the arms and involvement of the big powers - is a
new phenomenon which is not unconnected to the precarious nuclear
balance and the unstable security situation in the industrialized
countries. Small wars can lead to big wars and, should they keep
multiplying as such, they will leave behind death, destruction
and tensions. Excluding direct confrontation between the North
and South, therefore, does not mean the exclusion of war between
the East and West, nor does it mean the exclusion of destruction
and tension.

The confrontation between North and South, which no one wants, can
take different, undesirable forms. I was told by a distinguished
Western scholar in a public meeting that the Western countries
have the military and economic power to oppose any of the policies
or misgivings of the developing countries. I wonder if this is
still true, or whether it will ever be put to the test. It would
be useful to clarify and correct such ideas so that people and
nations in the North and South can identify for themselves a
future of prosperity, justice and peace. They may well also see
that the current difficulties which confront all of them are the
result of short-sighted, perhaps well-intentioned, nationalistic
or sectarian policies, and that the way out of their dilemma lies
in the application of the will to develop rationally. With this in
view, the developing countries will be happy if they see the
advanced countries successful in solving current crises for they
will be hoping for reasonable cooperation and understanding in
building the future. How to get such understanding and mutual
confidence? This is the most basic need: the will to develop
rationally.

The Search for Common Ground

Sartaj Aziz

Introduction

Despite many Conferences and meetings on the new international
order held in the past three years, it is painfully clear that
the international community is very far indeed, even from
visualizing, let alone implementing, a new and more equitable
world order. The North and South have very different views about
the inadequacy and shortcomings of the existing system; they look
at the future differently as if from different ends of a tele-
scope; the conflict of interests in relation to specific issues
is more visible than the convergence of interests and most
serious of all, the desperate urgency of the issues involved
and the range of choices facing the world are not even discussed
openly and seriously.

The Southern View

The Southern view of a new international order, already expressed officially and unofficially is now much clearer. The Third
World, it is emphasized, is not seeking more of the same concessions which provided some tenuous links between very affluent
and very poor nations under the old system i.e. a little more
aid, some technical assistance and promises of trade preferences.
What they are seeking is an end to their dependency relationship
with the developed world, through fundamental structural changes
in international institutions and political power structures and
equal opportunities for future progress. The present economic
system, based on a mixture of the so-called market system and
selective manipulation of that system, discriminate against the
poorer and the weaker nations. The evidence presented in support
of this contention seems very convincing and has been well
documented in recent years.

Underlying the evidence concerning the inequities of the existing
system are certain very fundamental issues which have not yet
been faced squarely. As some social scientists from the Third
World have pointed out, the existing international order is a
legacy of the classical economic thought based on perfect competition, free enterprise and free international trade, but
the theoretical and intellectual foundations of such a system
are no longer capable of supporting either national economic
policy or international economic relations. The first shock to
the "perfect world" of classical economists was dealt by the
Great Depression in 1929-31. Soon after they began to recognize
the need for government intervention through various kinds of
fiscal and monetary devices. Then agriculture was singled out
for special treatment and support prices because a large number
of farmers could not adjust supply fast enough or compete with

11

the organized industrial sector. The need for special protection
to certain industries or certain backward areas on social considerations was accepted in Europe and the U.S.A. in the 1950s.
The power of large corporations was also recognized in the
1950s and 1960s and nationalization of certain sectors or monopolistic enterprises was undertaken in many countries of Europe.

Today there is hardly a developed country in the world where
national economic policies are based on the classical equilibrium
model, but these very countries continue to advocate the principle of *laissez faire* in organizing economic relations between
nations. International markets, they would seem to argue, are
more perfect than national markets and trade will allocate
resources more efficiently among nations than within different
areas of the same country. Similarly, the need for protecting
the incomes of their own farmers is readily accepted but the
plight of farmers in other countries, particularly poor countries,
is generally ignored.

This divergence between the theoretical basis for formulating
national and international policies has so far been recognized
only implicitly and then also in a few areas that affected the
industrial nations themselves. The commitment to free international trade with fixed exchange rates could no longer be recon-
ciled with the objectives of full employment and collective
bargaining and as a result gold was demonetized and country after
country allowed its exchange rate to float. The West European
countries could not compete with a stronger trade partner like
the U.S.A. and formed their own regional groupings to increase
their bargaining power. Japan's exports excelled almost all
countries in free competition and she had to accept voluntary
restraints on her exports to allow the less efficient industries
of its trading partners to survive. But all these were piecemeal
adjustments of relations within the industrial nations, reflecting the reality of economic and military power. The developing
countries played no part in organizing the post-war economic
system nor have they had any role in changing it. In fact, many
of them have continued to suffer from the consequences of
adjustments made in the system by the industrial nations to
protect their own interests.

The most important impact of the existing international economic
system is in the gradual erosion of the real value of the goods
and services produced by the developing countries. In the past
30 years, the developed nations, with direct or indirect control
of an unduly large proportion of world resources, have enjoyed
unprecedented prosperity and have been able to generate a large
surplus for further technological development. The cost of
developing this technology has been paid by all users, but its
"scarcity rent" has been retained by advanced nations. The monopoly organization of technology is matched by almost perfect

competition in commodities and this is in turn reflected in a
constant deterioration in the terms of trade for developing countries. Despite reduction in production costs as a result of
improvements in organization and technology, the prices paid by
developing countries for manufactured goods have been rising in
relation to those received by them for primary products. The
workings of international monetary and financial systems gives
the developed countries an additional edge in international relations. Taking all these factors together, there is a continuous
and unmistakable bias in the present system in favour of industrial nations. It would therefore seem reasonable to argue that
the malfunctioning of the international economic system is at
least partly responsible for the poverty of developing countries.
For centuries rich people have blamed the poor for their poverty
and only in recent years is it being recognized that the socio-
economic system of a country can and does increase or reduce the
poverty of its under-privileged segments. It is time we recognized the validity of these arguments in the international discussion of causes of poverty.

The main thrust of these arguments is not to shift or dilute
the responsibility of developing countries for their own economic
and social development. In the past 30 years developing countries
as a group have achieved impressive rates of economic growth,
but this progress has not diminished the poverty of the bottom
40 percent in most of these countries. The task of meeting their
basic needs has emerged as the most important development
challenge of our time, but the developing countries cannot make
much headway in tackling this task without much greater international cooperation that will at least remove the limitations and
handicaps created by the existing international economic system.

Once these basic premises put forward by the social scientists
and official spokesmen of the Third World are accepted, the
debate on the practical implications of the new international
order would become much more meaningful.

The Northern View
International discussion of various facets of what is now called
the new international order began with the first U.N. Conference
on Trade and Development in 1964 and continued in many subsequent fora, but the concept was first presented coherently and
forcefully in the Sixth Special Session of the General Assembly
held in April 1974. The initial reactions of most developed
countries to the Declaration put forward by the developing
countries was negative and almost hostile. International cooperation for development, their statements explained, had been an
important element of their policies since the early 1950s. They
had all provided a great deal of financial and technical
assistance in the past two decades. As a proportion of their
gross national product, the flow of their aid had been declining
but this was due to their own economic difficulties.

There have been very few explicit statements on some of the
fundamental issues raised by the Third World representatives,
but in general there is an implied belief that workers in the
rich countries are inherently more efficient; that the world
system is more or less free and can distribute resources and
opportunities in an equitable manner; and that it is for the
developing countries to take advantage of these opportunities.
The first rude shock to those who had presented these lines of
argument came in 1973 when a group of developing countries - the
oil exporting countries (OPEC) - were able, by a unilateral
decision, to raise the price of petroleum. In effect this
decision, apart from helping to conserve a scarce and non-
renewable resource, had only restored the price of petroleum in
relation to manufactured goods to a level that prevailed 30
years earlier. It also helped to underline one major injustice
of the existing system: that a continuous decline in the price
of primary commodities, in relation to prices of manufactured
goods, was but need not be a permanent feature of the system.

In September 1975, at the Seventh Special Session of the General
Assembly, the developed countries accepted, with some hesitation,
the concept of a new economic order but have not yet faced the
broader implications of this concept or accepted the three main
points put forward by the Third World:

● that the existing system discriminated against the weakest
members of the international community through trade barriers,
limited access to technology and capital, and inadequate monetary
and financial arrangements;

● that the developing countries deserve at least an equal opportunity to participate in the world economic system without losing
control of their natural resources or their freedom to follow
their own priorities or policies;

● that this opportunity could be provided only through a gradual
restructuring of international institutions and a reorientation
of policies governing relations between developed and developing
countries.

Many institutions and eminent individuals in the North have now
begun to acknowledge the inadequacies of the existing system
and have presented many useful proposals for reform of the system.
But the official Northern view has remained reticent, for example
at the U.N. Conference on Trade and Development in Nairobi, and
the two Western Summits held in Puerto Rico in 1975 and in London
in May 1977. Both the latter Conferences expressed satisfaction
at the degree of success attained in tackling the monetary strains
created by the 1974 economic crisis, in evolving contingency
plans for energy shortages, and in "dealing with the problems of
developing countries". In contrast, the Third World leaders, in
their meetings in Manilla (February 1975), Colombo (August 1976)

and Mexico (September 1976) and the U.N. General Assembly (September 1977) have expressed grave misgivings about the present state of the world economy, the worsening economic situation in many Third World countries and the weakening commitment of developed countries to evolve a new international order.

The advent of a North-South dialogue at Paris in 1976 under the simplified title of "Conference on International Economic Cooperation", soon after the Seventh Special Session, generated hopes that this might be the first honest attempt to translate the concept of a new order into some concrete steps and programmes. By June 1977, however, these expectations had disappeared into thin air. The developed countries, having successfully recycled the surpluses of petrodollars, were no longer interested in a new deal for the Third World. They were in fact seeking assurance of oil supply and stable oil prices for themselves. If they could obtain such an assurance they might hand out one billion dollars to the poorest countries, but only through the existing international framework.

Some of the apparent reasons for the attitude adopted by the developed countries are not difficult to seek. Many of the countries are plagued by growing unemployment and relatively high rates of inflation which have in turn led to serious social and political strains, forcing many governments to plead for inward looking policies in an effort to solve domestic problems in preference to international problems, without perceiving the links between these two sets of problems.

This is a sad commentary on the current state of international cooperation and on the ability of the international community to understand grave issues facing both developed and developing countries. It is also ironic that, despite the unprecedented growth of information and communication facilities, these issues should appear so different to the two sides and the prospects for a meaningful dialogue or a genuine search for acceptable alternatives should seem so remote.

Search for Common Ground
The starting point for any dialogue is a consensus on the nature of the problem. This can then lead, in the second stage, to a search for common ground on the basis of which certain agreed solutions can be sought. If there is no convergence of interests, there can be little hope of any consensus either on the problem itself or the solutions proposed.

The moral imperatives for a new and more equitable world order are fairly obvious but moral arguments can seldom change the realities of this world dominated by self-interest and power politics. Per force, we have to look for areas of interdpendence and common interests.

The first major area of interdependence springs from our common environment and common heritage of natural resources. Each country has the capacity to manage or mismanage the resources and biosphere of this earth and its oceans. The ecological future of this planet can be secured only through cooperation among all nations and the task of conserving scarce non-renewable resources requires much greater international understanding on objectives and priorities.

The second area is the common and continuing need for world peace and the related possibilities for reductions in wasteful expenditures on armaments. Development can help to reduce and eliminate the underlying causes for tension and conflict and thus directly contribute to the objective of peace and security.

The third area around which a consensus is rapidly emerging concerns certain new development goals geared to elimination of absolute poverty and meeting the basic needs of the poorest 30 percent of mankind. In the past 20 years, the benefits of development and of international assistance for development have gone largely to well-to-do members in developing countries and therefore failed to meet the real objectives of development. A new basis for international cooperation can be found only if there is a consensus on certain new and more meaningful development objectives.

And finally, the developed countries cannot solve their economic and social problems without integrating the majority of Asians, Africans and Latin Americans into a growing world economy. Today the industrialized world is facing a major crisis in its efforts to get out of the economic recession, to reduce unemployment and to curb inflation. Short term adjustments have helped some countries like the U.S.A., Japan and West Germany to stage modest recoveries, but this recovery has also adversely affected many of the weaker industrialized countries. Most of the countries cannot reflate their economies because big unions and big business are now too powerful to hold any reasonable price line and the distribution of a shrinking pie is a major political issue in almost all these countries.

The stark realities of the current economic dilemma facing the world have to be squarely faced. Legitimate demand for a whole range of goods for the production of which industrialized countries are more suitable is already saturated. As a result, Western Europe, North America and Japan are competing for limited markets and pushing each other towards protectionist policies that can only aggravate the problem.

As Barbara Ward has reminded us, the present dilemma is matched by two historical analogies. In 1927, recession spread gradually, without being noticed, and reached American farmers by 1929.

Nothing was done about the problem and the whole world suffered from an unprecedented depression. Twenty years later, in 1947, Europe was devastated and had no purchasing power. The response, as we all know, was the Marshall Plan - the transfer to Western Europe over a period of many years of 2 percent of the GNP of the United States which was then far less prosperous than it is today. The result was unprecedented expansion over two decades which changed the face of Europe.

A "Marshall Plan" for the Third World

The key question is whether the response to the inevitable but multi-dimensional crisis that is so imminent will be one of deliberate indifference or a bold new planetary bargain. What is needed is a 20 year "Marshall Plan" for the Third World with concepts and purposes much broader than the European Marshall Plan.

The centre-piece of the proposed Plan could be a new fund for basic human needs. Its purpose, however, could be to build on all the common objectives mentioned above and to provide an important starting point for evolving a new and more equitable world order. This can be accomplished by securing a part of the required resources from cuts in expenditures on arms and by exploiting the resources of the sea-bed. At the same time, the management of such a fund could set into motion certain new institutions and mechanisms which will give the developing countries a greater share in decision-making. Some concrete ideas on such a Plan are outlined below:

(i) It has been estimated that by investing about $10 to 12 billion a year, the basic human needs of the poorest 30 percent of mankind can be met within 20-25 years. This in turn will eliminate the worst aspects of world poverty before the end of this century. By raising the purchasing power of one billion people, now living below the poverty line, new resources will be released in areas where marginal productivity will be highest, and new markets and higher levels of trade will be generated for both the North and the South.

(ii) All countries, developed and developing, will be invited to contribute a certain percentage of their GNP (possibly 0.3) to the proposed *"World Fund for Basic Human Needs"*. Since the oil exporting countries are currently contributing a much larger portion of their GNP to assist developing countries, they can readily contribute 0.3 percent of their respective GNP to this Fund, either directly or through the OPEC Special Fund, for what can be considered the most important development objectives of the future. The developing countries would be expected to contribute on a voluntary basis but their contribution would naturally be considerably less than that expected from developed and OPEC countries.

(iii) If the current disarmament negotiations succeed, even a 5 percent reduction in expenditures on armaments could provide $10 billion a year for this Fund. The Soviet Union and other East Bloc countries would also be asked to join the effort, since the proposal is in line with the long standing Russian proposal for a 10 per cent cut in expenditures on armament to find new resources for development.

(iv) In the longer run, a part of the resources generated by reforms in the monetary system (through the growing use of SDRs as a reserve currency for example) or by the exploitation of the sea-bed resources could also be channelled to the proposed Fund.

(v) The Fund would be managed by a high level coordinating body or *World Development Council,* consisting of Ministerial representatives of developed, OPEC and developing countries, probably in equal number, which would become a kind of world finance ministry, receiving a certain percentage of GNP from each country for certain well defined objectives. The programme itself would, however, be implemented by existing institutions and agencies. The "basic needs package" would be split into subsectors like food, clothing, shelter, education, health, drinking water, employment and the responsibility for each sub-sector would be entrusted to one or more international or regional institutions, depending on their capacity and future plans. These would include the World Bank, the three Regional Development Banks and the specialized agencies of the U.N. system. Each will be expected to present its programme, with specific targets, for financing to the World Development Council which would only allocate resources periodically and monitor progress but not undertake any operational functions. It could be linked to the U.N. General Assembly through special arrangements. The need for a new Fund, managed by a high level body, arises from the fact that none of the existing institutions with their own peculiar governing mechanisms can manage all the segments of a basic needs package, nor can they undertake individually a meaningful dialogue with the recipient countries on changes in policies and institutions, which are in effect more important than financial resources for attaining the basic needs objectives.

(vi) The developing countries, on their part, would not only contribute to the proposed Plan but would also undertake to pay priority attention to the poorest segments of their population and to undertake the institutional and policy changes necessary to channel these resources to them. In practice, only countries which can make these changes will expect to receive substantial assistance from the proposed Fund.

The proposed Plan is not simply a plea for more aid in the traditional sense, but reflects a new cooperative approach to

pooling international resources for certain common objectives.
A major distinction between the old type of foreign aid and the
new approach is that, in the latter, the transfer of resources
is geared to the basic needs of the poorest population. The
transfer would also take place under international auspices in
which OPEC countries and developing recipient countries would
make their contributions and share decision-making powers. It
would not thus impose an unequal relationship on the developing
countries. The Plan also provides for certain minimum structural
changes in international institutions but these are gradual and
geared to shared priorities and agreed objectives.

Such a "Plan" is needed as much by the North as by the South and
should be acceptable to trade unions in the industrialized
countries once they are convinced that they require growing trade
opportunities in the world if they are to solve their inflation
problem without aggravating the employment problem. They must
also realize that the creeping crisis which the world faces will
not go away in a year or two. It will take many years before the
one billion underprivileged people of the Third World can be
pulled out of their poverty and gradually integrated into a
growing world market. At present only a small minority of developing countries is a faltering participant in world trade.

The Plan would not in itself remove all the inequities of the
existing economic system, it would at least, however, provide
some compensation to very low income countries and hopefully
prepare the ground for tackling some of the more fundamental
issues that underlie the relationships between North and South.
The impact of these fundamental issues is not of course confined
to developing countries. In the longer run, the developed
countries themselves need more viable development alternatives.
It is increasingly clear that the present pattern of consumption
and production are rapidly pushing the world towards its outer
limits - both ecological and social. There is a desperate need
for simpler life styles and a drastic cut in wasteful consumption
at higher levels, but that cannot be achieved without first improving the plight of the underprivileged, no matter where they
live.

But grand ideas can be launched only by the wisdom and vision of
world leaders. Perhaps President Carter will offer a new deal
to the Third World in the same way as Roosevelt offered to the
workers of America in the 1930s.

Lessons from DD2 for a New International Development Strategy

Henk C. Bos

The Nature of the Strategy for DD2

The International Development Strategy for the United Nations
Second Development Decade, the period 1971-80, was a very balanced and comprehensive policy document (General Assembly resolution
2626 (XXV)). It formulated the fundamental goal of development in
universal terms: Para (7): "The ultimate objective of development
must be to bring about sustained improvement in the well-being of
the individual and bestow benefits on all. If undue privileges,
extremes of wealth and social injustices persist, then development fails in its essential purpose..."

At the same time this Strategy attempted to give operational content to this broad goal by specifying concrete objectives and policy measures in various fields. Some of these objectives and
policies were quantified. The targets for the average annual
rates of growth of the gross product (6 per cent), agricultural
(4 per cent) and manufacturing output (8 per cent) for the group
of developing countries as a whole and the target for a financial
transfer in the form of official development assistance to a
minimum net amount of 0.7 per cent of the gross national product
at market prices for each economically advanced country are perhaps most well-known, but they are not the only quantified
aspects of the Strategy. Most objectives and policy measures,
however, were only formulated qualitatively.

The Strategy cannot be fairly criticized for a narrow view on the
development process and for recommending a development strategy
focused mainly on increasing the rate of growth of GNP, as the
following two quotations might illustrate:

Para 18: "As the ultimate purpose of development is to provide
increasing opportunities to all people for a better life, it is
essential to bring about a more equitable distribution of income
and wealth for promoting both social justice and efficiency of
production, to raise substantially the level of employment, to
achieve a greater degree of income security, to expand and
improve facilities for education, health, nutrition, housing and
social welfare, and to safeguard the environment. Thus, qualitative and structural changes in the society must go hand in hand
with rapid economic growth, and existing disparities - regional,
sectoral and social - should be substantially reduced. These
objectives are both determining factors and end-results of
development; they should therefore be viewed as integrated parts
of the same dynamic process and would require a unified
approach..."

The United Nations Committee for Development Planning in its pro-

posals for the Second United Nations Development Decade wrote
the following on the meaning of development:

"It cannot be over-emphasized that what development implies for
the developing countries is not simply an increase in productive
capacity but major transformations in their social and economic
structures. Their economies are characterized by dualism which
has often the effect of making technological and economic advances sharpen the contrast between their modern and backward sectors
and widen social and economic disparaties .....
Within this framework, an increase in output or income only
represents one of the indicators of development. It has to be
supplemented by other indicators which bring out more adequately
the other dimensions of development. Some of these other indicators are not available, however; for this reason some of the
basic objectives can only be indicated qualitatively." (1)

The Strategy distinguished not only concrete objectives and
policies, it also specified in detail policy measures to be taken
by the individual developing countries, the developed countries
and at the international level, both through the United Nations
system and through other forms of international economic cooperation. The Strategy made recommendations for the formulation of
policies, their implementation and for a review and appraisal of
objectives and policies. It also set a time schedule for the
implementation of the various objectives and policy measures.

Why the Strategy for DD2 Lost its Relevance
In spite of its comprehensive, balanced and operational nature,
the Strategy fairly soon after its launching lost its relevance
as the central policy document guiding action in the field of
development policy. Although the Second Development Decade has
not yet come to an end, and the available evidence of the achievements during this Decade cover a period of only 5 to 6 years,
the Strategy no longer plays the significant role in national and
international discussions on development for which it was designed. Several reasons have or can be given to explain this premature fate of the Strategy. For the formulation of a new international strategy it might be worthwhile to review briefly the most
important explanations given. These reasons will be discussed in
a framework applicable for the evaluation of any type of policy
implementation. The following causes can be distinguished.

Lack of sufficient support and implementation of the Strategy. The
Strategy was in many respects only nominally accepted in 1970 by
the partners concerned. The major industrial countries did not
(or not fully) endorse all recommendations directed at the developed countries, e.g. with respect to the transfer of financial
resources and to trade liberalization, and consequently failed
to take the policy measures the Strategy recommends. Many developing countries were reluctant or unwilling to carry out the
domestic structural reforms suggested. From its very conception,

thus, the Strategy was not whole-heartedly supported by developed and developing countries alike. Comparison between the proposals for the Strategy as formulated by the U.N. Committee for Development Planning and the resolution formulating the Strategy shows clearly how, in the final negotiating process, the teeth were taken out of the proposals: targets were reduced, obligations changed into desirabilities and dead-lines deleted or extended. But even so, the final result did not receive full support.

The occurrence of unforeseen exogenous factors. The major factor of this nature was of course the quadrupling of the oil price by the OPEC countries in 1973/74. Although one could dispute just how unforeseen and exogenous this price increase should in fact have been, given the long term decline in the real price of oil, what matters in this connection is that no responsible policy-maker at the beginning of the seventies anticipated an oil price increase of the magnitude witnessed.

This action by the oil producing countries is the most important single factor which affected the Strategy. Its impact has been manifold. It not only afforded energy a fundamental role in the relations between developed and developing countries, it also added a new dimension to international development objectives; it led to new policy proposals and brought about a greater differentiation among the developing countries. Above all, this action gave an impetus to a more self-confident - if not militant - attitude of the developing countries in international negotiations, because it served as an example of what developing countries could achieve through cooperation and the use of their "commodities power".

The Third World's view on the objectives of an international strategy has changed and new policy measures have been recommended. The Strategy for DD2 focused its attention on the sustained increase in the standard of living and recommended both national and international policy measures. The Sixth Special Session of the United Nations General Assembly shifted the interest of the LDCs from this broad development goal to the more narrow and international objective of a New International Economic Order, the newly introduced phrase covering a list of recommendations or wishes in the field of international trade, commodity markets, the international transfer of finance and technology, the international monetary system, transnational corporations. Most of those proposals are already included, at least in principle, in the Strategy for DD2, but they were given much more emphasis. Other proposed policy measures are new, such as UNCTAD's Integrated Commodity Programme, the Common Fund, an indexation system.

On the other hand, the ILO World Employment Conference and studies by the World Bank and others focused attention, in different ter-

minology, on the satisfaction of basic human needs, the elimination of absolute poverty, a more equal income distribution and
the creation of productive employment. Although these cannot be
considered new development objectives, they were put forward with
greater and more exclusive emphasis. Development policies at the
national level are formulated first of all with respect to the
achievement of these objectives. Some of these views are ambivalent and less explicit about how to stimulate economic growth.

Dissatisfaction with the development performance of the Strategy.
Evaluation of the implementation of recommended policy measures
must be distinguished from the evaluation of the actual performance and realization of the development objectives of the Strategy. With regard to the latter, there is no reason for only
negative conclusions. One might even say that it is surprising
that, in spite of the unsatisfactory realization of the recommended national and international policy measures, the progress made
during the first half of the seventies has not in all fields
been disappointing and far removed from the objectives set in the
Strategy. Positive results were obtained, for example, for the
overall growth of gross product (an average annual rate of growth
of 5.6 per cent), manufacturing output (7 per cent), exports and
increase in savings. Historically speaking, the overall growth
achievement has even been exceptional, as has been demonstrated
recently by Morawetz (2). In many other aspects, however, the
development record has been disappointing, in particular with
regard to the increase in agricultural production (2.1 per cent
per annum), and improvements in the social situation, although
in the latter field the quantitative information is less hard.

If we consider further how the overall growth performance is differentiated by groups of developing countries, the overall
achievements can be evaluated less positively: the poorest group
of countries not only grew substantially slower than the higher-
income developing countries, but the long term trend in their
rate of growth has also declining since 1950, as the following
table illustrates.

Per Capita Income Growth Rates (%)

	1950-60	1960-70	1970-75
Developing countries			
Poorest	2.6	1.8	1.1
Middle Income	3.2	3.5	4.2
All Developing countries	2.9	3.2	3.7
Developed countries	3.0	3.7	1.9

Source: Robert S. McNamara, Address to Board of Governors, World
Bank, September 26, 1977.

Is there a Need for a New International Development Strategy?

DD2 is not yet ended. First discussions about what should come after this Decade, however, have already - early 1978 - started, both within and outside the United Nations system. The answer to this question seems clear only in a negative sense: it cannot be an updated version of the Strategy for DD2. For a more positive formulation the following preliminary question must first be answered:

i) is there really a need for a new international development strategy; and
ii) what should be the nature of such a strategy?
Of course, the answers to both questions are not independent, but they can best be discusses separately.

To answer the first question it must be realized what is meant by an international (development) strategy or policy. Such a strategy consists of a set of agreed objectives and agreed policies to achieve, or at least to further, these objectives within a certain period of time. The objectives can, in general terms, express desired changes in:
● efficiency;
● growth (long term sustained increase in production and income as well as shortterm stability); and
● justice (or equity or distribution).

In national policies these aspects have been recognized in the mix of objectives and policy measures. Differences in policies among countries reflect differences in views about the importance of objectives and about the effectiveness of policy measures.

For international policies the cooperating governments must have common views about international objectives and related policies. This also implies a common interest in the situation outside the national borders of their territory. This interest can be motivated by economic, social, political, military, human or other considerations. Without the basis of common interests, no agreement about a common international policy can be expected to be feasible. When there is agreement about objectives, it should be less difficult to agree on the necessary policy measures, if such policies are chosen on the basis of their efficacy and not on dogmatic preferences, whether it is, for example, for a free market mechanism, public ownership of the means of production, or self-management.

While it might be possible for developing and developed countries to reach agreement on international policy proposals which can be expected to contribute to a greater efficiency of the international economic system or to an acceleration of international economic growth, it is hardly, if at all, possible to expect agreement on proposals which will in fact lead to an international redistribution of income, or a change in influence or participation to the advantage of the developing countries. Most developed and developing countries, for example, agree, at least in principle, on the desirability of more free trade, short term commodity price stabilization and schemes for compensatory financing - policies which are considered to be relevant for greater efficiency and stability of the world economic system. But there is no support from the developed countries for proposals to introduce an automatic international mechanism for the transfer of financial resources from rich to poorer countries, a measure clearly directed at international income redistribution.

At the national level, it has been accepted in all industrialized countries, as the result of a long process of social and political development, that national and local policies must be based, not only on considerations of efficiency and growth, but also of justice and distribution. The social legislation in these countries expresses a special concern for the lower and lowest income groups of their population. In international development policies, considerations of international justice might be recognized in theory, in practice this aspect plays a secondary and often negligible role.

While for these reasons the difficulties involved in obtaining agreement between developed and developing countries on a truly international development strategy often seem insurmountable, this is no argument against the need for such a strategy; it concerns only differences in views about its objectives. Elements of common interest between developed and developing countries clearly exist in many fields. Stable international monetary relations, sustained and stable world economic growth, free trade (although there might be short term conflicting interests), stable commodity markets and security of energy and food supply are in the long term interest of all groups of countries. The present global interdependence of nations, developed and developing, makes the formulation of international policies and international cooperation among relevant partners no longer a matter of choice but rather of necessity.

Issues in Formulating a New Strategy
If one accepts that a new international development strategy is needed for the years after 1980, a number of questions arise concerning the nature of a new strategy:
● should this strategy include only recommendations for international policies, a New International Economic Order, or should it also make recommendations about domestic policies?
● should the strategy set quantitative targets, where appropriate and feasible, or give only qualitative formulations?
● what should be the time horizon: a DD3 for the 80s, the year 2000, or an open-ended strategy without a time dimension?
● should the strategy systematically differentiate its recommendations between different groups of developing countries, or

neglect such differences?
● should the strategy be comprehensive or selective and concentrate on a package of crucial policy proposals to be negotiated
simultaneously in a given period?
● what should be the appropriate forum or fora for the formulation of the strategy and the implementation of its elements?

Whatever the answers that will be given to these questions, it
will be useful to profit from the experience obtained in the
past, and in particular from DD2. This experience has, in my
opinion, taught the following lessons:

i) The hard core of the development problem is to combat poverty,
to raise the incomes and standards of living of the large masses
of poorest people, to accelerate growth and to strengthen economic and social structures. These are basically domestic problems
and by far the most important contribution to their solution can
only come from domestic policies. Without strong and correct
domestic development efforts little can be achieved, while effective domestic policies might be successful in spite of unfavourable international conditions.

ii) International policies are an integral element in a development strategy, although their influence on the development process will as a rule not be dominant. In fact, the influence of
international relations will depend, among other things, on the
size and structure of the country concerned, on its level of
development; the influence will be different for agricultural and
rural development as compared to industrialization and export
promotion. The impact of domestic and foreign influences on the
development process will sometimes be difficult to distinguish.

iii) Development is an indivisible process and selective or partial policies, whether they were concentrated on acceleration of
growth, industrialization or agricultural development, have often
failed in the past to achieve fundamental development objectives.
This should be a warning against new and equally selective policy proposals, for example, aimed exclusively at the satisfaction
of basic human needs, employment or income distribution.

iv) Our knowledge concerning the development process, both factual and analytical, is very weak. Little is known about the
effectiveness of the various national and international policy
measures under discussion. Many new concepts, such as "new international economic order", "dependence", "self-reliance",
"de-linking", "basic needs strategy", lack analytical and operational clarity. They need to be analyzed more thoroughly before they
can play a useful role in the formulation of a new strategy.

v) It would be unrealistic to close our eyes to the increasing
differentiation between various groups of developing countries.
Differences in levels of development and in economic structure

create different development opportunities and needs for international assistance. These facts cannot be neglected if appropriate international policies are to be formulated.

vi) The choice of a time horizon for a strategy, or the quantification of targets, is not a matter of principle, but rather of planning techniques and pragmatism. A medium term (10-year) strategy with some quantification, where of operational significance, can be more concrete and specific, but might run the risk of becoming irrelevant as a result of major unforeseen events. A long term or open-ended qualitative policy declaration will be general and vague, but can concentrate on crucial structural changes. Both approaches are not mutually exclusive and could easily be combined, as is often the case in national development strategies.

Whatever the final outcome of the international political negotiation process, if there is any truth in the previous remarks then there can be no doubt that a new strategy will be quite different in character from the Strategy for DD2. This cannot be considered the consequence of the failure of the latter strategy; it is rather a reflection of changed economic conditions, new development experiences and a new international political climate.

Notes and References
1) *Towards Accelerated Development. Proposals for the Second United Nations Development Decade,* United Nations, New York, 1970, p.5.
2) David Morawetz, *Twenty-five Years of Economic Development, 1950 to 1975,* The World Bank, 1977.

The Prospect: Global Planning or Chaos

Silviu Brucan

Introduction

One of the merits of the RIO report lies in the *scope* of its
analysis: it views the issue of the new international order in
its global dimension. RIO recognizes from the very beginning that
the establishment of a new international order entails fundamental changes not only in economic relations but also in political,
social and cultural aspects of society. Indeed, one could not
account for the diverse and contradictory reactions of governments, nations and leaders belonging to the same geographical-
political region if one views the new order only in economic
terms. There are governments who find the envisaged economic and
financial promises of a more equitable world extremely appealing
but fear the political or social changes that may follow. As for
the great powers, whatever their geography, they seem to be
reluctant (if not hostile) to a new world order because they
perceive it as a challenge to the present structure of power
whose beneficiairies they wish to remain.

RIO also argues against the claim that the new order is an
exclusive North-South affair. Given the nature of present interdependencies, the North-South conflict does not and cannot exist
in isolation; it is part of the international system and, as such,
it is intersected by and interacting with the other international
sub-systems, whether East-West or East-South. Therefore, the
reshaping of the international trade and monetary system could
not be realized without the participation of the Second World.

Strategy and Self-Deception

Four years have already elapsed since the industrial nations were
gripped by the so-called energy crisis followed by rampant inflation and protracted recession. Although the diagnosis has been
quasi-unanimous that this stagflation actually involved a breakdown of the international economic and financial order created
in the aftermath of World War II, in practice the emphasis in
policies has been on a concerted effort by the industrial nations
to overcome the crisis. The recurrent summits of the six or
seven rich and the OECD Scenario for 1980 testify to the priority
given to this course of action.

Surely, this has not prevented modern political rethoric from
paying lip-service to the imperatives of global interdependencies. In 1975, Henry Kissinger stated before the Special Session
of the U.N. General Assembly: "The reality is that the world
economy is a single global system of trade and monetary relations
on which hinges the development of all our economies". One year
later, Zbigniew Brzezinski went even further and warned his
fellow Americans that at a time when global politics are becom-

ing egalitarian rather than libertarian, to ignore the global pressures for reform of existing international arrangements is to open up "the specter of an isolated U.S. in a hostile world".

And yet, ignoring both the global pressures and the specter, President Carter has been leading the way on a course that could be called *Trilateral Commission First*, namely the United States, Japan and Western Europe. Let us look at the results of this policy.

The OECD Scenario for 1980, which is half prediction and half guideline and which is accepted by most OECD members, represents a historical novelty: it is the first attempt *to plan the economic development of the capitalist industrial world as a whole*. This in itself is a recognition that the situation is too serious to be left to the vagaries of the market. It illustrates the proposition that in international economics political motives and political will are becoming predominant. Only a decade ago this would have been considered both heretical and unrealistic in the West. The present crisis has substantially enhanced the economic role of the state not only internally but also externally and one can safely predict that the 1980s will be marked by a *general politicization of world economics*. This is in fact the essential prerequisite of international planning.

The Scenario is based on the effect that annual *growth of output* in each OECD nation may have on the two most sensitive indicators today: *inflation* and *unemployment*. The Scenario calls upon the 24 capitalist advanced countries to grow at an average rate of around 5.5 per cent annualy. However, a thorough examination of the figures leads to the conclusion that even if the prescribed targets were attained, inflation for most nations will still be higher at the end of the decade than it was in the sixties, and unemployment even more so. Hence, the call for the United States, West Germany and Japan to go for higher rates of growth and pull them all out of the recession.

The data already available are not very encouraging. In fact, not even the original targets have been attained. Although 1976 and 1977 were happy years of economic upsurge, it is by no means certain that this will continue into 1978 or 1979. In 1976, U.S. growth was 4.7 per cent and about the same rate is estimated for 1977, which is below the target of 5.75 per cent. West Germany's growth slowed down to a real 3 per cent in the first half of 1977 and it does not look any better in this second half. As for the whole European Economic Community, its industrial production index on a month-to-month basis declined during the entire first half of 1977, after rising 2.2 per cent in January. Small wonder that inflation, though less rampant, is still riding high, while unemployment is worsening.

There is but one inescapable conclusion and that is that the developed nations alone cannot overcome the present economic and financial crisis by planning in a closed circuit. Whatever they do within this limited framework is bound to fail for the very simple reason that OECD countries are already saturated with industrial products. It's like cats chasing their own tail.

The ominous result of such a strategy thus far has been growing protectionist tendencies and the quarrel among the partners of the Trilateral Commission over import quotas and trade imbalances.

A different strategy seems to be indicated. The reclusive rich nations must emerge from their cozy shells and proceed not only in words but also in deeds to working out more global solutions to the present problems. For one thing, three continents are eagerly waiting for the industrial products of the First World, making for a huge market which could trigger a most vigorous economic expansion in the OECD countries, provided there is political will to do so and cautious planning on a global scale to avoid disorder and disruptive competition.

It is worth mentioning here the proposition advanced by Claude Cheysson, Commissioner of the European Economic Community, in a recent interview with *Le Nouvel Observateur* (No. 664,1-7 August 1977). He argues that since 36 per cent of the Community's exports are headed for the developing nations, the best way of getting out of the present slump would be to inject, over a period of 3 to 5 years, a massive financial flow into the Third World. He goes on: "If we inject (some) tens of billions of dollars in the economy of developing nations, all these billions will come back to us as orders for industrial equipment. By all means, the access to industrial development and to higher living standards for hundreds of millions of people in the Third World will turn into a gigantic impulse to global non-inflationary growth".

The French economist views the whole thing as a *contract* designed to organize interdependencies within the framework of a general plan aimed at avoiding competition coming from the new infant industries of the South whilst at the same time allowing the European nations to gradually implement their own policies of industrial restructuring. This would provide a good start for what in the 1980s could evolve into global planning. Actually, the axis of the projected global plan is the *new international division of labor* which, in the coming world order, will bring industrialization to all nations and ensure that those which are currently lagging behind will be brought into the modern technological era.

The whole idea may today sound utopian. But the alternative is chaos and we already have a glimpse of it in the present international trade and monetary system.

East-West Realities

RIO rightly points out that the Eastern European nations do
not live in a hothouse: they also have been seriously affected
by world inflation and economic dislocations. Once more, one dis-
covers that the East-West conflict is not exclusively ideological;
in fact it has an underlying economic aspect the origin of which
goes back to the times when the nation-states of Western Europe
fully benefited from the Industrial Revolution, Eastern Europe,
however, remained predominantly agrarian, with strong feudal
structures surviving well into the twentieth century. And since
the revolution started in backward Russia and expanded later into
less developed countries (except Czechoslovakia) they were all
faced with the enormous task of industrialization against the
background set by the economic and technological superiority of
the West. Indeed, in spite of the great strides made by the centrally planned nations of the East, there is still a great dis-
crepancy in the structure of trade, in financial potential,
productivity and standards of living between the two parts of
Europe. Evidently, we are dealing here with a *pattern of dis-
crepancy in development* and the best evidence that Eastern
European nations are also subject to the rules of unequal
exchange characteristic of the North-South system is the rising
debt now running into tens of billions of dollars they have
incurred to Western banks and governments.

Truly, unlike the North-South system, the gap in Europe is
closing. Eastern European nations stubbornly enforce their
development strategy based on the all-out mobilization of the
population and a regular allocation of a high percentage of their
national income (25-35 per cent) for development, chiefly industrial. Of course, the share earmarked for agriculture and for
consumption in general remains comparatively low. Here, I must
recall Leontief's conclusion in his recent U.N. study that there
is no way an economy can develop at any substantial rate without
rapid industrialization; he calculates that sustained growth
rates of 9-10 per cent cannot be accomplished unless the investment ratio goes up to 35-40 per cent of the national income.

The obtaining situation is that the average annual rate of industrial growth in Eastern Europe has in recent decades been twice
as high as that in Western Europe. This is gradually reflected
in the relative level of living standards. In 1970, while the
average per capita income in Eastern Europe was $1,564, the same
indicator in Western Europe was $2,574 (Leontief).

In forecasting the future, one must take account of various con-
tingencies (e.g. vacillations in Soviet-American relations, political developments in France or Italy versus those in Eastern
Europe, evolution of stagflation) that may affect European poli-

tics in one way or the other. However, if one insulates Europe's development dynamics from the other variables, one may anticipate some interesting political shifts in Eastern Europe around 1990.

By 1990, Eastern European nations expect to attain roughly the average level of development prevailing in Western Europe. I submit that this moment will be crucial because the whole political system of Eastern European societies has been created, adapted and geared to their development strategy with the ultimate objective of catching up with Western Europe. Once this objective is attained, the whole rationale of this political system and its legitimation are bound to become irrelevant. In other words, with the termination of the development requirements, those within a socialist society will begin to assert themselves. This will dictate a change in the political structure. Whether this change will be smooth or disruptive will very much depend on the new generation of leaders that will then come to the fore, a generation no longer brought up under conditions of "capitalist encirclement". But change there shall be, for a socialist society once taking shape cannot function with a political super-structure geared to development.

We see once more that the question of a new international order, far from being exclusively economic, poses perhaps the greatest challenge to the structure of power, both internal and international.

A World Authority

Global planning must eventually include the socialist nations. This is why the projection of a new world order is ultimately bound to face what seems to me the crux of the whole matter: the *world institution*.

Certainly, the United Nations is not equipped to deal with problems of such a nature and magnitude. A new type of international institution is required: a world institution with the authority to plan, make decisions and enforce them.

This item is already on the agenda for it is organically linked with every step towards a new international order. Any agreement reached in the North-South negotiations will come up against the issue of enforcement. Suppose, for the sake of argument, that an agreement linking the prices of industrial goods with those of raw materials is concluded. How would it be enforced? Who will ensure that all the parties involved observe its provisions?

The real choice is between a world authority and the laws of the market. And by now everybody knows that the laws of the market systematically work in favor of the rich industrial nations. Sooner or later, a world authority will become a *must*.

North-South Dialogue: Concessions or Structural Change

Mahbub ul Haq

Real Objectives

I believe that a stage has been reached in the North-South dialogue where we must examine afresh the real objectives of the
Third World demand for a New International Economic Order and its
negotiating tactics to advance towards its goal. The initial
shouting is over. The process of negotiations has begun, though
haltingly. Now is the time for a sober examination of the issues.

What are the developing countries really seeking? Are they
seeking a few more concessions from the developed countries, a
few more crumbs from the table of the rich, a little more foreign
assistance, a few more trade preferences, a freer access to the
sophisticated technology of the developed world, a vain effort
to catch up with the life styles of the rich nations?

Or is the objective entirely different? Is this an effort to
graduate out of a relationship of hopeless dependency to a new
status of equal partnership and creative self-reliance? Is the
real aim the elimination of the systematic discrimination against
the poor nations in the international market system as organized
today? Do they seek fundamental changes in international institutions and power structures?

I firmly believe that the North-South dialogue must be clearly
focused on longer term structural changes, not on short term
financial concessions.

Parallel Between National and International Orders

The parallel here between national and international orders is
stark and obvious. Whenever there are major imbalances in economic and political power, economic growth and opportunities do
not filter down to the poor, either nationally or internationally. The remedy is not to put the poor on short term and uncertain
welfare schemes. It is to make economic opportunities available
to them so that they can improve their own productivity over the
longer run. It is not *ad hoc* concessions that the poorer members
of the society seek in such a situation: they demand progressive
taxation, land reforms, fundamental changes in patterns of ownership, and access to equal employment opportunities.

At the international level, it is no different. Evolution of a
new order will require a similar evolution of international
institutions as has already taken place at the national level -
including international taxation, an international central bank,
a global planning mechanism, and a new division of labour based
on greater equality and self-reliance of nations. All this is

probably three to four decades away, perhaps even longer. We
are merely at the threshold of the negotiations for a new order.
But let us not in our anxiety confuse long term structural changes with short term financial concessions. And let us quickly move
to adjust our basic perceptions, our negotiating agenda and our
principal tactics if the North-South dialogue is to stay on
course.

Basic Perceptions

Our perspective on the real essence of the New International
Economic Order must change. It is equality of opportunity we seek
in the Third World, not equality of income. We do not wish to
hijack the accumulated wealth of the rich nations. We instead
seek a chance to make it on our own, without systematic and organized discrimination against us in the international market structures.

It is an historic process we wish to initiate, not a single negotiation - for economic liberation of the poor masses can only be
regarded as a continuous movement, not a dramatic event. And we
recognize that most of the changes in this historic process lie
back home, in our own backyards. We do not wish to offer soft
options to our own national orders since equality of opportunity,
like charity, must begin at home.

And we reject the concept of "catching up", for it is futile for
the Third World to imitate the life styles of the rich nations.
Instead, we must devise new development strategies which meet our
own basic human needs within the framework of our own cultural
values, building development around people rather than people
around development.

And we reject the proposition that the new order is a one-way
street, of benefit only to the developing countries. If equal
partnership is the long term objective, not "concessions", then
both sides must gain or else it will become either exploitation
or dependency.

Negotiating Agenda and Tactics

Not only the basic concepts and perceptions, but the negotiating
agenda itself must change. It is a mistake to seek *ad hoc* increases in foreign assistance: what we must work for is a different
system of international resource transfers which converts the
periodic and unwilling generosity of the rich into an internationally accepted and monitorable responsibility and obligation and
which gradually introduces some elements of international taxation.

It is wrong to work for selective preferences on manufactured
goods: what we must seek is a freer international movement of
labour and goods, as the presently developed countries enjoyed in

the eighteenth and nineteenth centuries, since such free mobility
is the best guarantee for greater equality of opportunity and
since the present trade and immigration barriers deny Third World
nations the opportunity to earn at least $30-50 billion a year
more from the sweat of their own brows.

It is only of limited benefit to negotiate stabilization of commodity prices: what the Third World needs is much greater control
over the destiny of commodities, from the production to the processing and the distribution stage, so that it does not lose
almost $170 billion out of the final sales proceeds of $200 billion
from its twelve principal primary commodities to the international
middle men because of its own weak bargaining position.

Similarly, it is irrelevant to seek marginal changes in the voting power of existing international institutions: what is at
stake is a fuller participation in the management and control of
international decision-making structures.

If the basic perceptions about the new order and the international negotiating agenda are so recast, then the industrialized
nations and the Third World must resign themselves to sitting
around the negotiating table for a long time to come. Some quick
breakthroughs are always possible, especially if there is a
triumph of political statesmanship over short term vested interests. But economic and intellectual liberation - like political
independence - is likely to span many decades and consume several
generations.

The central issue in choosing the negotiating tactics is how soon
and how best the Third World can strengthen its countervailing
power. Of course, the first two essential requirements for this
are reforms of national orders and political unity within the
Third World. But the next practical step on this road is that the
Third World can begin to organize itself, without having to
wait upon the rich nations. There are many avenues open here. None
of them are easy. To illustrate just a few:

● The Third World itself can set up a commodity fund (with $10-20
million from each member and more from oil producing countries).
This fund can be used to take selected initiatives in international commodity trade wherever the developing countries are at
present losing out because of their weak bargaining position;

● The food-deficit countries of the Middle East at present importing over 5 million tons of foodgrains annually can enter into a
bargain with those countries in the Third World which have enormous potential to increase foodgrain production: the former can
exchange some of their present surplus liquidity for future food
imports from the latter;

• The oil-surplus countries can consider establishing a monetary zone of their own, both to protect the real value of their assets and to invest some of the surpluses in the future of other developing countries;

• The Third World can establish its own substantive secretariats and intellectual forums to provide the background thinking for, and continuity to, their international dialogue.

These are not steps towards an eventual confrontation with the rich nations. Such actions are necessary to demonstrate the determination of the Third World to establish a new order and to provide at least the minimum of organization and power needed to change the old order.

I am convinced, therefore, that the Third World must pause a little in the midst of its present negotiations and take some time out to organize a South-South dialogue. This will help clarify the basic issues and the negotiating strategy which are currently in great danger of dissolving into a series of small negotiations on isolated items in diverse forums.

Focus on Ends or Means
I also believe that too much time and effort have been devoted in the first stages of the North-South dialogue to the means, rather than to the ends of this dialogue. This is not surprising. The same thing happened when national economic development was taken up as a battle cry. Too much attention was devoted to the growth of the Gross National Product (GNP), too little to the removal of poverty or to the meeting of basic human needs. Only recently is the balance beginning to be redressed and we are proceeding from the ultimate objectives (basic needs) to the intermediate means (growth).

The preoccupation in the North-South dialogue so far has been with the means - increase in ODA, debt relief, commodity price stabilization, technology transfer, codes of conduct for multi-nationals, etc. These means must be viewed in the perspective of the ultimate objective, both to examine their relevance and to establish their order of priority.

What are the long term objectives of the two sides? The Third World obviously desires the abolition of mass poverty in the shortest possible time, to meet the basic human needs of all of its population, to ensure accelerated and equitable world economic development, to seek equality of opportunity nationally and internationally, and to be able to participate in decisions regarding the future of a world where it is an expanding majority.

The developed countries - whatever broader aims they may have for

a peaceful world - also desire an orderly rate of economic
growth and employment for their citizens, unmarred by inter-
ruptions in the supply of key raw materials or lack of demand
for their output.

Areas of Mutual Interest

Are these objectives reconcilable? I believe they are. In fact,
without the accelerated development of the Third World, the industrialized nations' prospects for obtaining key supplies, or
expanding markets for their durable goods, or establishing an
environment of world peace, may be seriously threatened. And
without the continued growth of the industrialized nations, the
prospects for international capital or technology transfers and
the demand for the exports of the Third World may be adversely
affected. In the long run, advance towards a new international
order is not only in the interests of the poor nations but would
also serve the enlightened self-interest of the rich nations.

Then why this resistance from the rich nations to the demand
for a New International Economic Order? Simply because it does
involve an adjustment in the international balance of power -
however skillfully worded, however gently negotiated, however
gradually introduced, however carefully camouflaged. And it
involves a short term cost, even though the long term benefits
may more than compensate for it.

When the New Deal was introduced in the United States in the
1930s by President Roosevelt, elevating the labouring classes
to partners in development and making them an essential part
of the consumer society, many in American corporate management
circles thought at that time that it marked the demise of capitalism and that President Roosevelt was a raving maniac. Yet
forty years later, it can be analysed calmly as a visionary
move which probably saved capitalism though it also changed
its very character.

This is the essential dilemma. How to reassure the present generations in the rich nations which will inevitably have to give
up some power and a few of their privileges, at least in the
short run, so that a new partnership for development, a new environment for peace, may emerge over the long run? Who will play
the role of President Roosevelt internationally? Where are the
sources of leadership? Where are the international intellectual
lobbies?

The best appeal may well be an appeal to history. Economic liberation of the developing countries will come just as surely as
their political liberation has, but tactical necessities may
force many compromises on the trade union of the poor nations. We
are familiar with the ebb and flow of these events from our movements of political liberation. But principles should dictate

tactics; tactics should never distort principles. We must reject the strategy of seeking various "concessions", as it sym-
bolizes the extension of the old order. We must work for equality of opportunity, domestically and internationally, and participation in decision-making. This is what will make it a new
order. It is often difficult to keep these distinctions clear in
the heat of the battle. But it is absolutely imperative that we
do so.

The Dilemma of Our Time

Fereydoun Hoveyda

A Crisis of Structures

The bold explorer of the problems of our time who is lucky enough
to escape sound in mind and body from the proliferating jungle
of political and economic writings is caught on the horns of a
curious dilemma. On the one hand, everyone knows, to a greater
or lesser extent, what is wrong and what should be done. On the
other hand, no one thinks of taking the measures required. I
intend here to try and answer the two questions which naturally
arise in the face of this dilemma: how we can explain this contradiction and how can we resolve it?

It is generally recognized that the economic order which has
ruled us for a long time is ill-suited to the present needs of
our world. From the beginning of this decade, a certain number
of symptoms have accumulated that prove it.

First of all, the failure of the First Development Decade (1960-
1970) initiated by the United Nations left the Third World in a
disquieting state of underdevelopment. Far from closing, the
gap between the industrialized and the other countries widened
alarmingly. The developed world after experiencing an unparalleled period of rapid growth following the Second World War went
into a recession comparable in extent to that of the '30s. At
the same time, there was growing almost universal realization of
the limit to natural resources and the deterioration in the
quality of the environment. Finally, the oil producing countries,
on whom abnormally low prices had been imposed by their western
customers, at last reacted to preserve their patrimony.

It was against this background that the need for a New International Economic Order took shape in 1974 and 1975 after the
Sixth and Seventh Special Sessions of the United Nations General
Assembly. The very abundance of literature on the subject
relieves me of the need to labor the point here. It is enough
by way of illustration to quote a passage from the excellent
report drawn up under the guidance of Jan Tinbergen (Reshaping
the International Order - RIO).

"The inequities in the international system are of tremendous
significance. They have given rise to essentially two worlds
and the disparities between them are growing. One is the world
of the rich, the other the world of the poor, united by its
heritage of common suffering. A poverty curtain divides the
worlds materially and philosophically. One world is literate,
the other largely illiterate; one industrial and urban, the
other predominantly agrarian and rural; one consumption
oriented, the other striving for survival. In the rich world

39

there is concern about the quality of life, in the poor world about life itself which is threatened by disease, hunger and malnutrition...

"Both the rich and poor worlds have pressing, unparalleled problems. They are not separate; they cannot be solved independently. Mankind's predicament is rooted in its past, in the economic and social structures that have emerged within and between nations. The present crisis, in the world economy and in the relations between nations, is a crisis of international structures. What both worlds must come to grips with is basically a sick system which cannot be healed by expeditious economic first aid. Marginal changes will not be sufficient. What is required are fundamental institutional reforms, based upon a recognition of a common interest and mutual concern, in an increasingly interdependent world. What is required is a new international order in which all benefit from change."

The Tinbergen report also contains detailed proposals for remedying the current situation. Many of these proposals have been the subject of heated debate during the eighteen months of the "North-South" dialogue within the framework of the Paris Conference on International Economic Cooperation. After an enthusiastic beginning, the conference closed on a pessimistic note with no agreement on the corrective measures to be applied.

Rearguard Action and Protectionist Decisions
In truth, it is not the Third World that is holding back. The developing countries ask no massive redistribution of the advantages and wealth acquired by the industrialized nations. They seek neither charity nor equal incomes. What they look for is only "equality of opportunity" and their rightful share in future growth. The co-president of the Paris Conference, Mr. Perez Guerrero, put it as follows at the resumed thirty-first session of the United Nations General Assembly in September 1977:

"We, the countries of the Third World, are aware that the major responsibility for our development lies with us, and that national, regional and interregional efforts - the so-called "collective self-confidence" - are basic and essential. But we are also aware, as we must all be, that without a process of deliberate transformation in international economic relations, developing countries cannot make sufficient, self-sustaining progress.....

"Our interdependence, which has become clear to all and which we wish to organize, must be based on a lesser disparity of forces between the various sectors of the international community. This is the only way to make the concept of interdependence compatible with the concept of the greater economic independence of the developing countries. We wish not only to be masters of our own destiny but also to participate effectively in decision-making at the international level."

The question then arises of why the "rich" of our world are fighting a rearguard action to delay the entry into operation of machinery for a new international order. The answer may be perhaps summed up in the famous saying of William Pitt to the British Parliament in 1774: "We will never tolerate the American colonies producing manufactures which would be in competition with those we produce on our own soil."

Yet America has become the greatest industrial power in the world and colonialism is surely on the way out. But the state of mind reflected in Pitt's statement has not entirely disappeared. We may see it in all protectionist decisions taken by the industrialized countries against each other and against the Third World. Its spectre looms in the trade policies of the rich countries. Its influence can be perceived whenever the transfer of technology is discussed. There was more than a faint echo of it in Henry Kissinger's statement in November 1976, to the American National Congress of Science, Technology and Global Development. He observed that "What we need is a global concept which would answer questions such as: what technology is it in our interest to transfer? How should the transfers be carried out so that the developing countries can benefit from them without the industrialized countries being penalized?..."

The fact is that competition between industrialized countries is multiplied by competition from the Third World. By way of illustration one can recall the situation prevailing a few years ago in the field of textiles - the rivalry between Japan and the USA and Japan and Europe. One can also recall the situation in the shoe industry or the ongoing competition between the developed and developing countries in textiles and many other fields. Accordingly, the entry into the market for iron and steel products of new producers, particularly from the developing countries, has brought about serious overproduction just when demand is stagnating at a very low level. And this crisis will not stop at steel: the race for industrialization pretty well everywhere will not fail to produce new bottlenecks in the industrialized world. The new producers, in whatever field it may be, will be forced to look for outlets for their products. On the other hand, the processing of raw materials is tending increasingly to be carried out on the spot. And sophisticated technology is being more and more speedily transferred. No quota system, no protectionist trade policy can halt the inexorable march of history. There can be no doubt that the situation in the Third World cannot be improved under present circumstances without affecting the privileged position of the advanced countries.

The least that can be said is that we are heading for unpreced-

ented world disorder which the industrialized countries,
whether they have a market economy or not, will be the first to
feel. Not only is the crisis not over; it is likely to reach
disastrous proportions, which will make the events of the 30s
look like a mere molehill. In these circumstances, the "rich"
have even more to gain than the "poor" from promoting the
establishment of a new economic order. However, the ups and
downs of the world economy take them in quite the opposite
direction; they seek to shelter in the wreckage of the old
order, and are content to plaster over the cracks of a doomed
system.

Public Opinion in the Industrialized Countries

Clearly, there are economic and political motivations behind
such an attitude. I have already mentioned the "protectionist"
mentality which still pervades the industrialized world. In
addition, a reform that aims at achieving a "modest and balanced
type of society" (Sicco Mansholt) is scarcely likely to win
votes in consumer-oriented societies. More than ever before, the
"short-run" is taking precedence over the "long-run". The truth
is that public opinion in the advanced countries is for the
most part unaware of the reality of the economic problems of
today's world.

The man in the street lives through change without gaining a
clear perception of its scope and extent. From time to time,
he is frightened with the spectre of overpopulation or the continual rise in cost of energy. When it is necessary to cope with
the most urgent needs of the developing countries, an appeal is
made to his compassion instead of making clear the inescapable
requirement for this transfer of wealth. No one dares tell him
openly that sooner or later he will have to reduce his consumption, that is, lower his "standard of living". This does not
mean going back to an economy of want, but simply calls for a
more "reasonable" attitude which excludes waste and carelessness.
However, everything is made to look as though an effort was
being made to force him to accept a more limited way of life,
without his consent.

In international bodies, the representatives of the industrialized countries constantly bring up the difficulty of convincing
their parliaments and public opinion at home of the need to
grant large scale concessions to the Third World. Although the
representatives of the developing countries show understanding
of the difficulties of their privileged partners, this cannot
serve to make them overlook the pressing problems assailing
them on all sides. If this dialogue of the deaf continues, mankind will be condemned to go round in a vicious circle for many
long years. A vast information campaign is urgently needed. It
involves nothing less than bringing the word "interdependence"
from the conceptual level to the level of contemporary fact.

The Responsibility of Economists

The responsibility of the economists is quite clear. After their earlier optimism, their pessimism of today leaves the public completely at a loss. Inflation is not only monetary. It is also verbal: the man in the street is drowning in a rising sea of contradictory positions. Galbraith of course likes to say that you should never trust the forecasts of economists. It is none-theless true that they are behind the decisions, right or wrong, taken by all governments. Their mistake, in my opinion, lies in the fact that, by seeking to make an exact science of their discipline, they have cut adrift from reality. Hardly ten years of "stagflation" have left little of the theories of Keynes or of Marx. Today's economists seem powerless to produce formulas against the disorders which are overwhelming "rich" and "poor" alike. Shall we not smile on seeing the Swedish Academy grant the 1977 Nobel Prize to Professors Bertil Ohlin and James Meade for their "pathbreaking contributions to the theory of inter-national capital movements" in a world where trade and capital movements in no way meet mankind's needs and even bring on dis-order? What use have complex mathematical models been in econo-mic reality?

I am certainly not casting doubt upon the value of the work of today's economists nor on the need for further research. All I am saying is that ever higher specialization in the various aspects of economic science takes the experts farther away from everyday reality. The divorce of theory and practice no doubt began before our time. But now when a clear explanantion is needed of the kind of effort required to set up a more equitable order for all, each day seems to see the economists further removed from taking on that task. They delight instead in building "models which reassure the mind as it watches them function *in vitro* but which leave one non-plussed when it comes to going into action"(Pierre Drouin). And when they must deal with real problems, they are usually content to find scapegoats to blame, as witness the case of inflation and the price of oil. It is as if economic theory were doing its utmost to set up a screen between ordinary people and the practical problems besetting them.

Indeed, the vast mass of specialized commentaries risk concealing totally from our view what is at stake in the New International Economic Order itself. Certainly, only the experts can draw up the measures which will make this new order a reality, but it will be the ordinary people who will have to bear the cost. And it is no use to go on trying to hide from them the sacrifices (albeit relative) which they must make.

The Way Ahead

I think that the "North-South" dialogue must continue at every possible level. In fact it is going ahead in the United Nations,

in the International Monetary Fund and in bilateral and multilateral relations between States. Slow progress is being made
and will continue. But such progress will be minute if nothing
more is done. Our side continues to deplore the lack of "political will" among the industrialized countries. I think that here
again we are talking in the abstract. The political will of a
government is nothing if not the consent of the people it
governs.

Now, observing the reactions of the taxpayers, one cannot help
noticing a certain reticence when it comes to the fundamental
issues of the transfer of "wealth" or the "international division
of labor". What in France in the 60s was called *cartierisme* is
a general feature of the industrialized countries. Even though
selfishness is characteristic of the individual, this does not
excuse inaction! And if the leaders in the rich countries have
difficulty in overcoming the hesitations of their public opinion,
why should we not think about how we might help them? An international information and education program does not seem to me
to be especially out of place.

The Tinbergen report ends with the following words:

"The past few decades have brought prosperity to some nations
and a complex array of problems to all. They have brought the
need to question many of the values, ideas and concepts upon
which the relationships between and within nations have been
forged. They have linked nations in a complex network of interdependence from which no nation, however powerful, can realisti-
cally exclude itself. They have placed mankind on the threshold
of new choices and opportunities and exposed it to unprecedented
dangers.

"The purpose of this report is to sketch the kind of evolution
in human institutions which could best ensure greater equality
of opportunity between people and nations. This is a challenge
for the entire human race. We can only hope that we, as individuals and as nations, have the wisdom, the courage and the fore-
sight to meet this supreme challenge."

We must take up this formidable challenge before us and work
quickly and thoroughly towards implementing the measures which
will make a reality of the New International Economic Order. The
continued "North-South" dialogue cannot and must not preclude
action. Otherwise we shall manage only to worsen the dilemma I
referred to at the beginning of this statement. One thing peculiar to dilemmas is that they cannot perpetuate themselves.
Sooner or later they break down under the very weight of those
trapped on their horns. We have all the necessary elements to
get out of the situation without too much upheaval. It is no
longer a case of looking to see who is responsible for prevail-

ing injustices. We may not be able to forget the past, but we must put it aside in order to get down to the problems of the present and the future.

If we do not make a clearsighted and serious start along this road, we risk being engulfed in apocalyptic chaos.

An Assessment of Prospects in the Light of Recent Experience

Idriss Jazairy

Introduction

The issue relating to the establishment of the New International Order has finally come to a head through a long process of trial and error, of stress in the face of indifference, of hope and despondence over the quarter century following the end of the recovery from World War II.

Although the foundations of the New International Order were laid at the Cairo Conference of the Non-Aligned Countries in July 1962 and embodied in the principles governing international trade and policies conducive to development adopted by UNCTAD I in 1964, they remained of no avail until the time that the developing countries took the matter in their own hands by deciding to exercise their sovereign right over their natural resources. It was only then that the 'new order' was re-discovered and made the headlines. There ensued a flurry of grand international conferences, starting with the Sixth Special Session of the General Assembly of the United Nations and apparently ending with the Paris Conference on International Economic Cooperation. Self-righteousness and self-satisfaction coupled with rising concern over inflation and unemployment in the industrialized world then weakened the thrust of the dialogue, which receded into the doldrums of unending negotiations on 'implementation'.

Assessments of the international picture were nevertheless blurred by what has unfortunately come to be an emotional rather than a common sense issue. Thus, while the co-chairman of the group of eight developed countries in the North-South dialogue declared that "never has any international conference in the world done so much for developing countries", developing countries were trying to remain "cautiously optimistic" concerning future prospects so as to avoid being accused of being responsible for the stalemate which was obvious to all. Such a recognition was clearly contained in the blunt statement of the Director General of FAO at the opening of its 19th General Conference. The New International Order, this high international official observed, is progressing at the pace of a tortoise. This indeed seems to be a fair assessment of present trends. It might even be considered an understatement. While the prospects of an early recovery are dimmed by double-digit inflation and close to double-digit unemployment in the industrialized countries, the developing countries remain deeply affected by the monetary turmoil and are encountering record deficits in their balance of trade. Even the purchasing power of oil producing countries is now on the wane. It is thus abundantly clear that the present international non-system is sparing no one and that the world's economic horizon has not been so dark since the great depression of the thirties.

In order to get the process of development moving forward again at a proper pace and to achieve a minimum degree of stability, the goals of international development action should be reexamined. At the same time, the responsibilities incumbent on both the developing countries and the international community as a whole should be redefined.

Redefining the Goals of International Development Action

The goals of international development action should be redefined in the face of endeavours to "recycle" development concepts to make them subservient to the vested interests prevailing under the old order.

The New International Order implies a continuous process rather than an act to be accomplished in a predetermined period of time. It thus requires the organization of a permanent solidarity based on the complementarity and mutuality of interests among the partners involved in its construction. Today, none dare to openly defend the old order, even when it is invoked in the name of "natural" economic laws. Where, after all, is the "invisible hand" of Adam Smith in a world in which transnational enterprises control more than 20 percent of world G.N.P. and may well control more than 40 percent in 10 years time; where 300 such enterprises are responsible for 30 percent of global exports, of which 50 percent of the sales of primary products? Is not the characteristic of these enterprises precisely to be in a position to control the mechanisms of price inflation at the international level and, thus, to substitute themselves for the "invisible hand"?

How much longer will transnational enterprises be allowed to remain in an international legal no man's land? To be allowed not only to appropriate the riches of the Third World but also - because they constitute a global challenge - to vitually ignore the democratic control of their activities by the citizens of the rich countries? Is not one-third of the trade between the rich countries accounted for by the internal transactions of transnational enterprises? And what does the so-called invasion of cheap products of developing countries into the industrialized world amount to if not to a penetration of new markets by the same Western transnationals from their bases in Hong Kong, Singapore and elsewhere?

The old order is in reality not only unfair; it has also shown itself to be inefficient in safeguarding the interests of the industrialized countries as well as the developing countries. It is only recently, however, that the weaknesses and the dangers of the existing institutional structure have been recognized by its Western architects. This recognition has not been engendered by the fact that the present system has resulted in the continued impoverishment of the majority of mankind for the benefit of a privileged minority. Nor has it been brought about by the moneta-

ry reserves – the main cause of the unprecedented rates of inflation experienced in recent years. Clear awareness only emerged
after certain producers of raw materials sought to control the
production of their principal source of subsistance: oil, and
to readjust its price to the evolution of the prices of the products they imported. Thus, lumping cause and effect together,
most developed countries dubbed the world crisis – the crisis
arising from their own excesses – the "oil crisis". It was only
then that voices started to make themselves heard in the industrialized countries which, in the name of the growing interdependence
between States, appealed to international solidarity for development. This appeal could not fail to raise legitimate suspicions.

For was it not in the name of solidarity for development that the
refurbishing of an obsolete, unjust and inefficient order was
pursued for a quarter of a century? What have the two Development
Decades, solemnly proclaimed by the international community,
brought about if not the mere demobilization of the rich countries
and the bitter disappointment of the poor?

Did not the moment chosen to launch this appeal to human solidarity contribute to giving it too strong a smell of oil? It is,
therefore, necessary to throw light on the proclaimed goals of
development and on its real contents.

Has not the notion of international cooperation at a time of crisis
been put forward by the industrialized countries to preserve the
status quo and to avoid disturbing the course of "spaceship earth",
which they command? Thus, when the interests of these countries
seem to be at stake, this nobel sentiment is used as an alibi
designed to prevent the critical examination of the present system
and its structures of exploitation.

The solutions proposed to the opponents of the established order
are thus limited to an offer of integration into the traditional
circuits of the world economy. Not only their assets but also they
themselves are to be recycled so as to consolidate the established
order.

The offer made to certain oil-producing countries to increase
their participation in certain international financial mechanisms
and the invitation extended to join the restricted clubs within
which the great powers elaborate their strategies and define their
respective roles, seem to have no other aim. Such also appears the
case as regards the claim of the industrialized countries to the
liquid assets of the surplus developing countries. The latter are
compelled to freeze an important percentage of their surpluses in
long term deposits which are difficult to mobilize, and the interest which accrues is tied to procurements from the rich countries
which receive the funds. Thus, the industrialized countries accu-
mulate new means of applying pressure designed to ensure that the

oil-producing countries tow the line espoused by the industrial centres. The divergence of views within OPEC concerning oil prices - differences which fortunately tend to be overcome - are only one of the side-effects of this policy. The purchasing power of oil has, however, dropped by one half since 1974 and this can be considered no mere coincidence.

Facts bear out the short-lived character of this proclaimed solidarity. The consensus which was painfully achieved at the end of the Seventh Special Session of the General Assembly is in the process of being dissolved, as is borne out by the recent Conference on International Economic Cooperation, by the turn of events at UNCTAD, and in specialized conferences. Is not the reason for this to be found in the fact that the most powerful Western economies, having absorbed the oil price rise and recycled the increased added value in their own direction, seem to believe that the recession is over and that a call for solidarity, in the name of which they might have to make concessions, can therefore serve no purpose? On the contrary, the interests concerned have regained their self-confidence and are now in the process of reconquering the strongholds which they were compelled to abandon at the height of the crisis.

Nevertheless, development cannot remain tantamount to a policy of indiscriminate growth leading to the prosperity of an *élite*. Nor can the "trickle-down effect" result in an improvement in the well-being and welfare of the large masses of poor. History has rejected these false pretences; they are but a veil barely able to conceal the deep selfishness which inspires them. Development implies a genuine historical discontinuity, a break with the former political and social framework. It implies a recasting of the power structure and a reorientation of its impulses at the level of the planet. Thus construed as the launching of a historical process, development cannot be reduced to a matter of give-and-take within the context of a collective bargaining process.

It follows that the appropriate answer to the question "towards what purpose should this solidarity be directed?" can only be "to build a new society through the efforts of the peoples of the world and in their own benefit with a view to enabling them to achieve another development"; a development whose ultimate goal is man and which fits in a global and all-embracing view of economic, social and human factors; a development which aims at economic and social equity and efficiency, in which economic and international aspects are not the only ones to be given consideration; a development intent on meeting the basic needs of the great masses, whether it be survival, peace or self-fulfillment through the exercise of the right to education, adequate nutrition, health and housing. Whilst dealing with the most extreme cases of poverty, the proposed action should also aim at elimi-

nating the most obvious sources of waste. This strategy, it must
be stressed, should not preclude but rather encourage the active
search for a constant improvement in living-standards through a
genuine industrialization process established on a competitive
basis.

The new distribution of productive activities in the world, which
must be aimed at, should be based on an equitable sharing of the
value-added arising from world industrial activity and not on
biased or static interpretations of the concept of comparative
advantage as a guide to so-called international specialization.
In the light of such interpretations, industrialized countries
would withhold for themselves the field of production related to
high technology industries with sizeable value-added, while rede-
ploying over the rest of the world those industries which are
based on the exploitation of cheap labour or on the pollution of
the environment. It should be clear, however, that the Third
World does not intend to remain, or to become, a dirt- or tax-
haven or a manpower reserve for transnational enterprises.

The new international redeployment of industry will, however,
be "progress" oriented if, by favouring imported technology based
on science, it leads to a disregard for technology based on
observation from which the former originally emanated. This would
lead to the underrating of the creative genius of the peoples of
the Third World, and hence to a more rapid integration of their
newly created production sectors into the main foreign industrial
centres rather than in their own internal environment, a process
leading to new forms of dependency and not to economic liberation.

Indeed, the path to be followed should preclude any notion of
"de-focusing" sovereignty, as would be the case under the new as
well as the old forms of dependency, of which elitist forms of
organization are invariably a corollary. This path should lay due
emphasis on the principle of introverted, self-reliant development, which implies making the most of local resources, human,
economic and natural. Hence, it is the duty of the international
community to ensure a participatory and harmonious development
as between different regions and different countries. This development should meet the requirements of solidarity not only in
space but also over time: in view of the rate of increase of the
world population, which is to double by the end of the century,
the problem of the conservation of non-renewable resources and
of the protection of the global eco-system are most acute. In
this connection it should be kept in mind that only through a
genuine improvement in overall living-standards can one set the
preconditions for an effective population planning policy. Any
isolated attempt at curbing birthrates, as is most often the case
under the present "order", is bound to be to no avail.

Finally development should lead to an order which is at one and the same time economically and socially efficient, equitable and long-lasting.

In short, the approach should be global and include fundamental choices pertaining to the management of world interdependency as well as to the rules required to implement it objectively. It bears the name of "The New Order". It is unfortunate that some, being more concerned with one or other of its many facets, have coined the concepts of a so-called new social or cultural order or a new order in the field of information or the like.

Likewise, the New International Order is referred to at times without any reference to internal orders as if it did not emanate from the will of the peoples who have outlined, through their respective struggles, the directions of the New Order, States having but to negotiate thereafter its implications at the international level. At times also, when the internal order is mentioned as a precondition, it is only intended to apply to the Third World so as to free developed countries from their commitment to international solidarity.

The global and integrating character of the New Order tends to be weakened by such fragmentary approaches. These lead to piecemeal bargaining rather than to global strategies. Alternatively, they may be designed to play down the problems arising from the lack of internal systems conducive to development. Yet the concepts of justice, of emancipation and of economic and social promotion are indivisible at both the world and the national level.

Never has the international community been so concerned with its collective future than in recent years. The debate around the New International Order, advocated by President Boumedienne from the rostrum of the United Nations General Assembly, has broken loose from its traditional sanctuary of bilateral and multilateral diplomacy. It has come to be the concern of world public opinion. The term has sparked off the will for change, so long suppressed, moblized efforts and served as a banner under which have rallied the forces in favour of change in the world.

Third World Responsibilities and Solidarity

The responsibiliteis incumbent upon the Third World can only be successfully discharged if its component parts are tied by bounds of mutual solidarity in its common struggle.

The goal of self-reliance is none other than to foster, at the level of the Third World, new bonds of solidarity on definite issues or on the international projections of a global design subservient to the rights of peoples and to their deeprooted aspirations. It is through concerted and coordinated action that countries of the Third World will succeed in "internalizing" their sovereignty and cease deserving to be referred to as the "periphery" of the main industrial centres.

This of course implies, as a prerequisite, that such self-reliant effort be based on national systems which do not rest on relationships of exploitation. Otherwise, the fruit to be reaped from the common endeavour would only consolidate the national elites and thus prevent the country concerned from moving out of the orbit of the great powers. Such a process would unavoidably cancel out the effects of the joint action directed towards the developed world.

What would be the meaning of an approach aimed at serving the cause of greater justice in world relations when the solidarity between "fellows-of-arms" of the Third World is not based within each country on genuine solidarity between different socio-professional strata? This implies full participation of the masses in the development process. Indeed, the aforementioned approach can only be the external projection and expression of this internal solidarity.

Achievements in the field of collective self-reliance between countries of the Third World are progressing in spite of the renewed tension resulting from the recent endeavours of those committed to the old order to destabilize progressive regimes, particularly in Africa, and to check moves towards regional or subregional groupings in that continent. Intensified efforts are aimed at promoting joint thinking to fight the homogenization of values, of cultures, of models of development, of consumption, and of man himself. The thinking of developing countries, which should be autonomous, should discard patterns of analysis presented as dogmas by some economists who have made their conceptual capacities subservient to prevailing interests. Its aim should be to provide a doctrinal replica to the permanent ideological agression to which the mind of the man of the Third World is exposed.

The developing world must, therefore, seek to contribute to the elaboration of a new substratum of concepts and to the mobilization of a planning and research capacity aimed at enabling it to bring its intellectual tools up to date. The proposed approach should reject both the theories of integration of the Third World in the world market, or its total extroversion, and the theories of a paralyzing nihilism which stress the impossiblility of ever achieving a compromise, be it tactical, with the developed world and therefore advocate isolation or World Revolution. Rather than being an ex-post rationalization, this effort at joint thinking should tend to underscore action. It is in the name of this body of doctrine that one finds an increasing number of developing countries opposing exclusive relations with former colonial powers, challenging their exclusion from the main currents of science, technology and world trade, questioning their isolation from other developing or friendly countries, denouncing a world monetary and financial system subjected to the domineering arbitrariness of a reserve currency and, in general, a whole set of institutions imposed by the great powers at a time in which the Third World was all but absent politically from the world scene.

The solidarity of the developing countries in their struggle has developed year by year since its inception in the early sixties. What was initially a list of isolated claims was gradually integrated by the "Seventy-seven" into a strategy of action moving from the Charter of Algiers in 1967 to that of Manila in 1976. But a breakthrough was undeniably achieved through the determined action of OPEC following the 4th Non-Aligned Summit in Algiers (1973). This gave teeth to the pronouncements of the Third World and opened the way for the North-South dialogue. The latter would have been inconceivable in previous times.

The unity of the developing world was further enhanced by the OPEC Summit in Algiers of March 1975 which was followed by a sharp up-turn in the trend of financial assistance to other Third World countries. The following year, the 5th Non-Aligned Summit in Colombo devised the tools required to materialize the unity of, and provide collective economic security to, the members of the Group. Furthermore, the First Arab-African Summit, which met in March 1977 in Cairo, expressed its determination to give to the concept of solidarity an all-embracing meaning covering political, economic as well as cultural issues, and to make it the backbone of the long term strategy of the countries of the enlarged region.

The cardinal task of the Third World is now to keep up the momentum in the face of rising opposition from vested interests tied to the old order. The Arab-African summit did succeed in effectively proving, for a time at least, that the Third World could not be readily opposed to a so-called Fourth World, thus bringing out the ulterior motives of some advocates of this thesis. Furthermore, manoeuvres aimed at cutting off the oil exporting countries from their natural base, which is the rest of the developing world, have been defeated. Attempts at stirring antagonism between them by stretching economic data to give scientific weight to biased presentations of facts inverting the causal relations between world inflation and oil prices, were of limited impact since the prices of equipment imported by OPEC rocketed to reach a level four times higher in 1977 than in 1973, while a substantial drop in real terms in the price of oil was recorded over the same period. Even the divisive tactics applied by some advanced countries within OPEC, making bilateral arms deals or other commitments conditional upon positions adopted by some members of OPEC, have not yet succeeded in "breaking the back" of this organization. It is likewise to be hoped that the developing world will reject its division into two blocks: the coastal States on the one hand and the landlocked and geographically disadvantaged States

on the other. Without such rejection they will become mere pawns
in the hands of the main protagonists intent on sharing the
ocean resources between themselves.

More disquieting still are the loci of political tension which
are being kindled in the Third World, and in particular on the
Eastern, Southern and Western flank of the African continent,
for it is clear that they will be used as a stepping stone to
re-impose outside control over its resources.

Third World Solidarity and International Cooperation

*Solidarity within the Third World does not preclude but rather
should fit into a broader framework of effective international
cooperation.*

The unity between "fellows-of-arms" of the Third World implies
a joint struggle directed not, it should be stressed, against the
people in the developed world, but rather against a system of
exploitation which puts two-thirds of the world's population on
the fringe of humanity. It follows that harmonious global development can only result from cooperation between equal partners,
which is the most elaborate form of dialogue. Nor does the
latter preclude struggle, for struggle and dialogue are part of
the same dialectical process.

The purpose of the struggle is to identify all forms of shallow
solidarity whereby the advocates of the established order only
aspire to change insofar as it enables them to keep matters under
full control; who seek to improve the present order through
recourse to tactical solidarity in times of crisis. Yet it follows
from the Sixth Special Session that the genuine interdependency
then proclaimed has implications which cannot be derived and
applied unilaterally. Nor can it simply be taken to mean an integration of the poor countries into an order based on mechanisms
which lead to the impoverishment of the Third World in order to
assure the perpetuation of hegemonic positions.

It is therefore only through the resolute struggle of the forces
of progress in the world - the success of which depends as much
on the mobilization of Third World energies as on the emergence
of new forces in developed countries - that the rich countries
will draw the unavoidable conclusions with respect to cooperation
and to their own dependence on the resources and potential of
economic areas previously considered by them as being under their
influence.

In this way the concept of solidarity will be extended to cover
all States, including those which have remained, de facto if not
de jure, pawns rather than actors on the world scene.

The questions, then, which arise are the following:

• whether we think in terms of solidarity between the "civilized nations", as hallowed by nineteenth-century international law which conferred on a minority of privileged nations the right to regulate their own as well as the freedom of others;
• whether we think in terms of solidarity between big powers in a bi-polar world, as it took shape after the Yalta agreements;
• whether we think in terms of a banding together of the "haves" to face the rising tide of claims proffered by a world which has only just started to exist in world conscience; or
• whether the experience jointly acquired in the course of recent years and the shock resulting from OPEC's determination to obtain a fairer share of the value derived from its main resource, may now lead humanity to the only form of cooperation compatible with genuine development: a cooperation between peace-loving countries, including the strong as well as the weak. This may ultimately develop to arouse a sense of solidarity between the peoples of the world to which the United Nations had appealed more than 30 years ago but which, because of the egoism and short-sightedness of the great powers, remains unanswered.

Disregarding the concept of cooperation between "assisted" and industrialized nations, the Third World has fought to gain recognition for a form of cooperation more consonant with its dignity and which has to do with the principle of duality of norms, of compensatory discrimination as proclaimed by the Lomé agreements, even if there is an obvious hiatus between proclaimed principles and adopted mechanisms of implementation.

But this is only a transitional stage. One will have then to work for a new stage, by-passing that of redistribution and of stabilization of incomes, leading to the equalization of opportunities for all the members of the international community. Once the policy aimed at redressing inequalities has attained its goals, the way will be opened to the establishment of bonds of solidarity between equal partners, and thus to a democratic participation of all States concerned in international negotiations and decision-making.

Unless the concept of cooperation is revised one can hardly feel responsive to the exhortations of those who feel qualified to defend a free and united world while believing that democracy is compatible at the international level with the tyranny of a minority exercised through weighted voting (replacement of the principle "one Nation, one vote" by the principle "one dollar, one vote"), through the right of veto, through *diktats* which restricted clubs of rich countries seek to impose on the world, or through sectoral condominium, as is the case with nuclear and disarmament issues. Those who adopt such positions are ill-placed to oppose what they refer to as the tyranny of the majority, which is not more than the transposition at the international level of the principle "one man, one vote". And yet it must be clear that the Third World is by no means a third block attempting to impose its views on its partners. This was clearly demonstrated at the North-

South Conference when the South accepted parity-representation with the North.

The test of the real desire of the big powers for democratization will lie in the position they will adopt concerning the future framework into which the components of the New Order will fit and, in particular, in the thrust which will be given to the Plenary Committee established for this purpose by the 32nd session of the U.N. General Assembly.

Democratization also implies the full participation of the developed socialist countries in the new institutional arrangements. These countries have an invaluable contribution to make at the conceptual and at the material level in view of the far-reaching experience they have acquired in the field of accelerated development. Quite rightly international cooperation should first aim at redressing the injustices of colonial and neo-colonial exploitation. But it must transcend this stage and become truly universal solidarity. In this connection OPEC countries, and in particular Arab countries, which were formerly colonized and not colonizers, have demonstrated a concrete proof of their solidarity with more disprivileged countries.

In the name of such genuine cooperation between equal partners, each country, or group of countries, will have to give as well as to take without attempting to balance its sacrifices by its gains at every point of time. For this form of cooperation draws the dynamism conducive to its perpetual renovation from the political will of its proponents. In this concern, the governments of the industrialized countries would give impetus to the New Order by fully accepting their responsibilities rather than hiding behind the fiction of non-interference in the activities of their enterprises. One might thus ensure, with the support of the Third World, that the world economy be governed by objective rules, the enforcement of which would be jointly controlled and sanctioned, whether through sectoral codes of conduct concerning transnational enterprises, or codes pertaining to technology transfer or to debt rescheduling.

This united approach to development could also materialize in the context of the concept of the "common heritage of mankind" as applied to oceans, outer space, knowledge, culture and to global ecosystems. Unfortunately, this concept has recently been used as a device to legalize attempts to deprive unilaterally the developing countries of their dearly-acquired sovereignty over their natural resources.

In this grand developmental design, the big powers need not necessarily lead the game. In many cases enlightened self-interest would draw medium and smaller developed countries closer to the Third World than to the super powers. Europe, and in particular

the so-called "Like-minded countries", have an opportunity to be
in the vanguard of the developed world by placing their creative
spirit and technical and organizational capacities at the service
of the New Order. Thus, Europe would derive a new sense of purpose.
Without this, what will this region represent in the future? Only
a few decades ago it presided over the destinies of more than 50
percent of the world's population; today it is the home of just 5
percent of humanity.

If this approach had been perceived more clearly by the European
representatives in the Arab-European dialogue, if instead of
haggling over incomplete and inadequate proposals ($3 million as
a minority European contribution to joint feasibility studies,
non-preferential trade agreements, etc), if the E.E.C. had integrated its cooperation with the Arab world in a grand Mediterranean design, then perhaps the scope of this dialogue would have
been commensurate with the real potentialities of a joint endeavour at the level of the two regions.

The Paris Talks

Such is also the case *mutatis mutandis* with the Paris Conference.
One may even be reluctant to talk about solidarity between countries at different levels of development so soon after the end of
the Conference. Whatever may be said about it, it failed to produce palpable results. Whilst recognizing the inadequacy of Third
World conceptual and analytical tools, one can but note that the
group of 8 was not prepared to make the minimum concessions to
ensure the success of this meeting. No wonder, therefore, that
the unity of the Third World was preserved; the fact that the rich
countries stood firm on the initial positions was the best way
of guaranteeing this unity.

Would not some surplus oil exporting countries have supported even
more openly the creation of an international energy institute
- aimed at restoring indirectly the control of importing developed
countries on price-fixing mechanisms - had the latter accepted to
provide guarantees for the former's external financial assets?
How would the poorest countries have been able to resist pressure
excercized by industrialized countries to withdraw support to
price indexation for oil exports, if, instead of being offered $1
billion to allegedly alleviate their external debt, they had been
faced with a proposal commensurate with their real level of indebtedness, reaching $200 billion.

Furthermore, developing countries even went so far as to agree not
to discriminate between investments made by transnational enterprises and their own national investments. Yet this policy is
rejected by the developed countries themselves, and by Japan in
particular, as far as their own economies are concerned. Hence,
one might legitimately ask whether the Group of 8 would not have
been able to steam-roll through the meeting a code designed to

protect the investments of transnational enterprises in the Third World had this group accepted to accede to requests for minimum guarantees concerning the operations of the enterprises and for the adaptation of the Witteveen facility to bring it in line with the interests of the poor countries. This is no figment of the imagination since the elements of a code favouring transnational enterprises had been adopted at the committee level and were only rejected in plenary at the last minute.

It is also uncertain whether some relatively industrialized countries in Latin America would have continued to support the Common Fund within the Integrated Programme on commodities if they had been granted freer access for their processed products to Western markets and if more than lip service had been paid by the Group of 8 to measures of structural adjustment in the industrial sector.

In any event, there remains precious little of the Common Fund - the acceptance of which was in principle construed by the Group of 8 as a major concession - after the adjustment on 1.12.1977 of the UNCTAD Negotiating Conference. On this occasion, the Western countries refused to accept an autonomous fund which would be a key instrument for carrying out the objectives of the Integrated Programme, and a central source of financing covering a broad range of commodities.

Thus, in view of the disappointing results of the Norht-South Conference, the unity of the Third World, which has hardly been put to the test, does not have any particular significance.

It has been said that the North-South Conference was neither the beginning nor the end of the dialogue. One can legitimately ask, however, whether the dialogue has moved forward at all during this Conference, bearing in mind that discussions were held up in other fora for over 18 months awaiting the hypothetical results of the Paris debates on the same subjects. At times, the view was held in the Conference itself by some countries that the very same issues should not be settled because they were being debated elsewhere.

One must also recognize that the North-South Conference was the culmination of a process of erosion of the positions acquired by the Third World at the 6th Special Session and of its attempted recycling in the system of the old order.

This can readily be illustrated by the reinforcement of the IMF as it now operates; the Conference suggested that the IMF would run the Common Fund of the Integrated Programme and, likewise, the new oil and other facilities aimed at trapping the surpluses of the oil exporters while not increasing their voting rights. The fact that UNCTAD has been kept out of the study to improve the scheme of compensatory finance managed by the IMF, the maintenance of the *conditional* drawing rights providing an opportunity for big powers to interfere through the IMF in dependant economies, and the new powers conferred upon the IMF to control the access of the developing countries to capital markets, all confirm this assessment.

We are also left with a series of unanswered questions concerning the protection of the purchasing power of primary exports, access to markets, control over the activities of transnational enterprises and the renegotiation of the external debt of the poorest countries.

As for the redeployment of industrial activities CIEC leaves the problem untouched. It is thus increasingly difficult to reconcile advocacy of the "free play of market forces" and for comparative advantage with recourse to the arguments of inflation and unemployment, propounded in the same breath, to oppose this indispensable restructuring. How is it that those advanced countries which denounce, and often rightly so, the spirit of passive dependency on external aid in developing countries, stimulate this same spirit in the retarded sectors of their own economy through protectionist measures.

The blame should not, as is now the case, be placed on low-price imports from poor countries(which would certainly not object to obtaining better value for their exports!) but on the lack of structural flexibility in the industrialized countries. After having so improved the tools to protect the strong from the weak, it is high time to find the ways and means of protecting the latter from the onslaughts of the former, not by searching for the free-trade phoenix but rather by framing a system of active discrimination in favour of the poor countries, with the exception of those which have become the extra territorial bridgeheads of transnational enterprises.

As for the CIEC format, it has turned out to have major drawbacks. In particular the renegotiation of resolutions already adopted, with a view to achieving consensus on positions falling short of those initially adopted, tends to introduce a dangerous precedent in international law. It might be said that, henceforth, only resolutions adopted by consensus would have force of law. The very principle of the sovereignty of states *inter alia* would thus be called into question.

Towards the Rational Management of Planetary Resources

Hence, the search for a minimum common denominator between all the governments of the planet cannot invariably lead us to the structural revolution which is called for by the implementation of the New International Order. The search for consensus should, therefore, not be pushed too far and a clear distinction should be made between a forward- and a backward-looking consensus.

The U.N. framework and decision-making process are particularly
well suited for the pursuit of the dialogue. Meanwhile, the Third
World should review and renovate the intellectual framework which
underpins its actions in order to avoid sclerosis and demobilization. It should militantly pursue action to strengthen its position in the resumption of the dialogue and seek to impose on those
of its advanced partners who remain adamant the language of cooperation.

Cooperation between States should be seen as a stage of transition
between the present stage of non-cooperation and the projected
cooperation between peoples. Its achievement calls for the creation
of new coalitions which would seek to enlist the support of workers,
scientists, politicians, business circles, consumers and, in particular, youth movements, in Western countries, and to bring out the
long term complementarity of interests between the North and the
South.

This, of course, requires that problems be put in their proper
perspective. At present only a distorted picture can be seen
through the prism of the transnational enterprises which control
the world system of press-agencies, intent on using information
for the preservation of the status-quo. The "europeo-centric"
(for want of a better word this also refers to North America)
character of information is reflected by the fact that flows
from North to South are estimated by UNESCO to be 100 times more
important than those in the opposite direction. These media have
presented the subject of development as a bone of ideological
contention between North and South which would partially supersede
the East-West conflict. The man in the Western street is given the
impression that the fruit of his labour is to be turned over to
the poor countries. The truth, of course, is quite different:
it is a matter of putting an end to present inequities whereby
the workers of the poor countries are deprived of their rightful
share of the value-added derived from their own labour.

If they are thus enlightened, the people in the rich countries
may be ahead of their governments and provide a strong impetus
to the search for a common "higher"(rather than lower) denominator between North and South which will be progressively raised
to lead to a concerted, economically and socially sound, management of the resources of the planet.

The North-South Dialogue: Background and Present Position

Don Mills

Changing Geo-Political Realities

The concept of the New International Economic Order was presented
in comprehensive form at the Sixth Special Session of the United
Nations General Assembly in April 1974, in the Declaration and
Programme of Action. But the call for fundamental change in the
structure of the international economic system, and in the economic relationships between developed and developing countries,
was made well before that time. Moreover, many of the proposals
and ideas embodied in that document had already been the subject
of discussion and negotiation in the U.N. system.

The presentation of the full range of proposals in 1974 took
place in the context of a particular and unusual set of circumstances. Some of the developments which gave rise to the events
of 1974 are outlined here.

In this century the world has seen many far-reaching developments
and events which have shifted the balance of economic, political
and strategic forces in the international community. With the
growth of the economies of the Western industrialized countries,
their rivalries led from time to time to destructive economic
policies and practices and to wars of global proportions. While
they struggled, and as they sought to establish some element of
order and security in which they would enjoy the prospect of
growing prosperity, there emerged two major political and social
phenomena - first, the Soviet Union, and later, the People's Republic of China - which have added new dimensions both to the global
political and strategic situation and to the perception of national, social and economic development.

At the end of World War II, the Bretton Woods institutions were
established as the centrepiece of the economic system. They were
dedicated to the enhancement of the functioning of the market
system and to the promotion of international trading and economic
relations in general, with reconstruction of the economies of the
Western industrialized nations as their primary concern at the
outset.

The United States came to achieve a position of supremacy in
terms of economic and military power in the world and in more
recent years a reconstructed Western Europe has become a major
force in international economic affairs. The search by these
countries for a common approach to global problems is now a significant element in the economic dialogue.

Finally, the past twenty years have seen the virtual disappear-

ance of the great empires of the Europeans, which reached across
the world. Scores of countries which were part of these colonial
holdings achieved their independence and have become a new and
increasingly significant element in world affairs. These countries have come to realize that, inspite of the achievement of
political independence, they faced a world organized for the
most part, and particularly in respect of economic affairs, very
much in the interest of a small group of industrialized countries.
They have learned that only by way of structural change in the
international economic system will they have the opportunity of
playing a full and active part in global economic activity and
decision-making and share equitably in the benefits of such activity.

All of these developments have had considerable implications for
the global community. They have resulted in dramatic changes in
the international distribution of power and influence - whether
military, political or economic. Along with technological advances - not the least in the field of armaments - they are forcing
upon the world a gradual realization of the meaning of interdependence and of the fact that military and economic strength are
not now sufficient to insulate any country from the impact of the
actions of others.

Of the 51 members of the U.N. in its first year of establishment,
30 were developing countries, and of these 20 were from the
Latin American region. Particularly through the late 1950s and
early 1960s, large numbers of developing countries joined the
U.N. and shifted the balance to a point where in 1977 these
countries represent more than two-thirds of the total membership
of that body. This has had a profound effect on the U.N. system
and on discussions on development and international economic
cooperation. The newly independent countries rapidly established
a sense of unity and common purpose, particularly in regard to
economic issues. With the establishment of the U.N. Conference on
Trade and Development as a permanent organ of the U.N., came the
formation of the Group of 77 - the caucus of developing countries.
The Group became over the years the primary means by which these
countries have formulated and presented their proposals on economic matters and through which they negotiate in the various sectors of the U.N. system.

Thus, the unity and effectiveness of developing countries in
international affairs and their advancing perceptions about the
need for major changes in the relationships between themselves
and developed countries became more and more apparent.

The *United Nations system* has gone through a process of evolution
since its establishment and has contributed significantly to the
examination and understanding of the processes of national and
international development. Through the 1960s, new U.N. institu-

tions were established, including the United Nations Development
Programme, the U.N. Industrial Development Organization, and the
basic framework for what would later be the Committee on Science
and Technology and the appropriate division of the U.N. Secretariat in this subject area.

Over these years, in the various meetings of the U.N. bodies in
New York, in Geneva and elsewhere, the pressure increased for
greater accommodation of the interests of developing countries
in such matters as the level of official development assistance,
trading relations, industrial development and the transfer of
technology, and the operations of transnational corporations.
This movement coincided with a growing realization that aid by
itself could not bring the desired internal development, or alter
the structural relationship between developing and industrialized
countries.

It became increasingly clear that a much broader approach to the
problems of development than that of the 1950s and early 1960s
was necessary. Out of this came the establishment of the *Development Decades,* first, the decade of the 1960s and then that of the
1970s. The International Development Strategy adopted in 1970
represented an ambitious undertaking which has been described as
a comprehensive and integrated programme of national and international action to achieve a series of inter-related economic and
social objectives. It sought to establish targets for the growth
of the economies of developing countries and for social sectors,
and outlined a series of policy measures designed to improve the
position of developing countries in such fields as international
trade, the transfer of real resources and science and technology.

The role of the *Non-Aligned Movement* in the process of developing
perceptions and attitudes over the years has been a significant
one. At the first Conference of Heads of State or Government of
Non-Aligned Countries in September 1961 in Belgrade, the 25 countries represented called for the closing, through accelerated
economic, industrial and agricultural development, of the ever-
widening gap in the standards of living between the few economically advanced countries and the many economically less-developed
countries. They called for just terms of trade, for elimination
of the excessive fluctuations in primary commodity trade and for
effective application of the fruits of the scientific and technological revolution in all fields of economic development to hasten
the achievement of international social justice.

At its second "Summit" in Cairo in October 1964, almost ten years
before the Sixth Special Session of the United Nations General
Assembly, the leaders of 40 Non-Aligned countries observed:
". . .that economic development is an obligation of the whole
international community; . . . that it is the duty of all countries to contibute to the rapid evolution of a new and just economic order under which all nations can live without fear or

want or despair, and rise to their full stature in the Family
of Nations; . . . that the structure of the world economy and the
existing international institutions of international trade and
development have failed to reduce the disparity in the per capita
incomes of peoples in developing and developed countries or to
promote international action to rectify serious and growing imbalances between developed and developing countries . . . ".

At this and subsequent conferences at different levels the member
countries of the Non-Aligned Movement continued to stress the
need for structural change in the international economic system,
and their demand for full participation of developing countries
in global economic activity and decision-making, as well as the
principle of collective self-reliance on the part of developing
countries.

Growing Disillusionment

The post World War II years were a period of great change in
national and international political, social and economic affairs.
They saw the most rapid economic growth and technological progress. For the industrialized countries - whether victors or
vanquished - they have been years of unparalleled prosperity.
Developing countries reaped some benefit from this. But the
economic gap between rich and poor countries continued to widen
and the population of the latter grew rapidly, opening an increasingly wide gap in that area.

The passage from the era of the Cold War to that of detente did
little to offset the great preoccupation with the accumulation
of armaments, and the annual expenditure on these rose to present
levels of something like $350 billion. The contrast between this
huge and increasing expenditure of money and material and human
resources and the decline in the proportion of the resources of
the developed countries flowing to developing countries became
more and more evident.

The Pearson Commission on International Development appointed by
the President of the World Bank in 1968 spoke of the situation
at the time as having reached "a point of crisis". They concluded
that "if the developed nations wish to preserve their own position
in that world, they must play their full part in creating a world
order within which all nations, and all men, can live in freedom,
dignity and decency . . .". This view was based on the very
limited results obtained after two decades of effort, mainly concentrating on development assistance or aid, in the field of
international economic cooperation.

The early 1970s saw the growing disillusionment of developing
countries as their efforts at the national and international level
failed to bring significant change in their circumstances. In the
1970s, clear signs emerged of the deterioration of the interna-

tional economic system - with the collapse of the monetary system
and the persistence of inflation and recession in the industrialized countries and, more recently, the trend toward protectionism.

It is in this context that the OPEC countries took action in
regard to the supply and price of oil - action which underlined
sharply the dependence of most of the world on imported oil, the
waste of non-renewable resources and the extent to which these
were produced in developing countries and consumed in industrialized countries, and the low returns in prices and revenues
received by primary producers in developing countries. Oil provided in large part the political leverage necessary to force
industrial countries to face up to the long-standing demands of
developing countries.

The Central Issue

Since the Sixth and Seventh Special Sessions of the United
Nations General Assembly, the subject of the New International
Economic Order has become more and more the central theme in international discussions. The many conferences and negotiations
inside and outside of the U.N. system have had some very positive
effects. They have resulted in a greater understanding of the
issues involved and of the nature of the international economic
system and the relationships surrounding it. A considerable
amount of work has been done both within the United Nations
system, in other international institutions, and in the agencies
of governments of many member countries in the effort either to
throw further light on these issues or to prepare various participants for the discussions and negotiations which have been
taking place.

Universities and other private bodies are becoming more and
more interested in the issues and are promoting conferences and
seminars and other discussions on the subject. Such discussions
often include persons who are involved in dealing with these
matters at the governmental level or as representatives of
governments at the U.N., as well as officials from international
institutions. Particularly important is the development of
research programmes on the New International Economic Order outside of the official bodies. Outstanding work in this direction
has been done by the Club of Rome and by the group of specialists
responsible for the study entitled *Reshaping the International
Order (RIO)*. Such efforts are of particular significance in the
light of the absence of any specific official research agency
working directly with, and in the interest of, Third World
countries. Both the Non-Aligned Movement and the Group of 77 have
studied the possibility of the establishment of some institutions
which are taking a positive and constructive interest in the proposition concerning the establishment of the New International
Economic Order.

A number of institutions of this nature working directly in the interest of Third World countries have been established in recent years. These developments are of particular importance in the light of the great advantage which the industrialized countries have had in this area by reason of the existence of the OECD and other bodies which service these countries in their negotiations with developing countries. The extension and deepening of the process of examination and analysis of the issues related to the proposal for the New International Economic Order is therefore one of the most interesting and hopeful developments of the last three years.

The central issue in this matter is the call by developing countries for structural change in the international economic system and in the relationships in this area. Their case rests both on the injustice of the existing and past systems - taking into account the present state of affairs in which what is left of the old system no longer serves the interest even of the industrialized countries - and the fact that a restructured system would serve the interests of all countries in an equitable manner.

Clear evidence is increasingly being put forward that the economic system is proving incapable of providing for the assured and continued growth and stability of the industrialized countries. These fears are being expressed within the industrialized countries themselves. The conclusion is being drawn by some that the future prosperity of those countries will depend on the establishment of a balanced and equitable relationship in economic terms with the Third World. This can be regarded as a modulated and partial acceptance of the need for some fundamental changes in the economic system in the interests of developing and developed countries.

The strong support for the New International Economic Order expressed by a number of industrialized countries from the outset continues to be one of the very important developments in this situation. This support is based not merely on sentiment but on a practical and constructive view of the requirements of global economic justice and of the benefits which all countries would derive from an economic system which provided in a realistic way for the abolition of poverty and the elimination of the inequities which exist between developed and developing countries in economic relations.

Disappointing Results
But as far as developing countries are concerned, the results of all the discussions and negotiations to date have been very disappointing. Industrialized countries as a group have come to recognize that it is in their interest to make what they regard as greater "concessions" to the developing countries in the face of the pressure from the latter. But on the matter of structural

change in the international economic system, which is the very core of the proposal for the New International Economic Order, a number of these countries remain unwilling to move in any constructive manner. The results of such meetings as UNCTAD IV and the Paris Conference on International Economic Cooperation clearly indicate this. The resumed negotiations on the Common Fund, held in November and early December 1977, were seen by many as having the greatest significance in this respect. It was the view particularly of developing countries that the outcome of those discussions would represent a clear indication of the willingness or unwillingness of the industrialized countries to accept the need for major structural changes in the interest of an orderly and just system in the field of commodity trade, which is vital to the development of Third World countries.

In other areas negotiations have produced very limited, if any, progress. In spite of the continuing signs of deterioration in the international monetary system, the talks on the question of reform in this area have failed to produce adequate results, certainly from the point of view of developing countries. The question of the crushing burden of indebtedness of developing countries still presents major difficulties for most industrialized countries insofar as the approaches proposed by the developing countries are concerned. But the action taken recently by such countries as Sweden, Canada and the Netherlands by way of the cancellation of the official debts of a number of countries has been a positive factor, but one which has created some misgivings in other industrialized countries.

One particular matter stands out because of its crucial importance to the whole process of national and global development, and in the light of its major significance from a political viewpoint. This is the question of energy. There is a growing realization that the global community must find some means of dealing, on a coherent basis, with the question of energy and the issues which have emerged as a result of OPEC action, since energy is the lifeblood of economic activity. It is widely realized that the United Nations system must play an active role in this field. But such a role must take account of all the varying interests and must contribute significantly towards establishing a situation in which national and global development can continue satisfactorily; in which the interests of the oil-exporting countries can be adequately protected, and in which the crushing burdens on oil-importing developing countries can be relieved.

Collective Self-Reliance
An aspect of the New International Economic Order which has received increasing attention over the past three years relates to the efforts of developing countries themselves in the pursuit of their own deployment. One of the major principles listed in the Declaration on the Establishement of a New International Economic Order is, "the strengthening, through individual and collective

actions, of mutual economic, trade, financial and technical cooperation among the developing countries ...". The Programme of Action
speaks of "collective self-reliance and growing cooperation among
developing countries (which) will further strengthen their role in
the New International Economic Order".

Such inter-action between developing countries has been extremely
limited. In the field of trade, the situation is illustrated by the
following table:

Direction of Exports by Value, 1970 *

Exports from	To North %	To South %	Total
World	79.8	20.2	100.0
North	80.2	19.8	100.0
South	78.2	21.7	100.0

* Market economies only
Source: *U.N. Monthly Bulletin of Statistics*, December 1971.

Trade between rich countries is not only greater but has also increased faster than has trade within the Third World. The reversal of these trends, and the opening up of opportunities and
contacts between the countries of the South, represent a major
undertaking. It includes the processes which come under the
heading of technical cooperation between developing countries.
All of this is now the subject of increasing attention within and
outside the United Nations system. More and more developing countries are coming together in an effort to establish contacts and
relationships in the field of trade and investment and in other
areas. The establishment of Producer Associations is a special
manifestation of this development. But on a regional basis, as
well as between individual countries, there has been significant
growth in economic and technical cooperation.

Internal Orders
Where internal development particularly within the developing
countries is concerned, a number of new perceptions are emerging.
First, there is the growing realization on the part of developing
countries themselves that the restructuring of their own economic
and social systems is an indispensable element in the process of
obtaining economic and social justice for their peoples. A number
of countries are in fact taking very active steps in this direction.

At the same time, a number of industrialized countries have
developed ideas and approaches which would seek to create an
element of conditionality in the matter of global restructuring.
The idea is that developing countries would have to show clear
evidence of their movement in the direction of internal economic
and social justice as a condition, or perhaps a pre-condition,
for movement by developed countries on restructuring of the

global economic system. In some cases the issue of human rights has been injected as a part of the condition - so that developing countries would have to have an acceptable record in that area if they are to qualify in particular for bilateral assistance.

It is on these considerations, and because of a recognized inadequacy of conventional approaches to development, that the concept of basic needs has gained so much favour in recent times. That concept is now becoming a major element in the approach of many industrialized countries to the question of global development and economic relations. The danger which lies here rests not so much on the ideas themselves but on the manner in which they might be introduced into the dialogue on global restructuring.

Developing countries view with increasing concern what is regarded by many of them as an attempt to divert attention from the issue of global restructuring by focusing on internal conditions in those countries, and by raising the issue of conditionality. Such a move could lead to very serious difficulties in a dialogue that is already fraught with danger.

The issue of basic needs presents other complexities. No one disputes the great and beneficial changes which would result from a system which provided for all of the people of the world, whether in rich or poor countries, the basic requirements for living. Certainly, many developing countries will argue with justification that the primary purpose and aim of their approach to development is the meeting of the basic requirements, both in material and in other terms, of all their peoples. The proposition relating to basic needs is one which would identify in specific terms the major elements in these requirements, and would seek to satisfy them on a conscious and planned basis. So far there is not too much difference in the approaches.

But the provision of these requirements cannot be separated from the broad and complex processes of development and the use of resources within a community. There is a great element of oversimplification, in political and social terms, as well as in economic terms, in some of the proposals concerning basic needs. The process of trying to divert the resources available to a country towards a form of development that seeks first to remove the pressures and indignities of poverty and deprivation, consists of far more than the identification of specific and sometimes quantified requirements in particular areas and the provision of programmes for meeting them. There is great need, therefore, for the concept of basic needs to be brought into a realistic relationship with the facts of political and social and economic organization and development so that its intrinsic value can be preserved without it becoming a philosophy of development, or the ultimate aim of the development process.

Altogether, the present situation concerning the move towards establishing the New International Economic Order is not an encouraging one. But the price of failure is too high to be contemplated seriously. Moreover, developing countries have maintained their unity in spite of all the difficulties facing them and are determined to persist in their efforts toward arriving at the necessary agreement with the industrialized countries in the interest of real progress toward establishing the New International Economic Order.

A New U.N. Development Strategy for the 80s and Beyond: The Role of the "Third System"

Marc Nerfin

A Changing World

Preparations have begun within the United Nations for a new development strategy which will probably cover not only the next decade but also the years beyond that. Since the adoption of the International Development Strategy for the Second Development Decade, in October 1970, the world has changed in many respects. Politically, economically, conceptually, things are no longer the same. Also, the discussion on development and international cooperation has extended well beyond intergovernmental organizations. Any new United Nations strategy will have to reflect the changes which have taken place, and its elaboration should be seen as an opportunity for widening the discussion through the deliberate participation of individuals, institutions and social forces outside the formal United Nations system.

The turning point was the autumn of 1973, marked as it was by the Fourth Summit Conference of the Non-Aligned Countries held in Algiers in September, and the OPEC decision to increase the price of oil in October. The peace in Vietnam, in April 1975, was a third major indication of change.

The OPEC decision, whatever the immediate circumstances, was, as observed in the 1975 Dag Hammarskjöld Report on Development and International Cooperation (*What Now - Another Development*), a "historic" reversal. In October 1973 the oil-exporting countries put an end to an era which had begun with what the West calls the "great discoveries". For the first time since Vasco da Gama, mastery over a fundamental decision in a crucial area of the economic policy of the centre countries escaped their grasp as certain peripheral countries wrested it from them. (1) The rules of the game, four centuries old, had been changed at once.

The outcome of the events in Indochina, after decades of foreign interventions, showed for its part that political will and organization can overcome the display of military and technological might.

In Algiers, the Non-Aligned countries had decided to take joint action at the United Nations "with a view to extending the Organization's security system to include economic security, as a pre-requisite for promoting (...) all-round development (...) and the well-being of the people of the developing world". They called upon "the international community to restore the development objective to its rightful place in the functioning of the United Nations system and to establish a new system of world economic relations based on equality and common interest of all countries". Noting "the continued inadequacy of the internal structure of the United Nations", they invited the Secretary-General "to convene a special session of the General Assembly at a high political level devoted exclusively to the problems of development including the revitalization of structures". (2) This led, through the Sixth and Seventh Special Sessions, to the decision to establish the New International Economic Order (NIEO).

The process of change which has been set in motion over the last few years is thus due to three principal factors: the political vision expressed by the Algiers Summit; the mutation in international economic relations implied by the OPEC decision; and the leadership provided in the United Nations by the Non-Aligned countries, especially that of their chairman, Algeria. In retrospect, the Fourth Non-Aligned Summit appears clearly as a landmark on the road of Third World liberation, itself a condition for an authentic planetary inter-dependence and for a real development of all societies.

A Challenge to the "Third System"

"In preparing for the future", said the then Dutch Minister for Development Cooperation, Jan Pronk, in his address to the United Nations in October 1976, "the first task (...) is to review, rethink and re-assess the past. The next step is to go beyond the horizons of today and to start formulating the strategy for the last quarter-century. We must assign and distribute these tasks in a coherent and logical manner among international secretariats and institutes of research and learning. We may call on the wisest and most experienced among us, teachers and thinkers of today, to advise the world on the future. More than in the Sixties, the world community has at its disposal a variety of institutes and centres of excellence in developed and developing countries. (...) They must now be set to work".

Indeed, there is no reason to leave exclusively to governments and intergovernmental machineries the elaboration of the strategy for the future. Societies in their diversity are too rich in values and aspirations to allow governments and organizations, even when democratically established, to represent them fully. The intergovernmental system, which in the context of international relations may be called the "first system", is only one part of reality. The transnational power structure, which represents the major barrage on the road to change, could be seen as a "second system". It is time to give the "third system", that is, one which is closer to people and social forces, a better chance to have its voice heard in the debate. (3)

Individuals and institutions outside the United Nations system are in a privileged position to endeavour to open up new approaches, investigate new themes, and experiment with new methods of work. They could address themselves to the "white spots" which are taboo to intergovernmental organizations - especially the structural transformations at national level; they could formulate

alternatives to the national and international conventional wisdom; and they could be more free to tackle the stumbling blocks
which have so far prevented the implementation of the NIEO.

Clearly, however, being outside the United Nations system does not
immunize the "third system" from elitism and bureaucratization.
Its contribution would, as a matter of fact, be meaningful and
useful only to the extent that it would succeed in establishing
contact with real social forces. New ways and means have to be
found and employed to foster mutually educating dialogues between
researchers, social actors, and statesmen.

In this sense, the challenge - and possibly the radically new
element in the elaboration of the strategy - would be the
participation of researchers and social organizations - those
constituted by workers, women, youth, political parties, religious
groups, consumers, ecologists, and others - whose natural allies
are the progressive statesmen, the "like-minded" countries in the
North and democratic ones in the South.

Legitimization of New Approaches to Development

The re-assessment of the past includes that of the International
Development Strategy for the 70s, of which the Secretary-General
of UNCTAD had this to say: "There is now widespread recognition
that existing international development policies have largely
failed to achieve their stated objectives. The hopes that were
placed on the International Development Strategy for the Second
United Nations Development Decade, when it was adopted by the
General Assembly in 1970, have been essentially frustrated. It
could be argued, with the benefit of hindsight, that the existence of the Strategy has had no significant positive impact on
the pace of development of the Third World. Indeed, it now appears
evident that the policy measures envisaged in the Strategy, even
had they been fully implemented, would not have provided an
adequate basis for the long term development of the developing
countries". (4)

The results - or rather the lack of results - of the present
International Development Strategy could be ascribed to a number
of conceptual and political shortcomings. But, since its adoption,
there has been a process of rethinking the development *problématique* which, at the intergovernmental level, is reflected not
only in the Sixth and Seventh Special Sessions of the General
Assembly, but also in the series of major United Nations system
conferences: Environment (Stockholm, 1972); Population (Bucharest,
1974); Food (Rome, 1974); Industry (Lima, 1975); Women (Mexico,
1975); Health (Geneva, 1976); Trade (Nairobi, 1976); Habitat
(Vancouver, 1976); Employment (Geneva, 1976); Education and
Culture (Nairobi, 1976), as well as, at a more technical level,
Water (Mar del Plata, 1977) and Desertification (Nairobi, 1977).
The process also included, prominently, the Charter of Economic
Rights and Duties of States.

To different degrees each of these contributed to legitimizing, through intergovernmental declarations, plans of action and resolutions, a number of concepts which had often been generated outside the intergovernmental system.

In the "third system" as we know it, a number of studies have also been undertaken, notably the Tinbergen Report: *Reshaping the International Order* (5); the Bariloche Report: *Catastrophe or New Society* (6); the Dag Hammarskjöld Report: *What Now - Another Development* (7). These are only beginnings. There are groups, already known or yet to be identified, which could contribute further to the process of thought, conceptualization and formulation of the new strategy.

A detailed analysis of the existing texts - intergovernmental or emanating from the "third system" - would be outside the scope of this paper. However, and at the risk of over-simplifying a complex conceptual re-orientation, one may venture to suggest that the most significant result of the process is the emergence of a new set of development parameters and goals which could perhaps be summarized as follows:

● development should be *need-oriented*, that is, being geared to satisfaction of the needs, material and "non-material", of human beings, beginning with the basic needs of the majority poor;
● development should be *endogenous*, that is, stemming from the heart of each society, which should define in full autonomy its values and the vision of its future. This implies that development cannot be a linear imitative process, that there could be no model, and that only the plurality of development patterns can answer the specificity of each situation;
● development should be *self-reliant*, that is, implying that each society relies primarily on its own strength and resources in terms of human creativity and environment. Self-reliance should be exercised at national and international (collective self-reliance) levels, but it acquires its full meaning only if rooted in local contexts;
● development should be *ecologically sound*, that is, utilizing rationally the resources of the biosphere in full awareness of the potential of local eco-systems as well as the global and local outer limits imposed on present and future generations. This implies careful, socially relevant and controlled technologies;
● development will require *structural transformations*, both nationally and internationally.

Such a development, clearly, cannot be reduced to economic growth, as necessary - if purposeful and socially sound - as that may be. Economic growth refers to things; it is an instrument. The activities suggested by the term "development" mean development of each man and woman, for and by themselves, individually and socially. Its goal is the humanization of men and women through their struggle for liberation from oppression, exploitation and alien-

74

ation. It is thus a holistic process encompassing political,
cultural, social, economic, technological as well as psychological
elements.

From Concepts to Implementation

The new international situation, the self-assertion of the Third
World, the fate of the present International Development Strategy,
the conceptual advances of the past six years and their intergovernmental legitimization, all declare that the forthcoming
strategy and subsequent policies are bound to be different from
those of the 70s. The participation of the "third system" in
their elaboration, discussion and implementation could hopefully
contribute to this.

It is certainly too early, when preparations are just beginning,
to go beyond a few suggestions concerning what the next United
Nations strategy could consider and perhaps include.

The consensus of governments, as expressed in the documents
referred to previously, shows essentially two things.

On the one hand, there is no dearth of ideas on what development
and the New International Order (NIO) should be. The approved
positions certainly provide a basis from which it should not be
overly difficult to derive, after consolidation of their
constitutive elements, a pertinent United Nations strategy - even
if, as noted by Majid Rahnema in connection with the Medium-term
Plan of Unesco adopted in Nairobi in 1976, and this an essential
qualification, we are "fully aware of the fact that we are living
in an epoch where power structures are increasingly in a condition
to take over those ideas which they deem dangerous and then to
make use of them for purposes which are sometimes diametrically
opposed to those originally foreseen". (8)

On the other hand, and most important, there is still a major gap
between decisions already taken and their implementation. It may
thus be seen that the first task in the years immediately ahead
is to move towards the implementation of what has been agreed
upon. In this context, three remarks seem in order.

First, at the societal level, whilst the "five pillars" sketched
out in the preceding section may help in re-defining the goals
and parameters of the real processes, they still have to inform
the latter. A first necessary, if not sufficient, condition is
that the former be articulated in *strategies of transition* to be
worked out in the specific context - natural and cultural - of
each society, be it at a high or at a low level of productivity,
in the industrialized world or in the Third World.

Second, virtually no society can now afford, or is left, to live in
isolation. There are unavoidable linkages or reciprocal ramifica-

tions - beneficial or harmful to different partners - between whatever local measures are taken. This is the essential motivation for the NIO, meant to provide a favourable or, at least, a non-antagonistic environment for national development. Thus, the NIO cannot be achieved through verbal consensus. On the contrary, the different partners involved, be they governments, economic organizations or social actors, must recognize, analyse and overcome contradictions or, having faced their responsibilities and accepted the necessary trade-offs, reflect them in *contractual arrangements* capable of giving substance to the NIO.

Third, any discussion of restructuring for positive change would be devoid of operational validity without consideration of the question of power. The present "order" is the result of oppression and exploitation, as long as history itself nationally and going back to four centuries of colonialism and imperialism internationally. It benefits the national and international *power structures*, which are more often than not intertwined: the centre's power structure has maintained and/or created, in spite of the political emancipation of the Third World, its accomplices and appendices in the periphery. In such a situation it is essential to understand better how the present power structures operate at national and international levels. Further, the only possible response of those who suffer from them, those who have been pauperized, exploited, dominated, alienated, is in their *organization* to give effect to their projects, be it through strategies of transition from the present to orders they would prefer, or through the negotiation and implementation of mutually beneficial arrangements (as far as people are concerned) of world affairs.

This would be facilitated if it were realized better (a) that national and international changes are only different facets of the same restructuring process, and (b) that what is at stake is no zero-sum game, not a matter of simply sharing what exists, but of changing it, of creating new, more equal, societies and new societal relations. The principal political working assumption of the forthcoming strategy may thus be formulated as follows: there could be no meaningful and sustainable restructuring of international relations without concomitant restructuring at national level, in the North as well as in the South.

Areas of Work for the "Third System"
A number of specific activities, be they policy-oriented research or conscientization actions, could be envisaged in that light. Some of them are mentioned below by way of illustration. They are grouped, for the sake of convenience, under three principal headings which may well be the three major components of the next United Nations Development Strategy and of its implementation, that is:

(i) *strategies of transition* towards a need-oriented and self-

reliant development through restructuring, in the North as well
as in the South;
(ii) *Third World collective self-reliance*, seen as a critical
instrument of re-equilibration of international relations and as
a condition for an authentic planetary interdependence; and
(iii) movement towards *contractual arrangements* in fields where
they could be mutually beneficial.

Clearly, however, key themes such as the analysis of how the power
structure operates and could be fought against, or the linkages
between national measures, pertain to each section as well as to
the whole list of examples.

Strategies of Transition. "Global" models do not really help
much in formulating strategies of transition, whereas examples
and exchange of operational information on experiences are useful;
there is as much to learn from failures as from successes. In
this context, policy-oriented *Third World* research institutes
could undertake case studies of current or recent efforts to
design and carry out development strategies aiming at the satisfaction of human needs through self-reliance, new patterns of
education, innovative health systems, increased productivity and
production, autonomous technological choices, transformation of
socio-economic structures, wealth and income redistribution,
popular participation. The implications of the links with the
centre's power structure (economic, social, cultural, ideological,
military) could also be investigated as well as the scope for
"de-linking" partially or totally from it. In particular, the
experience of countries having chosen to "de-link" may be of
interest. Generally speaking, the experiences of the following
countries – at different moments in time - could be studied:
Algeria, Burma, Chile, Cuba, Egypt, Iraq, Jamaica, Kampuchea,
Madagascar, Peru, Somalia, Sri Lanka, Tanzania, Tunisia, Vietnam.

National institutions or individuals could also attempt to sketch
out alternative strategies of transition towards another development for selected Third World countries - such as Bangladesh,
Brazil, India, Indonesia, Mexico, Nigeria and Pakistan, i.e.
those with a population of 60 million and over, as well as for
some of those just mentioned.

In the North, on the assumption that any proposal for change
should stem from what people want and sometimes do, it would be
important, first, to know more about their perception of the
crisis, their aspirations and their capacity to organize for
change, and to understand better the on-going process of social
transformation in such countries as Holland, Norway and Sweden.
What are the real trends? What is the experience of the "provo"
movement in the Netherlands? Are movements like that of Norway
Damman ("Ny livsstil") typical or marginal? Could the reactions
of the Swedes to "How much is enough - Another Sweden" be
analysed? (9) What policy lessons could be derived from the U.S.

grassroots movements for greater equity? (10) What is the significance of the ecological movement, especially among the youth?
What is the role of the unions?

What alternatives can be worked out to either unemployment or
alienating work? What is the potential for the reduction of unemployment through a general reduction of working time? Of improvement of conditions of work (e.g. the Volvo experiment)? More
generally, what is the scope and feasibility of increasing free
time? Is it not astonishing that the tremendous increase in labour
productivity over the last thirty years has not been matched by a
significant increase in free time? Is the improved material
standard of living the only explanation for this, or was not a
major part of the added surplus diverted into the consumption of
non-necessary goods and services encouraged by socially
irresponsible advertisement, into the growth of public and private
bureaucracies, into military expenditures? What are the internal
"terms of trade" between time use and need-satisfaction? What
kind of restructuring could be envisaged to improve them?

Second, a number of critical aspects of the implementation of the
NIO for the industrialized countries could be analysed. As a
point of departure, one could attempt to work out, at least for
a few selected countries, some balance-sheets of the actual economic relations between each of these countries and the Third
World (covering trade in commodities, manufactures, and
invisibles; financial flows in both directions - investments,
profit repatriations, royalties, aid, brain drain, workers'
migration) with a view to representing the facts to the opinion
and gauging the possible implications of the NIEO as far as
trade (in both specific and financial terms), balance of payments, production and employment are concerned. Precise figures
may be impossible to ascertain, but such an exercise could at
least suggest the orders of magnitude, and become an important
conscientization tool for the opinion in the industrialized
countries.

In the same manner, attempts could be made to prepare and present
some well-documented studies - again on a country basis -
comparing real gains, if any, and the costs, for the economies at
large and the people in the North, of the activities of the transnational corporations in the South.

What would be the potential implications for, and necessary
adjustment in, the North of the industrialization and economic
growth of the South through both import substitution (e.g. capital
goods versus consumption goods) and production and services
substitution (e.g. the steel industries or shipping)? In
particular what would be, for selected countries, the implications
of various scenarios of implementation of the UNIDO Lima
Declaration, taking into account the conflicting interests of
transnational and national enterprises? The objective would be to

formulate the specific measures which would avoid or minimize social costs such as unemployment or brutal relocation of industries and workers.

Finally, could future-oriented groups devise, for selected industrialized countries, strategies of transition towards another development which would provide for a better use of the existing productive capacity, reflect the adjustments required by the NIO and the internal aspirations to change?

In both North and South, what are the possibilities of curbing the existing power structure and democratizing the concrete exercise of power, whether at national level, at work (e.g. participation in decision-making, workers' control, self-management) or in human settlements (at the level of the region, the city and the housing block)? What is the scope for, and political implications of, redistribution of wealth and income in order to finance change without increasing inflation? What are the alternative patterns of consumption among the affluent groups, principally in the industrialized countries, but also in the South (the "elites")? What are the alternative means of providing the goods and services which are really needed whilst minimizing alienation and waste of resources (including time)?

Would it be possible to throw more light on the militarization of economies and societies? What is the impact of armaments R&D and expenditures on patterns of production and technological choices in the economies at large? How could disarmament and development be really linked? How is the military sector related to the centre-periphery domination?

Third World Collective Self-Reliance. The present "order" clearly benefits those who are stronger, and harms those who are weaker. The NIO, aiming as it does at a more equitable world, implies the strengthening of those who are weaker. The Third World can achieve this through a much greater collective self-reliance. Its potential could be investigated further by Third World institutions, groups and individuals on the basis of an analysis of past experience (both positive and negative), especially at regional and sub-regional levels as well as between countries in different regions facing similar problems. This could cover Third World cooperation measures for development as well as for strengthening Third World bargaining capacity.

The former could include the formulation of such concrete measures as:

● coordination of industrial and agricultural development aimed at securing greater collective economic balance and productive efficiency, with trade among members as a necessary supporting means to achieving these gains;
● reinforcement of autonomous financial capacity in Third World

countries and movements towards a Third World monetary system;
● strengthening technological capacity through innovation, and
internalizing the processes of knowledge creation, adaptation and
use;
● strengthening autonomous – but not necessarily governmental –
channels of communication among Third World countries and between
them and industrialized countries to help create new patterns of
communication and cultural cooperation, thus contributing to
mental de-colonization and re-affirmation of cultural identity.

As for the latter, there are obviously contradictions among different aspects of the NIEO. These contradictions, as well as,
conceivably, the lack of relevance of certain of its aspects, or
missing elements, could be identified and studied further by
research institutes in the Third World with a view to presenting
a coherent and consistent plan of action designed to promote the
implementation of a really new international order. In particular,
it would be important to elucidate the links between the NIO and
collective self-reliance.

Such options as "de-linking" from, or selective participation in,
the centre-dominated system could also be examined from a Third
World point of view. One may also consider, as an alternative to
an international development strategy, the possibility of a
"moratorium" in the North-South "dialogue" to be replaced, for a
period of time, by a South-South dialogue geared to strengthening
and furthering collective self-reliance.

Towards Contractual Arrangements. Conflicts and confrontations
are, in certain areas, unavoidable. The challenge is to minimize
those and to search for mutually beneficial solutions wherever
possible. The process of negotiation of contractual arrangements
to this effect could be facilitated by the cooperation of action-
oriented institutions, groups or individuals from both the North
and the South who could contribute to a better understanding of,
and approaches to, such issues as:

● how the prevailing power structure operates and the linkages
between its North and South components with a view to formulating
concrete and workable proposals for change;
● a new system of trade relationships, supported by the appropriate
institutions, in commodities, industrial goods, shipping,
technologies and other invisibles, with particular reference to
access to markets and resources and to purchasing power of the
Third World and prices indexation;
● a new industrial geopgraphy of the world providing for a significantly larger share of the transformation of its raw materials
(especially to satisfy the needs of its people) by the Third World
itself, taking into account the problems of the migration of
workers and the brain drain as well as the interest of industrialized countries to halt pollution resulting from excessive
industrial concentration;

• revisions of contracts, leases and concessions entered into with TNCs under conditions of inequity;
• acceptable arrangements for the utilization of the seabed;
• new aid and cooperation policies and pratices (both bilateral and multilateral);
• a fresh look at the tourism industry with a view to limiting its negative impact, increasing its economic benefits for the Third World and making it an element of real contacts between people;
• last, but not least, a new information structure able to promote a better understanding between people and to contribute to the cultural cooperation which is an essential element of the NIO.

More specifically, since different industrialized countries react in different manners to the NIO challenge, one could thus investigate, on the basis of illustrative contractual arrangements, the feasibility of possible long term pilot agreements between selected pairs of forward-looking industrialized and Third World countries, aiming at comprehensive cooperation through mutually beneficial trade, financial, technological and cultural relations。

If it is true that out of the US $ 200 billion paid by the final consumers in the North for commodities imported from the South only $ 30 billion remain in the South (11), the analysis of such a margin would help in identifying the scope and methods of concerted action between producers (in the South) and consumers (in the North).

Of relevance would also be an investigation of various forms of automatic mobilization of resources for development transfers through, say, use of the seabed benefits, levies on high-sea transport, re-allocation of resources now devoted to armaments, etc.

Finally, the NIEO does require a new structure for negotiation and cooperation. Whatever the recent decisions on the restructuring of the development sectors of the United Nations system, they are likely to fall short of what is required, especially if the time-horizon is the 80s and beyond. Much remains to be done to understand the functioning of the United Nations system, to streamline its functions and organizations, and to formulate alternatives covering the entire system (i。e. not only the General Assembly organs and the specialized agencies but also the World Bank and the International Monetary Fund)。

Further, the elaboration of the next United Nations Development Strategy could be seen as an opportunity to facilitate the participation of the "third system" in discussing, negotiating, making decisions and implementing it since it is, as significantly as the intergovernmental and the TNC systems, an essential part of the real world。 Indeed, the activities described above could be carried out in such a manner as to contribute to building up, on the basis of aspirations shared by loosely related institutions, groups and individuals, a real "third system" which would be a meaningful factor of international cooperation.

Whether all this could be undertaken, or has a chance to be reflected in the United Nations Development Strategy for the 80s and Beyond, is another problem. At this stage what is essential is that those who constitute the "third system" spare no effort and work towards as meaningful as possible a strategy, thus living up to their social responsibilities. Beyond that, and whatever the formal success in the General Assembly, the process itself would be the result, because what does matter in the final analysis is the conscientization and the self-mobilization of the forces which do need and want change.

Notes and References

(1) The 1975 Dag Hammarskjöld Report on Development and International Cooperation: *What Now - Another Development*, The Dag Hammarskjöld Foundation, Uppsala, 1975.

(2) United Nations document A/9330.

(3) For a discussion, see Johan Galtung: "Nonterritorial Actors and the Problem of Peace", in Saul H. Mendlovitz (ed.) *On the Creation of a Just World Order, Preferred World for the 1990s*, The Free Press, New York, 1976, pp. 151-188.

(4) United Nations document TD/B/642.

(5) Jan Tinbergen (Coordinator): *Reshaping the International Order, A Report to the Club of Rome*, E.P. Dutton & Co., New York, 1976.

(6) Amilcar O. Herrera (Director): *Catastrophe or New Society? A Latin American World Model*, International Development Research Centre, Ottawa, 1976.

(7) Op.cit. (cf. note 1) and its two companion volumes, William H. Matthews (ed.): *Outer Limits and Human Needs, Resource and Environmental Issues of Development Strategies* (1976), and Marc Nerfin (ed.): *Another Development, Approaches and Strategies* (1977).

(8) Majid Rahnema: "An Open System Geared to the Future", *For Endogenous Development, Bulletin of the Committee for the Furtherance of the Medium term Plan of Unesco*, No. 1, 1977, pp. 9-11.

(9) Göran Bäckstrand and Lars Ingelstam: "How much is Enough? - Another Sweden", in *What Now* (op.cit.), pp. 44-54. See also Stig Lindholm: "Another Sweden: How the Swedish Press Reacted", *Development Dialogue*, No. 1. 1976, pp. 68-81.

(10) See, for instance, Hazel Henderson: "Citizen Movements for Greater Global Equity", in *International Social Science Journal*, Vol. XXVIII, No. 4, 1976, pp. 774-788.

(11) See Mahbub ul Haq: *The Poverty Curtain*, Columbia University Press, New York, 1977.

We Must Build a Better World Together

Manuel Pérez Guerrero

Leaving Distrust Aside

No one can be satisfied with the present world situation, neither
from an ethical, nor from a rational standpoint. It is, therefore,
difficult to understand why, in spite of the awareness of the
world's fundamental wrongs, not more has been done to right them.
We all know that the time for a change has come, and no one wants
to think of war as its instrument. War has never worked for the
benefit of the international community and today it would mean
the destruction of mankind.

However, where we have been spending most money is on the art of
war, pushed by the lack of a climate of mutual trust and by mer-
cantilist strivings. This situation has clouded, hopefully only
temporarily, the common perception we all have of the future.
Time is of the essence. We are in dire need of a true negotiation
that encompasses all countries and all major issues. What is at
stake is so important that we must leave distrust aside and dedi-
cate ourselves to the solution of the problems that affect mankind, each country assuming its responsibilities. And we could
not ask any country to do more that it can.

We cannot continue to work along the lines of the U.N. Development Decades, limited in scope and to be largely forgotten when
the time for implementation comes. Growth cannot be a substitute
for development. This course was corrected with the approval of
the Declaration and Programme of Action on the Establishment of
the New International Economic Order. But having tried and, to
a great extent, failed in Paris it is now time to give the North-
South negotiations a new dynamism. Within the framework of a
far-sighted outlook that takes into consideration the general
interests of mankind, we cannot set aside the various arguments
in support of the different positions. But we must all approach
the conference table in good faith, with the determination to
solve a common problem and not with the intention of having
another round of largely sterile discussions. Not dialogue for
dialogue's sake.

To reach this goal we have to prepare our public opinions and
make them understand what is at stake. It seems paradoxical that
the countries that have a larger share of responsibility and
that, it could be said, have more to lose, should be those that
have the greatest difficulties in establishing a constructive
position to deal with the structural reforms that a structurally
sick economy demands. This, of course, can be explained by the
inertia of those that have benefited most from the old economic
order and their hope for its continuation. Yet, no one can be
sure of what might happen in the coming years. The prevailing

uncertainty leads us to think that it would indeed be a dangerous and ungratifying task to attempt to prolong the life of an order, unworthy of that name, with repairs that would not make it last, but only retard the real task ahead of us, whilst making it more difficult and hazardous. The validity of this judgement is increasingly accepted. One way or another we will have to move towards a new world. One that - we all hope - would be just and rational.

But if in the long term the need for this change is generally admitted, in the short term the measures necessary to pave the way towards this goal are not taken. This contradiction, between reason and action, must be eliminated: our long term goal must find its support in decisions concerning the short and medium terms.

A Turning Point

If we are, as it appears reasonable to suppose, at a turning point in mankind's history, and if we recognize that to achieve our goal a fundamental change is required, we must take the curve that will enable us to bring that change about in a deliberate and orderly manner. To this end, it would be necessary to proceed at what could be called "a critical speed". If the vehicle is driven at too high a speed, the risk is great that it would miss the curve and end up in rough and intractable terrain. If we take it too slowly, events will overtake us and we would lose control. In both cases, the way back to the road would be difficult, if not impossible.

We all share the responsibility of making this transition towards the New International Economic Order as smooth as possible. Inertia is the great enemy. The alternative would be to recognize the validity of the historical determinism approach, allowing mankind to be subjected to mutations that take time to be conceived and born until a different order reflecting new power relationships emerges. Accompanying this vision is the trauma of war and other commotions, as happened in the first centuries of the Chirstian era following the decline and fall of the Roman Empire. But at present more than at any other moment, it would be irresponsible to abandon ourselves to this passive attitude; it would clearly magnify the danger of self-destruction and, at the same time, prolong mankind's sufferings which we could otherwise reduce, if not altogether eliminate.

There is thus only one way of viewing, as rational beings, the solution to our problems: we must use the reason with which we are endowed; we cannot allow ourselves to be simply guided by the instincts of greed and power, nor to permit the present situation to go unchanged.

There is urgent need for measures designed to redress present

inequities and disequilibria, to avoid further distortions and
to alleviate the sufferings of many people. Yet, we should not
deceive ourselves into thinking that these measures alone will
initiate the transformation that is required.

Admittedly, man has, with many costly mistakes, endowed himself
with technical and, to a lesser extent, spiritual resources of
a wide variety, many of which could be put to very good use in
the search for new ways of pursuing our common goals. It cannot
be repeated too often that only by advancing on a broad front of
issues can we make lasting progress towards these goals.
Fragmented and uneven advances can only be consolidated if timely
action is forthcoming to maintain the balance through mutually
supporting and reinforcing measures.

The Question of Raw Materials

In this context, action on the question of *raw materials* holds
a central position. For the great majority of the developing
countries, the export of raw materials is still the principal
means of earning foreign exchange. The inadequacy of this situation is evident; constant uncertainties with respect to these
earnings due to erratic and exagerated price fluctuations, with
a general depressing effect on prices resulting in a deterioration in the terms of trade. The consequence has been market dis-
organization with speculators playing a major role in the price-
setting function. The latter have been the only real winners in
this global casino. The producers, to a great extent the developing countries, have been the constant losers.

It is, therefore, generally admitted that, with the exception of
the limited number of beneficiaries of the present system, both
producers and consumers stand to gain from a scheme designed to
limit price fluctuations within previously agreed ranges. The
greater stability of world prices for raw materials would contribute effectively to bringing inflationary pressures under control
and to stimulating the necessary investments. These are among the
objectives of the Integrated Programme for Commodities agreed
upon at UNCTAD IV in Nairobi, the adequate functioning of which
depends decisively on the establishment of the Common Fund. For
this reason, it remains essential that the coming session of
the Negotiating Conference on this issue should produce the result
that is expected in furtherance of the agreement that was reached
in Paris at the Conference on International Economic Cooperation.
The advantage of the Integrated Programme is that all the parties
that have a real stake in commodity trade would have an important
say in the decision-making process of the Programme. In such a
situation, the producers' associations that may exist at the time
would play a cooperative role in the negotiations on prices and
other related matters within the broader framework of the Integrated Programme.

To ensure the effectiveness of the Programme, it is indispensable

that positive results be forthcoming within an agreed timeframe
in the negotiations concerning individual commodity agreements
or arrangements. All the various interests of the international
community, not least those of the weaker partners,would have to
be adequately taken care of if we wish to have, as is the aim,
a balanced and well-functioning scheme. This is what would make
it work and stick.

These efforts will have to be carried out in keeping with such
established principles as permanent national sovereignty over
natural resources and within a broad framework encompassing the
resources from the ocean floors. In the case of those resources
outside the national jurisdiction of states, the two basic pillars of a sound policy must be in the first instance the management through an international mechanism which will ensure the
participation of all members of the international community in
the decision-making process and, secondly, the avoidance of disruptive competition with the raw materials produced by sovereign
states, which is referred to as the principle of complementarity.
It is only in this way that these great resources of the seabed
would respond to the concept of the common heritage of mankind.

Another basic principle worth stressing, due to its conceptual
and practical importance, is that of the conservation of raw
materials especially those of a non-renewable nature. In the case
of agricultural products, the basic concern must be the conservation and improvement of soils combined with efforts aimed at
the optimalization of productivity and their utilization, which
is common to both renewable and non-renewable sources. The greater awakening to the dangers arising from the wastage of raw
materials, including its impact on the environment, reveals the
great significance of this problem as a point of confluence of
current responsible thinking, even though the awareness is as yet
inadequately reflected in current policies and practice. The
example of oil is undoubtedly the most dramatic, although obviously not the only one.

It is no exaggeration to afford oil this importance: the world
economy will continue to depend on it to a decisive extent in the
coming decades since there is still no substitute in sight. Along
with the active search for new sources of energy, suitable to
mankind's needs, and the expansion of conventional sources, particularly in energy-deficient developing countries, there is a
great need to advance rapidly towards a rational pattern of consumption. At present, we must aim at both a deceleration in the
expansion of demand for energy, and oil in particular, and at
stimulating the development of the new sources. This would entail
changes aimed at creating new patterns of consumption.

It may appear as if producers should concentrate their attention
on just prices and consumers on secure supplies. In fact, it
stands to reason that these issues cannot be separated and that

it is in the common interest of all that a workable agreement
should be reached on the general principles governing these
issues, together with adequate solutions to the other questions
pertaining to the New International Economic Order and which
have been the subject of the North-South dialogue. The lack of
consistency between the domestic and international approaches in
some industrialized countries in this field, however, is particularly distressing. The manipulation of internal taxes could be
continued as a way out of this conceptual inconsistency. In fact,
such a practice would make even more evident the injustice of
trying, at this juncture, to insist on the old pattern of raw
materials exploitation as a source of subsidy to the lopsided,
so-called world economy. It will help no one and hurt too many.

Other Problems

The particular significance of raw materials should not make us
lose sight of the fact that developing countries should be encouraged to take advantage of their potential for *processing and
manufacturing* an increasing range of goods. Although the insis-
tence on adequate prices for raw materials will remain valid,
exports thereof should increasingly take the form of processed,
semi-manufactued and manufactured goods. This is the best way
of creating employment in the countries of the Third World, meeting their local consumption needs and, at the same time, increasing and broadening their external purchasing power, making them
more active partners in international trade. As is understood in
the industrialized countries, an adequate distribution of income
cannot be reached without providing stable and well remunerated
employment to the people.

Access to the markets of industrialized countries is an
essential prerequisite, although not the only one, but one which
is still beset with obstacles of many kinds. The Generalised
System of Preferences has been a step in the right direction but
further improvements are necessary and it requires a broader and
firmer basis. Furthermore, there are countless non-tariff barriers
about which a great deal has been discussed but nothing achieved.
Reasons always exist for inaction or increased protectionism,
without considering the consequences for the people of the developing countries. The same holds true for another key aspect of
the same problem and one which goes to its very core, namely
adjustment assistance. Such assistance, which has been used only
in a few cases, would permit the orderly redeployment of the
resources in the non-competitive sectors in the industrialized
countries, allowing developing countries to make better use of
their comparative advantages. With the increased purchase of the
latter's products the consumers of the industrialized countries
would receive a direct benefit from an increase in the purchase
of the products of the developing countries. It is difficult to
conceive of any approach on the part of the developed countries
which could be more important than this one: to bring about a new
international division of labour which would do justice to the

developing countries by giving them a real chance of playing
their full part in international trade and thereby earning their
own living.

Technology is another important chapter in the North-South relationship. In the last few years efforts in this field have
addressed two main lines of action. The first concerns the transfer of technology. This has to be facilitated through the elaboration of a number of rules embodied in a code of conduct. Obser-
vance of these by the technology-transmitting agents, such as
transnational corporations, should help safeguard the interests
of the developing countries, especially with respect to the conditions concerning the provision and use of technology. The other
line of action aims at the adaptation of technology to local
conditions and the promotion of indigenous technology. The transfer of technology cannot be considered as just another form of
business to be carried out in a haphazard way. It has great potential significance since it touches on the type of development and,
consequently, on the life-style of the people. Although cooperation from outside is, to varying degrees, required, what is at
stake is a reduction rather than an increase in the links of
dependence on the nations that have already developed a technological capacity of their own, in keeping with a soundly understood
and practiced concept of interdependence.

Another area of special concern to the developing countries - and
to the international community as a whole - is the creation of a
new and effective *international monetary order*. As in other matters,
the countries of the Third World are prepared - and indeed have
consistently requested - to share here in the decision-making.
Yet, clearly, the main responsibility belongs to the major countries whose intentions at times suggest a desire to follow the
line of least resistance and to keep alive for as long as possible
the old and decaying monetary order.

Monetary management at the international as well as the national
level cannot take the place of required structural change. A
monetary order, responsive to new international realities, is,
however, an integral part of such structural change. The reinforcement of Special Drawing Rights as a central monetary asset cannot
be delayed without risk. Moreover, Special Drawing Rights carry
the seeds of balanced and equitable monetary management. It is
admitted that only through the adoption of such an approach will
it be possible to prevent the recurrence of the international
monetary upheavals that have occurred in the past decade. This
does not preclude - on the contrary, it presupposes - greater and
better coordinated efforts to bring inflationary pressures under
effective control, while laying the basis for the New International Economic Order. Such development is a necessary, although not
sufficient, condition for an equitable agreement on foreign
investment and other flows, attuned to the new international situation.

This order does not only refer to the relations between states in a North-South context. It also implies changes within states, both developed and developing, and promoting of the same principles of social justice. It also has inherent in it the concept and practice of *self-reliance* - national and collective - which is basic to the aspiration of playing an active and respected role in the world community. Collective self-reliance has been understood by the Third World as a militant demonstration of the solidarity of the developing countries, however diverse their stages and patterns of development.

While the process of addressing the structural problems inherent in the system of international economic relations is underway, certain traditional approaches to North-South problems will have to be pursued. This is particularly true in the case of *development aid and debt relief*.

Although a few developed countries have a praiseworthy record in respect of official development assistance, most major industrialized countries are still far below the O.D.A. target of 0.7 per cent. It remains to be seen to what extent the picture will improve as a result of the agreements reached at the Paris Conference. The efforts of the OPEC countries with respect to international resource transfers cannot in any respect be placed in the same context as those expected of the developed countries; they certainly do not relieve the rich countries of their responsibility in this regard. Unlike the situation of the industrialized countries, OPEC's present liquidity is the result of the sale of a non-renewable resource.

The other face of the same problem is the question of the external debt of the developing countries, amounting to around $200 billion and owed mainly to private banks. Although the debt problem has become a very real one, it is the underlying situation - mainly the erosion of the purchasing power of the unit value of their export earnings - that has forced developing countries to reach this level of indebtedness. Some industrialized countries have already taken the enlightened step of cancelling a substantial part of the official debt owed to them, and President Pérez of Venezuela has proposed steps, within OPEC and other fora, to deal effectively with this, the most pressing problem confronting the international community today.

Not only the developing countries but the industrialized countries also stand to gain from measures that promote debt relief. The misgivings about the precedent that such measures would create are *not* wellfounded since we are not witnessing isolated cases of emergency, but rather a situation which encompasses a large number of countries and which calls for decided and courageous action of a corresponding magnitude. Should such a situation again present itself in the future we would have to concede that all our efforts

towards a fundamental change in international economic relations have been to no avail. We should view it as an important
way of making it possible for all countries concerned - creditors
as well as debtors - to reflect more freely and constructively on
the changes they may see fit to introduce in the light of their
own internal circumstances. In any case, the world economy would
be stimulated by the increase in the external purchasing power of
the developing countries and by the improvement in the international financial situation.

Emerging Awareness
In these few pages it has only been possible to call attention to
what appeared to be the main lines of action which have to be
pursued to achieve our aim of a new, just and rational system of
international relations. They are all interrelated. None can be
left out without endangering the whole. They presuppose a general
consensus on certain social objectives of great significance such
as, for instance, the satisfaction of basic human needs, which,
in turn, presupposes the existence of a dynamic structural framework within which every one would have an active role to play.
In the end, our ultimate goal is the promotion and attainment
of life-styles among all peoples which, although diverse in their
expression, would be equally committed to fundamental human
rights. This is a cooperative effort: it not only involves governments, it also involves peoples whose strivings we have to inter-
pret objectively. As all countries, large and small, should have
a say in these far-reaching and momentous matters, so should all
human beings in all walks of life, since they are, after all, the
central subject and object of our common endeavours.

The great obstacle before us is the absence of a sense of urgency
and political will. The support of public opinion is, therefore,
indispensable as is an enlightened mass media which helps to
form it. The RIO Report, sponsored by the Club of Rome and coordinated by Jan Tinbergen, has shown how a group of people from
many countries can contribute to this challenging enterprise. We
understand that this task of forming public opinion is the main
concern of the recently created Brandt Commission.

The awareness is already emerging that we cannot afford to miss
the present opportunity to resolutely undertake the building of
a better world. This cannot be accomplished in a short period of
time. Yet we must give from the outset the required decisive
impetus to this challenging task. We still have a long way to go
before we reach the critical speed necessary to take the curve at
this turning-point in mankind's history.

Let us remind ourselves that there can be no lasting prosperity
without justice; and let us hope that we will not be found wanting
in vision and courage.

To address ourselves to overcoming the inequities and absurdities

of the present situation at this crucial juncture is the best
tribute we can pay to a personal friend and a leading thinker on
what we could well call the art of living in the face of our
common hopes and apprehensions. To one that helped to provide
economics with the tool of mathematics without losing sight of
the social and human reality and goals, we owe a great debt.

What Next? A Mandate for the Developing Countries

Shridath S. Ramphal

Matching Rhetoric With Action

Nearly four years after the world community, in the snap of
realism induced by OPEC policies, took its first timorous step
in 1974 towards a New International Economic Order, the path
still remains untrodden. That the world should take that path is
the foremost challenge of our time to rich and poor alike. But
it is a challenge that presents the developing countries with a
specially compelling mandate for action.

The frustrations of UNCTAD IV; the failure of CIEC to agree even
on the character of its disagreement; the negligible progress
being made at the Multilateral Trade Negotiations after four
years of intensive dialogue; the bogging down of the negotiations
on individual commodity agreements and on the Common Fund in
spite of verbal agreement on the Integrated Programme for Commodities; the perpetuation of disorderly conditions in the international financial system; the inability of the international
community to agree even on a forum for coming to grips with the
staggering debt problem of the developing countries; these set-
backs are not only disappointing in themselves, they are positively dangerous. To put it at its most charitable, this record
of continuous dialogue and consistent inaction suggests that the
realism which produced the promises of the Sixth and Seventh
Special Sessions has passed, and that the rich have returned to
their accustomed complacency with an unequal world – with all that
that implies for a world at war with itself, even though all the
evidence argues that "surviving is the only war we can afford" (1).

The task now facing the international community is to match
rhetoric with action, concern for human 'rights' with improvement
of the human condition, the promise of a new order with its
reality. New ways must be found to accelerate decision and action,
and the developing countries have to be in the forefront of the
search. To dwell on the need for specific and urgent action by
the developing countries does not, of course, imply that the
solution to world poverty is the responsibility of the poor alone.
Far from it; in a world of unequals, to require even equality of
effort would be to perpetuate inequality. The industrialized
countries have a major responsibility for making the necessary
quantum leap, in the areas of ideas and of action, to enlarge the
probability of survival for all on the planet at tolerable levels
of existence. But while the industrialized countries have much to
lose from a collapse of dialogue, the developing countries have a
world to win from a new international order and, therefore, a
primordial responsibility for sustaining dialogue and ensuring
that it leads to change.

And the developing countries have a responsibility for action in their own right. After so much frustrated effort, they will almost certainly feel the need to reappraise their strategy. In doing so, there are four levels of action that should not escape attention:

First, the introduction of changes within their own economies, giving greater emphasis to strategies designed to satisfy basic needs and to mobilise the creative ability of the whole population.

Second, bringing home to the people of the developed countries the realities of interdependence and of the mutuality of benefit involved in introducing orderly change in existing economic arrangements.

Third, enlargement of trade and economic relations between the developing countries and the centrally planned economies.

Fourth, increasing functional cooperation among developing countries themselves, and especially with OPEC countries, and strengthening their capability to negotiate structural change with the West and the East.

The Necessary Action at Home
Self-reliance must be the underpinning of an action-oriented strategy for the developing countries. But self-reliance does not imply autarchy, it does not mean pulling down the shutters on the world outside. On the contrary, it presumes global cooperation and provides the most secure basis for it. Self-reliance must mean, therefore, that developing countries individually must do as much as possible for themselves on the basis of their own resources. And it must mean, also, that collectively they must exploit every possible advantage for development from dynamic cooperation among themselves - including the mobilisation of a global effort for beneficial change. Self-reliance is nothing if not a multi-dimensional strategy for development. By adopting it and, above all, by implementing it, developing countries will be acknowledging what the developed have long known, namely that dependence, both material and intellectual, is no basis on which to pursue effective negotiation, and that consensus is rarely, if ever, achieved except in circumstances where confrontation is recognised as a feasible alternative.

The new order which the developing countries seek is intended to facilitate a direct attack on the central issue of our time - widespread poverty. But such an order could be without any impact at all on the majority of people in many developing countries unless those countries themselves installed national arrangements both to optimise their gains from an improved external regime and also to bring about an equitable internal distri-

bution of the increasing national product. It is true that many
of the measures which are required to improve the internal economic order depend upon improved international arrangements in
trade and finance. For example, it would be difficult to envisage
significant and sustained improvements being made to the quality
of life of producers of export commodities in the developing
countries in the absence of a new regime for commodities. Nevertheless, improved internal arrangements need not await external
changes in every case; there is a good deal which the developing
countries individually can and must do to alleviate the conditions of their own poor, not only with a view to giving credibility to their demands for a more equitable international order,
but also because economic development will not proceed at its
most rapid rate or produce results of any significance unless it
is spurred by the full commitment of all the people and is clearly directed towards improving the conditions of life of the
poorest.

It is customary to define the actions which the developing
countries must take in terms of economic aggregates, such as
increasing the savings ratio and controlling public expenditure
on non-essentials. These, however, do not go to the heart of the
matter. What is required is the adoption of poverty-oriented
strategies which have the satisfaction of the basic needs of the
people as their centrepiece. It means establishing institutions
to mobilise the creative energy of the whole population and
directing an equitable share of the national product to the disadvantaged. Each country will have to tailor its policies to
accord with the mores and culture of its population and the
resources which it has for exploitation. All the evidence suggests, however, that most developing countries will derive
benefits from specific policies designed to widen the basis of
their economic growth.

A primary sector in this connection is rural development. For too
long, in too many countries, the rural areas have been required
to subsidise the urban areas at the pain of their own impoverishment; the results have been almost wholly bad: the creation of
urban slums deriving from the rural/urban drift being one of its
main results. The reversal of the deteriorating internal terms of
trade between primary producers in the country-side and the
producers of other goods and services in the urban areas through
the adoption of new pricing and credit policies is an urgent
priority. The benficial impact this can have on both income growth
and distribution and on food supply will be enhanced by the dis-
mantling of feudal structures (which in some places do persist)
or by curtailing fragmentation through appropriate programmes of
land reform. Developing countries can also take steps to achieve
a better distribution of their limited social services. Small
community-oriented education and health facilities designed to
meet basic needs can perhaps make larger contributions to nation-

al welfare than major urban structures with the most 'modern' (and expensive) equipment; and they can be catalysts in mobilising the creative talents of the people in the development process. They will give some semblance of meaning to 'human rights' among those for whom the phrase is now almost entirely devoid of significance. Finally, the sometimes all too ready acceleration of expenditure on arms (not always in an external context) by some developing countries in the face of national impoverishment is not only grotesque but grossly inefficient in terms of the developmental goals they set for themselves.

The installation of a new internal order will require hard political decisions; in some cases it will certainly call for policies that weaken the privileged position of elitist groups in the country. The difficulties involved cannot be underestimated and the implementation of such policies is often not assisted by the tendency of the Western media to attach ideological labels, with cold war overtones, to such essential efforts. Further, international financial institutions often require departure from the essence of such policies as pre-conditions for access to international finance and support. Despite all this, if the developing countries are to press successfully on the industrialized countries for change in the international order, given the hard political decisions involved in effecting such change, then they must themselves demonstrate a preparedness to take the necessary steps at home requiring similar courage and commitment.

Besides, there are examples in the developing world where the basis of a new internal order is being laid; they include large as well as small countries, countries under different socio-political systems; countries rich in natural resources and countries which have no known natural resources other than their human ingenuity. The common factor in these cases of successful emerging transformation appears to have been a determination to use self-reliance as the vehicle for achieving development aspirations. It has been customary to treat these examples as exceptional and arising from special or unique circumstances; yet every country is unique and each has its potential. The experience of developing countries which appear to be making the breakthrough (including mistakes made along the way) could provide valuable guidelines for other countries determined to exploit their own potential.

Reaching the People of the Developed World
International poverty is an international problem requiring an international solution. A solution is necessary and urgent because it is wrong that millions should be afflicted with the scourge of poverty when the world has the capacity to eradicate it; this is the moral imperative to action. But a solution is necessary and urgent, also, because upon it depends, in large measure, the maintenance of the very standards which the rich

countries now enjoy and which they rightly seek to preserve;
this is the imperative of survival, deriving from the linkages
of interdependence.

The plight of the poor in the developing countries has hitherto
evoked a positive, though inadequate, response in wealthy countries largely in the form of tied aid. But aid, in any event,
is the soft option. It is not a substitute for new international
arrangements to enable developing countries not only to produce
more but also to sell more, to earn more and to acquire through
these earnings more of the things which they require and which
the industrialized countries have the surplus capacity to
produce.

It is the creation of these arrangements that lies at the centre
of the new international order on which the world agreed (however grudgingly in some quarters) three years ago. Now is the
time for implementation. The moral imperative by itself has
failed to provide adequate motive power for basic change. Nor
should this occasion surprise. Centuries of experience have
shown that, both within and between nations, the moral imperative, however strongly it may dominate polite conversation among
the affluent, is never sufficient to convert dialogue into
decision and to sustain decision through action that changes
the power structure. While, therefore, the unacceptability of
the existing distribution of world income provides a strong base
for urging action at the level of the rich and poor countries
alike, it has to be faced that the morality of the Third World's
case will not be sufficient to generate political will in industrialized countries and lead to the introduction of those substantive structural changes in the world's production, trade,
technological and financial arrangements which alone will yield
equality of opportunity to the developing countries.

In this implementation phase, in transforming the structures on
the ground, conflicts inevitably arise. The hard-headed recognition by all countries, and by all peoples within all countries,
of their own self-interest in the necessary changes to existing
arrangements is the only reliable way of ensuring progress. As
we move from dialogue to decision and, more especially, to action,
it becomes increasingly necessary to reach the people of the
industrialized world. People, not just governments alone, need to
be convinced. The new order cannot be imposed by even the most
enlightened Western government on an unprepared and an unconvert-
ed people.

That task of conversion must be undertaken, and there is no
shortage of convincing evidence. It is easy to demonstrate, for
example, that sustained growth in income and jobs in the 'North'
depends critically upon enlarging purchasing power in the
'South'. The non-oil developing countries, with 63 percent of

the population of the world (excluding the centrally planned economies), earn barely 17 percent of the income generated (2). Increasing the incomes of this large majority can only enlarge the market they provide. In fact, the development of this undeveloped part of the world is the final frontier for long term expansion of the developed countries, where the affliction of weak recovery from deep recession now threatens to become chronic and where, in the constricting atmosphere that prevails, reflation is forever haunted and held in check by the spectre of uncontrollable inflation.

Recent studies carried out in international institutions, in the industrialized countries, and elsewhere, have all thrown additional light on the mutuality of interest between rich and poor in structural change. Significant perceptions are emerging; among them:

(i) The developing countries are becoming increasingly important as markets for the manufactured goods of the industrialized countries as well as for the services they produce. Some 38 cents of every additional export dollar earned by North American manufacturers and 44 cents of every additional export dollar earned by Japanese manufacturers during 1969-75 came from the developing countries. (3)

(ii) During the 1974/75 recession the continued imports by developing countries had "a perceptible impact on business trends in the developed countries. Their balance of payments deficit has sustained demand (in the developed countries) as much as say a vigorous German demand expansion". (4)

(iii) A stimulation of demand for manufactured goods in developing countries could provide the least inflationary method of recovery in OECD countries. (5)

(iv) Low cost, labour intensive, manufactured imports into the industrialized countries - the type now subject to the most pernicious forms of discrimination in these countries - can play a significant role in cooling the forces of inflation. (6)

(v) Commodity price stabilisation through a new deal for commodities - a major plank of the developing countries' programme for international reform - is important for economic management in the industrialized countries. Over the past 100 years every recession in industrialized countries has coincided with a collapse in commodity prices and earnings in the developing countries. (7) Under certain assumptions, the stabilisation of the prices of the ten core UNCTAD commodities over the decade of 1963-72 would have increased incomes in developing countries by $5 billion and yielded economic gains to the US alone of $15 billion a year. (8)

(vi) Europe in particular, and other industrialized countries as well, face the prospect of disruption to their economies because the industrial materials they need are likely to become scarce. (9)

(vii) The necessary expansion in mineral exploration and exploitation in the developing countries - where the ultimate solution has to be found - will not come about through new demands for guarantees of the investments made by transnationals. Such an approach will produce confrontation but will not enlarge the supply of materials and the goods which derive from them. (10) The more lasting solution will arise when developing countries earn the resources they need to participate on acceptable terms in all phases of such ventures. No nation, rich or poor, can afford or will any longer accept arrangements which deny it an equitable return from the exploitation of its national patrimony.

These realities and prospects are generally discounted or ignored when localised difficulties threaten to arise in the industrialized countries in the process of introducing change. We witness a growing trend towards reversing the laws of economics which argue the special need for protection to infant industries. More and more, the argument of the developed countries is that senile industries should be the prime candidates for protection. And recent attempts at trade liberalisation show little liberality towards the developing countries. Cheap imports of manufactures, efforts to maintain the purchasing power of commodities and expensive oil are castigated equally in the decision-making centres of the West; the role which the industrialized countries still perceive for the developing nations is fully revealed in this picture. This negative approach, though widespread, is not all pervasive in industrialized societies. There are signs that the perception of interdependence and the need to translate it into operational policies and programmes is being recognised. The British Minister, Frank Judd, reflected this awareness when he said (to an American audience):

"If the lot of the world's poor is to be alleviated then there will need to be a redeployment of economic activities across national boundaries. Countries like Britain, for example, will need to concentrate on industries which have a high input in skills, leaving many of our traditional industries to the Third World. We may have to accept that a change in roles, a blurring of the traditional concepts of nations divided into primary producers and industrialized countries, will call for changes in international institutions. The challenge to the dominance of the developed countries in these institutions can-cannot be shrugged aside. If they cannot be adapted, they will lose their relevance to the ordering of international relations" (11).

It would be naive to believe that these views are widely shared
in the developed world; indeed, they do not form part of the
literature for general practitioners in the field of policy. The
developing countries would therefore miss a great opportunity
if they did not help to ensure that the voices of those in the
industrialized countries who have a perception of the needs of
poorer countries are in fact widely heard and, at the same time,
that those who are told by other voices that the development of
the poorer countries is being sought at their expense are made
fully aware of the realities of interdependence.

It is now well established that a sustained expansion of industry
- which must include agro-based, agro-supportive as well as other
types - holds the key to future growth in the developing countries. Yet, the imperial connection not only assigned little
importance to industry in the developing countries but has
resulted in a host of barriers against their establishment. The
removal of these barriers is a major goal of the international
dialogue. But in this area, the voices of organised labour in
the industrialized countries are more often than not ranged
against the developing countries; organised labour is made to
see structural change solely in terms of the loss of jobs. The
other side of the coin - the growth of new jobs flowing from the
increase in import demand from the developing countries - is not
demonstrated. What is more, policies in the industrialized
countries tend to reinforce this negative perception. Adjustment
policies to relieve transitional hardship even when officially
agreed tend to be implemented with such lack of vigour that they
often fail to convince organised labour that adjustment is a
credible path to follow or even that it is one to which the
government of the day is committed.

The research needed to demonstrate the several aspects of interdependence and widen its acceptance at the various levels of
policy-making and execution is now being started - much of it in
the developed countries themselves. But this is not a process
that should be left to a handful of those already converted in
the West. Developing countries, at all levels of advocacy, and
there are many, must carry this message to the people of the
developed world whose governments, however enlightened, need
informed popular support if they are to take the decisions
involved.

That support must come from the labour movement who must see in
the struggle for real development at the international level a
reflection of their own successful struggle for social and
economic justice at the national level - and who must also see
economic growth in the South not as a threat to Northern jobs
but as an enlargement of Northern job opportunities. It must
come from the consumers - convinced that there are gains in a
new system which does not deprive them of access to the products

of the Third World at prices uninflated by artificial barriers.
It must come from the businessmen and industrialists - understanding that their long term interests, both in terms of access
to materials and their capacity to sell, lie in the restructuring
of the world order and that they would do well to make an investment in it now. It must come from the political parties and
political movements impressed with the urgency of bringing governmental policies into line with human needs and their own basic
principles. It must come from the many ordinary citizens whose
instinct of survival tells them that the present system does not
serve their own countries well and who are searching for the
values and concepts of a just global society. And it must come
from the youth as a reflection of their rejection of contemporary values and the economic structures that perpetuate them.

It is heartening to see how much is being done within many
developed countries by individuals and associations and institutions in this regard. The effort, however, has barely begun
and current economic difficulties - some, themselves, the aftermath of the collapse of the old order - do not create an altogether propitious climate for drawing attention to international
poverty, even on a basis of enlightened self-interest. All the
more reason, therefore, for a vigorous effort by the developing
countries to alert the people of the developed to the predicament which international poverty implies for rich and poor alike,
and to convert them to the cause of change.

A more Positive Role for Centrally Planned Economies

In establishing the new order, a major responsibility rests upon
industrialized Western countries; together, they dominate world
trade, international finance, technology and industrial production. But the obligation does not rest on them exclusively. All
industrialized countries, of the East no less than the West,
share the obligation for contributing to the eradication of
international poverty. The East, no less than the West, must
recognise that the security which they seek has an economic
dimension; that it will be found not mainly in escalating
expenditures on weapons of destruction but also in the elimination of those human conditions which, through the frustration
and despair that they generate, lead inexorably to conflict.
And it is a wholly inappropriate response for the centrally
planned economies to justify a laggard role in the quest for
improved living standards in the developing countries with the
plea that they had no part in the colonial exploitation of the
Third World and bear no responsibility for its reconstruction.
Restitution or reparation forms no significant part of the quest
for the new order on which a more just global society can be
established.

The adversary system that was an inevitable concomitant of the
cold war has frustrated the logical development of trade and

economic relations between the developing countries and the
centrally planned economies. Yet, paradoxically, it has not
prevented a veritable explosion in trade between the principal
protagonists in the cold war. Indeed, the chief sufferers appear
to have been the developing countries who have been affected by
the fall-out of the contest, as they have not only experienced a
relatively small increase (in both absolute and relative terms)
in their export trade with the centrally planned economies but
have also witnessed a decline in the amount of official development assistance from them.

Thus, of the $64 billion increase in imports by the centrally
planned economies between 1969-75, $30.6 billion (or 47.8 percent)
came from other centrally planned economies; an almost similar
amount, $27.5 billion (or 42.9 per cent) came from the industrial-
ized countries, the growth being almost equally divided between
primary and manufactured goods; the developing countries supplied
barely $5.6 billion (or less than 9 percent) of the total in-
crease, the larger share of the total being petroleum. (12)

The centrally planned economies can enlarge the opportunities for
development open to the developing countries - all the developing
countries: they can certainly enlarge their purchases of the
primary, processed and manufactured goods which these developing
countries can produce, as both the aggregate imports of these
commodities and the share which they obtained from the developing
countries are extremely low. At the same time, the developing
countries can only exploit such opportunities as may arise by
establishing the institutional and other arrangements which are
needed to undertake such trade under the special circumstances
which prevail. The fashioning of these instruments will take
time, and may even cause some conflict with vested interests both
in and out of those developing countries. Yet in the face of
the phenomenal expansion of trade between the industrialized
countries of the East and the West, the even more substantial
growth in financial relationships (Eastern bloc countries'
indebtedness to Western Banks is estimated at $29 billion at the
end of 1976) (13), and the clear scope for a substantial increase
in consumption in the centrally planned economies, it would be a
mistake for the developing countries to allow relics of ideological conflicts to stand in the way of accelerating their development through measures designed to enlarge their trade with the
East. The asseverations of 'Eastern' commitment to the goal and
objectives of the developing countries need to be more systematically tested.

Cooperation, Solidarity and Organisation
Functional economic cooperation between developing countries has
been generally acknowledged to be an important instrument for
accelerated growth and development. But experience with such
efforts has not been encouraging. Many integration movements

have failed to bloom; others have withered on the vine. But it would be wrong to conclude from this limited experience, which has been essentially regional, that the value of regional and inter-regional cooperation is minimal. What the events of the past do emphasise is the need for new forms of cooperation, not tied to the traditional forms of preferential trading arrangements, but directed to pragmatic ways of increasing production jointly, taking advantage of available complementarities.

The joint establishment of individual production units may be one route to follow, as some countries are now doing. New scope is offered also for joint ventures in the exploration for new mineral resources in continental areas, as valuable economies of scale are to be gained; and a whole new area for effective cooperation in the exploitation of the resources of the seas is being opened up through the discussions on the Law of the Sea. It would be a pity if the integrating function in the developing countries were assigned, by default, to the transnational enterprises alone when the developing countries are in a position to do a great deal for themselves.

In the promotion of greater cooperation among developing countries, a special responsibility falls upon two categories of countries - the relatively large and industrially advanced developing countries and the OPEC states. If global economic development is assigned a high priority by all countries, both rich and poor, there is a strong case for the relatively large and advanced developing countries to be prepared to extend to their smaller developing neighbours, especially contiguous ones, favourable conditions of access to the markets, the technology and the managerial capability they possess. These large countries themselves are in the process of seeking improved conditions from the industrialized and centrally planned economies, and it would not be unreasonable to expect them as their economies grow stronger to extend similar benefits to those less fortunately placed than themselves. The impact which the extension of such facilities would have on the donor countries would in most cases be negligible and is unlikely to cause any more transitional disturbance to their production system than would be involved by the changes being required of the industrialized countries. On the other hand, the impact would be dramatic on the smaller developing countries and open new horizons for production and cooperation. This step by step approach to promoting increasing cooperation among developing countries clearly requires further exploration. It is probable that such an approach will require modification to the existing rules governing international trade. But this need not prove to be an insuperable difficulty if there is the political will to act.

The OPEC countries have emerged as an important source of finance for both the industrialized and the developing countries. They have also markedly increased their aid effort - which in 1975 stood at over 2 percent of GNP as compared with 0.36 percent of GNP for the Western industrialized nations and 0.04 percent of GNP for the centrally planned economies. But a much greater contribution may be possible through closer cooperation between the non-oil developing and the OPEC countries.(14) Ever since the oil crisis broke in 1973 the question of complementarities between OPEC and non-oil developing countries has been mooted; it has been suggested that in designing their industrial base, the OPEC countries should take into account as a matter of policy possible backward and forward linkages with non-oil developing countries. However, this idea has not been pursued with any intensity and current indications are that the opportunities for such complementary development may soon be lost. An urgent responsibility falls on the OPEC countries to re-examine such long term possibilities; the granting of procurement preferences to the developing countries and the establishment of joint ventures with and in developing countries to supply inputs required by the OPEC countries may be among the ideas for examination.

The action taken by OPEC in reversing the long term deterioration in the price of oil no longer requires justification. At the same time these countries must recognise that the adjustment problems which developing countries now experience in the light of the higher price for oil are very serious indeed. If they acknowledge an obligation to inject new strength into the weakened economies of the non-oil developing countries - as it appears they do - they should urgently apply some of their resources to developing mechanisms for providing such support. Aid alone, welcome though it is, does not provide the answer to the long term development problem. The OPEC countries are in a position to make a substantial and lasting contribution to this problem on a basis of mutual gain.

To mention the potential of productive cooperation between the developing countries is sufficient to point to the inadequacies of the existing institutional mechanisms through which the developing countries can systematically research and explore their economic options. And this is quite apart from their needs in relation to negotiations with developed countries. The Third World is loosely organised in the Non-Aligned Movement and the Group of 77. But, periodic Non-Aligned Summits and Ministerial Meetings and ad hoc meetings of Ministers or officials of the Group of 77 alone are an inadequate basis for negotiating with the developed countries or for developing effective programmes of cooperation among the developing. Even among a cohesive group such discontinuities would be a threat to unified action. Within an inevitably disparate and multi-layered Third World grouping they provide an almost unanswerable challenge to organised effort. Some 592 professionals work full-time at the OECD Secretariat: 327 more than in UNCTAD itself.(15)

The need for a secretariat facility serving the developing countries specifically is now too urgent to be longer postponed.
There are enormous difficulties - not all at the level of
principle; but they are as nothing compared with the problems
and deficiencies attendant on inaction. The human resources
indisputably exist, much now deployed in the service of multilateral institutions. And such a facility will serve not only the
functional purpose of servicing Third World negotiators and
policy-makers but the even higher purpose of harmonising Third
World interests and strengthening Third World solidarity. All
the world will be the beneficiary - for all men have interest
in ensuring that the dialogue between the rich and poor is
effective enough to lead us to that other more equal world that
must assuredly be in this one.

Notes and References

(1) Margaret Attwood: *They are Hostile Nations*, 20th Century
Poetry and Poetics, Oxford University Press, Toronto, 1973.
(2) *World Economic & Social Indicators*, IBRD, Washington, D.C.,
1976.
(3) *North South Issues*; Presentation by the Commonwealth Secretary-
General to the Joint Economic Committee of the Congress of the
United States, Washington, D.C., April 22, 1977.
(4) John A. Holsten and Jean L. Wadbroeck: *The Less Developed
Countries and the International Monetary Mechanism*,. American
Economic Review, May 1976.
(5) Views expressed by Claude Cheysson and the U.S. Senate Budget
Officer. See James P. Grant and John W. Sewell: *The LDC Connection
- How do Events in Developing Countries Affect Inflation, GNP
Growth and Jobs in the United States*, Overseas Development
Council, August 1977.
(6) Ibid.
(7) *World Economic Interdependence and Trade in Commodities*, Her
Majesty's Stationary Office, London, May 1975.
(8) Jere J. Behrman: *International Commodity Agreements*, Overseas
Development Council NIEO series, 1977.
(9) 1977 Alastair Buchan Memorial Lecture delivered by Herr Helmut
Schmidt, Chancellor of the Federal Republic of Germany, October
1977.
(10) Address by Hon. Judith Hart, M.P., Minister for Overseas
Development, to Conference on "European Business in World Development", on 31 October 1977.
(11) *Challenges of the Rich-Poor Relationship*, Address by Hon.
Frank Judd, M.P., Minister for Overseas Development, to Congress-
ional Group for Peace Through Law, HMSO, 1977.
(12) International Trade 1975/76, GATT, 1977.
(13) Bank of International Settlements, Annual Report, Basle, 1976.
(14) Development Cooperation 1976 Review, OECD, Paris, 1976.
(15) Information obtained from unpublished sources in OECD and
UNCTAD.

Approach to a New Decade

Philippe de Seynes

Emergence of a New Philosophy

Those of us who worked closely and, if I may say, ardently with
Jan Tinbergen in the preparation of the international strategy
for the 1970s, should be the first to take stock honestly of what
has happened since those days of confidence and hope. Jan Tinbergen's vision was that of a world gradually evolving towards
the widening of the area of international decision-making and an
incipient measure of global planning and management. The "Grand
Design" embodied in the International Development Strategy was
the expression of that vision in the United Nations. Within its
framework, goals as well as means could be defined with a degree
of specificity, a model of coherence elaborated, and performance
periodically monitored, so that changes in the course prescribed
could be introduced in time. These views were strongly held and
seemed the natural outcome of the most extraordinary phase in the
"ascent of man", which humanity had yet experienced. They were
sustained by a good deal of optimism, although a widespread
"malaise" was already noticeable in the parts of the world which
had most benefited from the "miracles" of the last quarter century.

How quickly the scenery has changed! First, the lack of performance in regard to the prescribed policies, whether good or bad,
then doubts about the validity of these policies; the prophesies
of "physical limits", however misjudged and ill-documented; the
discontinuity introduced by the oil strategy whose significance
as a "transforming event", a point of departure for a necessary
mutation in international relations failed to materialize; finally the severity of a prolonged economic recession, pointing to a
malfunctioning of the world economic system. Perhaps the most
important phenomenon of this malfunctioning was the irrefutable
and cumulative evidence of persistent and, in some areas, increasing poverty against the backdrop of spectacular world-wide growth;
the realization that growth, based as it was on capital, technology and trade, was not producing equity, while stimulating the
need for it. The "Grand Design" began to disintegrate as its main
ingredients were called into question. One began to suspect that
the tools which had served to construct it, the targets and the
modelling, might have themselves contributed to bias it in the
wrong direction.

A new philosophy was emerging. It was expressed in many different
versions but there was a kind of common denominator, embodied in
the most frequently evoked watch-words, Self-Reliance and Basic
Needs Strategy. The apostles of the new creed were often de-empha-
sizing the concept of inter-dependence, deprecating strict

involvement in the international system and outward-looking development policies. They were rather advocating action at the grass
roots, "do-it-yourself" pragmatism, and the popular ethic of
"small is beautiful".

This sharp and rather sudden reaction was emerging mostly from
academic circles, and it must be viewed as a healthy sign attest-
ing to the resilience of what Dudley Seers once called "the com-
fortable ghetto of development economists". The assault, inevitably indiscriminate in its total impact on so many cherished
beliefs, may leave the United Nations in an awkward and embarrass-
ing position at a time when it is actively preparing for the
advent of a new decade. It exposes the organization as largely protected from important currents of thought. A new "Grand Design"
of some sort, to be launched in 1980, seems almost inevitable as
part of the ritual which sustains the pulse of institutions. Its
absence would be viewed, in the light of historical precedents,
as a dangerous lowering of the sights, perhaps a confession of
impotence. Grand designs, in spite of slow progress toward their
objectives, have an operational function. But their symbolic value
is even more decisive, as it carries, within a well articulated
frame of reference, a meaningful message directly related to the
aspirations of the International Community. Yet, unless a new design embodies some of the major elements of the conceptual changes
which are now in process, it will lose credibility in many
sections of the world community, whose assent and active support
is desirable.

Challenge to the United Nations
There is not, at the moment, any real evidence that United Nations
governmental bodies are willing to venture much beyond the analytical framework, and the set of prescriptions which have constituted its conventional wisdom, and which in fact were codified as
far back as 1964, at the first UNCTAD Conference. Even the resolutions proclaiming as more notable for a change in the *context*
rather than a change in the *concepts*, a new and more vigorous formulation at a time when the OPEC strategy had reshuffled the cards
of the international game, and hopefully improved the negotiating
power of Third World countries, a hope which still has to be con-
firmed.

The stability of concepts in the United Nations must be well
understood. It is largely the result of years of frustration at the
failure to implement policies on which agreements on principle had
been repeatedly registered. This has probably bred a suspicion of
every novelty which might divert or distract from obligations
unfulfilled and could even be construed as deliberate tactics to
that effect. Such reactions were already noticeable in the beginning of the 1970s, when the United Nations failed to come to grips
in a systematic manner with the problem of possible "physical
limits". Admittedly the findings of the Club of Rome were grossly

erroneous, but the questions were valid, important, and drama-
tically presented. In the face of highly unequal resources
endowment and the increased price of an essential component of
development, the organization has not, up to now, responded by
launching a bold energy programme which might be of assistance
to so many countries, both industrial and developing.

Perhaps more enduring, and therefore creating more severe problems, is the reluctance of the United Nations to bring the
social dimension, in a meaningful way, within the scope of its
research, its debates and its legislation. There are, it is true,
in official documents and resolutions, well rounded and elegant
statements about employment, distribution, participation. But
they appear somewhat perfunctory as the difficult problématique
which they raise, the conflict with other objectives and the
mechanisms whereby social goals may be effectively pursued, are
not integrated in the conceptual analysis. The history of social
reporting in the United Nations is not encouraging. Factors label-
ed as "social" come too close to the political component of
development, to the causes and effects of sociological stratifi-
cation and to other aspects in which the sovereignty of nations
is intimately involved. Meaningful reporting, not surprisingly,
can be viewed as an invasion of privacy. Beyond the periodic
recital of labour, education and health statistics and the factual description of social welfare programmes, it is difficult to
go in any depth in the analysis of the real forces at work, the
entrenched interests, the rigidity which they impart to the institutional structures and the conduct of governments. Even the ILO
conference, which pioneered in the emergence of the new creed,
has mostly shyed away from real class analysis.

Incomplete Diagnosis and Ambiguous Language

To be quite honest, there are also problems with the new creed
itself, or rather with some of its high priests and "true
believers". The diagnosis has certainly not always been correct
or complete. For instance, the more radical thinkers who have
been instrumental in bringing the new creed to life have constantly, in their analysis, overlooked or underestimated the demographic factor. To recognize its impact,, seems essential, not necessarily for the purpose of promoting birth control policies (which
can only be successful or useful within a narrow range of given
circumstances), but because numbers make a big difference in the
choice of policies. Attention to the demographic evolution might
have at an earlier stage focused the attention on surplus labour
rather than on final demand and the need for capital.

The language is also often ambiguous. Under "Self-Reliance" or
"Basic Needs Strategy" there is a whole range of discernible
approaches, from the clever but deceptive upgrading or adjustment
of traditional concepts, to the revolutionary scenarios of rupture,
not to mention the flowering of so many pastoral utopias which
may already influence the choice of investment or technology. The

recurrent use (as a kind of incantation) of derogatory expressions such as "trickle down" does needlessly conceal that traditional approaches have produced results. Too slow and lopsided, but still generating a capacity to move forward. For instance, it is somewhat ironical that in the current discussion about Basic Needs Strategies, longevity is frequently proposed as the best single indicator of social progress. In this respect the performance has been rather remarkable, even in countries which are quite derelict in their policies towards the eradication of mass poverty. Other watch-words charged with subjective emotion such as "dependencia" or "alienation" belong to the mobilizing language and have a useful function in the process of raising consciousness. They do not, however, provide practical guidance to the planners and policy-makers.

One should not begrudge the iconoclastic zeal which characterizes so much of the current literature. It is probably a necessary stage. Historically, the new creed has not emerged so much from systematic analytical work, but rather from a protest, a revolt against the failure of the International Community to come to grips with the problems of poverty, the "sense of horror" which Friedrich Engels experienced at the plight of the workers in Manchester; it stems from the intuitive repudiation of an approach to the development problem, viewed as both too complacent and misdirected, and from the will to reinstate social justice at the centre of the development syndrome.

Basic Needs - Basic Questions

However, one of the problems with the blanket condemnation of the policies of yesterday is that it leads to insulate Self-Reliance and Basic Needs Strategies from the requirements of total development. They appear as a neat package, a self contained paradigm whereas any desirable strategy of the new type will have to start from a context where a considerable amount of modernization has already taken place, for good or for bad. The infrastructure thus created, the levels and patterns of education, the stock of capital goods and many other existing factors, will condition and often constrain the options open and the margins of freedom of any voluntarist, normative new strategies.

It must also be realized that the new canons will not be acceptable if they appear to abolish or displace some of the most enduring and strongly held ideas, prevalent in almost all countries in the process of development. Among these, the ideal of industrialization remains paramount. Not only is it, *in the long run*, the element *par excellence* of modernization but it also conveys an "image of the future", which probably has no equivalent in terms of propulsing a vigorous development effort. Therefore, one must be ready, in pursuing Basic Needs Strategies, to cope with trade-offs and with the necessity of choices. While food and health confronts us with physiological survival which suggests absolute priority, the same is not necessarily true of housing and education, which may come in some kind of conflictual relationship with other development goals, at least within a perspective of some duration. The acceptability and success of Basic Needs Strategies require that the benefits as well as the costs of alternative policies be carefully examined. Paradoxically, situations where the problem is the more forbidding are perhaps those where the choice is clear. When demographic pressures are already paramount, which is the case in a number of countries comprising some of the largest populations, a policy of capital accumulation organized around the mobilization of surplus labour would seem to be the *only* effective strategy likely to reconcile both the satisfaction of Basic Needs and the pursuance of industrialization. In other circumstances, it is probably helpful - if hazardous - to plan for successive strategies the sequence of which depends on preferences as well as constraints.

In the current literature about Basic Needs Strategies the *final product* is usually more emphasized than the process. Much useful work is done in regard to the definition of a basket of goods and services which, if delivered to all sections of the community, would meet its most elementary requirements. If food rationing appears necessary, for instance, either through administrative action or through the price system, refined indicators, valid under different climatic conditions and for different occupational structures, should help. Given the time needed for the building of a full-fledged medical corps, research about the optimum training and minimum knowledge programmes required in the interim is essential. Yet all this work should be placed in perspective. It is unlikely that those governments which have successfully pursued policies aimed at the satisfaction of basic needs have relied on a smiliar amount of effort and ingenuity as that which is at present lavished on such studies.

In fact, it is the *process* through which new strategies can be promoted that is the more difficult and essential to elucidate, the mechanisms, the obstacles, the constraints. "Delivery system" is very much part of the jargon of a Basic Needs Strategy. But the terminology is here very misleading, for it conceals the problems deeply rooted in the political and social fabric of societies.

Basic Needs Strategies and Power Structures
On a rough approximation, it appears that Basic Needs Strategies have been successfully pursued within two different types of societies: one pre-capitalist (or patrimonial), the other socialist. The first is best exemplified in the experience of Japan and countries which have been under its influence, such as South Korea and Taiwan. Their experiments antedate the era of large-scale modern industries and, to some extent, also the era of exhaustive sociological investigation so that one can be tempted to "idealize" them. It seems probable, as Norman McRae has shown in one of the

Economist's surveys, that the development effort was, from the origin, deliberately directed towards the achievement of full employment in the rural areas. Increased productivity in agriculture was assisted by public investments, and small-scale industrial enterprises, closely linked with the agricultural set-up, and located in the rural areas themselves, gradually absorbed the surplus manpower resulting from a still fast growing population. These industries did not require sophisticated skills; they rather relied on training by doing, but they did impart to the workers a minimum of technical education and of new attitudes which enabled them to enter naturally the labour force of large-scale modern industries when those required it. Such a scheme represents a far more harmonious process than the abrupt transition from primitive farming to the new environment of mechanized and automated plants on which contemporary industry is based.

It also had another effect; the patrimonial context frequently evolved mechanisms devised for social defense and social improvement which were able to survive during the industrial transition and to protect the new societies from some of the worst aspects of wild capitalism which were not avoided elsewhere. Looking at such an evolution, again provided that one is not idealizing it, an important lesson emerges. It is futile to talk about "a" Basic Needs Strategy. It should rather be viewed as a transitional stage which should be carried out in such a way as not to jeopardize future phases of development. The concept of "reversibility" is a neglected area of economic and social research and yet it may hold some useful clues for the choice of development patterns.

It is obviously easier to begin in the way exemplified in the patrimonial model for it implies a kind of "virtuous circle" which produces cumulative results both for economic growth and social welfare. But most countries have missed this opportunity. It is a big handicap, now more recognized, to start, as so many countries did, by privileging industry largely through the operation of adverse terms of trade for agriculture. Reversing the rural-urban population movements when the need for food self-sufficiency is finally recognized is one of the most difficult feats of social engineering. It can probably only succeed under scenarios of rupture.

It is now known that even in such circumstances, Basic Needs Strategies were able to succeed, and in a relatively short time, within a socialist model of society. Most observers now agree on the achievements in this respect registered by China, North Korea, Vietnam and Cuba. And going back to an earlier period one should also recall that, starting from a higher level of development, the Soviet Union was very successful in ensuring to its large and varied population within a short period the elementary goods of individual consumption as well as advanced services in the health and education fields. It is also known that these experiments have not followed a smooth linear progression. Rather, they have been subjected to successive periods of drastic reappraisal - sometimes painful - and correction. One fundamental element of the policies pursued seems to have been the bending of the individualistic frame of mind towards the search for a collective identity. The techniques used to that effect could not succeed without a high degree of social discipline, requiring specific institutional systems. These are readily accepted under conditions of extreme poverty, if there is widespread confidence that the State, however authoritarian, is relentlessly and efficiently working toward the objective moves forward towards greater dynamism and specialization, collective discipline is more difficult to enforce. Once the worst problems are overcome, it may begin to be felt as oppressive; the cultural consensus which had been forged may then disintegrate. The system may have to rely more on coercion and develop a political and administrative apparatus, strong enough to perpetuate itself even when the conditions which made it necessary have dissipated.

How much of a Basic Needs Strategy can be attempted within different power structures and systems of social organization? How, within these different power structures, can the pursuit of Basic Needs Strategies be appropriately combined with the other objectives of society, such as rapid industrialization? These anguishing questions are more crucial than those raised by the exact composition of the ideal food basket and they should be faced squarely in the ongoing debate on alternative approaches to development. At a symposium recently organized by UNITAR and IDEP to explore the answers to these various questions, a significant section of the participants were of the opinion that Self-Reliance and Basic Needs Strategies would not be possible except under a revolutionary process, a scenario of more or less complete rupture with the existing institutional framework. This is not very hopeful for a majority of countries where it is hard to see how such scenarios could come about. According to the very teachings of Karl Marx, there is a right moment and a right set of circumstances for the success of revolutionary undertakings. Otherwise a backlash is almost inevitable. Where policies of Self-Reliance have been introduced, it has been mostly in the wake of severe traumas, foreign or civil wars, or a "long march", an armed insurrection sustained over a long period. This should not be surprising, for not only do such events create conditions favourable to a large scale overhauling of the institutional system, but they bring with them a direct experience of something very close to the desired strategies. Armies in the field, or guerilla forces, must by necessity live largely from the land which they occupy and mobilize to the maximum extent the local resources.

Self-reliance and the application of do-it-yourself ingenuity, public works through the mobilization of available labour and elementary technologies are a matter of survival. There must also

be a measure of egalitarian distribution of the goods and services at hand, for the levels of living of the chiefs under th
conditions of war cannot be so very different from those of the
troops. In such circumstances, all the right attitudes come naturally and without too many questions being asked about Marxism-
Leninism. How many revolutionary situations in the sense defined
by Marx are in existence today? In so many countries a well
entrenched coalition is in command which would preclude the success of a scenario of rupture or promise a severe reaction if
it were to succeed momentarily. However sincerely we espouse the
ideal of Basic Needs and Self-Reliance, there is a danger in a
certain absolutism which colours much of the discourse today.

Nevertheless, there is much to go by. It is not completely a
shot in the dark. There is already some solid evidence from which
we can see that progress towards welfare objectives need not
always wait for an increase in average income.From an important
study on the State of Kerala commissioned some years ago by the
Committee on Development Planning, (The "Tinbergen Committee"),
we clearly see that calorie intake has moved faster than income,
in line with local food production. We also see that one of the
poorest states in India has the lowest mortality rate, and,
looking further at the population problem, we find correlations
which lead us to believe that demography can be viewed as an
endogenous factor influenced not just by the rise in income, but
by the deliberate pursuance of social policies. The improvement
in empirical knowledge which comes from such studies may gradually give us a better basis for inserting Basic Needs Strategies
within different development patterns.

Basic Needs Strategies and the International System
Conceptually, one of the difficult questions inherent in the
current debate is the insertion of economies geared to Basic Needs
Strategies within the international economy. Disassociative policies or, for short, "delinking", feed much of the debate today,
as many feel, not without reason, that the type of linkages which
have been created between industrial and developing countries
through capital transfers, export-led industries and international production have had themselves a corrupting effect, and would
inevitably thwart any self-reliant scheme. It is one thing to
realize that the policies which have produced or condoned increased inequality and the persistence of mass poverty have been part
of outward oriented policies of development more attentive to the
demand of the world market than to the domestic needs of the economy. But it is a rather gratuitous assumption to believe that
by severing their links with the international system the developing countries would be more prone or more able to pursue in a
sustained way the desired social policies.

Soft states (to use Gunnar Myrdal's terminology) naturally choose
a soft approach. Others, however, learn to develop the machinery

needed to direct the profits of exports and other dividends
accruing from the international system towards their war against
poverty. Different types of political coalitions and administrative regimes have learnt to break in this respect an old fatali-
ty, as the traditional type of class analysis proved misleading.
The assumption that extreme austerity produced by "delinking"
would presumably be accompanied by the required changes in the
balance of social and economic power may be another "trickle
down" fallacy.

This is not to say that the modalities for integrating Third
World development efforts within the world economy should not
undergo changes, sometimes drastic. This is fundamental to the
preparation of a new "Grand Design" which would give real meaning
to the war against poverty.

There is a lot to be said, for instance, for a new approach to
capital transfers which, in their present mode, too often reflect
and perpetuate the inheritance of colonial days. Aid, as we know
it, should fade out within a specified period, but international
liquidity remains a necessary ingredient of the progress of poor
countries, particularly some of those most attentive to social
improvements, which may require a larger and more steady flow of
foreign exchange. Cuba, for instance, offers a good example of a
country which has pursued most of the policies advocated in the
new creed of Basic Needs and which, thanks to the support received
from the Soviet Union, has been able to avoid the foreign currency bottlenecks which have defeated so many development efforts.

It is a great pity that the idea of using the creation of monetary reserves for development purposes, which had made steady
progress even within the ranks of the more recalcitrant, seems
to have evaporated during the recent monetary upheavals. It is
true that, with floating exchange rates, the need for the creation
of new reserves has to a great extent vanished, at least in those
countries of the industrial world whose financial and economic
systems respond naturally to fluctuations in exchange rates. But
some other device for "deficit financing" of development could
be constructed for implementation in the 1980s and beyond. A
scheme of this sort should be assured of continuity, for its very
meaning is to ensure that the burden of fighting world inflation,
when it occurs, does not bear on that part of the liquidity created for development purposes.

The Response of the North
Perhaps the most difficult problem will be that posed by the
world-wide *redeployment of industry*. This is likely to be one of
the major claims of developing countries at the time of negotiation of a new "Grand Design". The targets which have already been
proposed by UNIDO for the distribution of industrial activities
should now be worked out in such a way as to allow redeployment
in conformity with the policies of self-reliance and basic needs.

This means that the redeployment cannot be based exclusively, or perhaps mainly, on the traditional criterion of comparative advantages. The optimum mobilization of productive forces in developing countries must be the guiding principle and this would require, in most cases, a simultaneous advance of consumer and capital goods industries. The new international specialization on which one should now begin to speculate should therefore be substantially different from that implicit in the conventional wisdom, and which still permeates international action. The response of the North to new approaches in the South must take into account the complex set of requirements of self-reliant policies, the political and sociological as well as the economic.

Is the North likely to respond? The U.N. through some kind of strange tropism, has never systematically scrutinized the operating mechanism of industrial societies, being rather content with prescribing policies of trade and aid and technology transfers which were, it was thought, susceptible of being pursued within a voluntarist approach, independently of what happened to the basic structures of the economies and the societies. But industrial redeployment inevitably calls into question these basic structures, and the attention of the United Nations should now be directed to them. Advanced societies, either through self-deception, or through calculated occultation, have often left out of their political discourse some of the major flaws which they tolerate. In almost all the rich countries there is today a Third World of disadvantaged minorities, old people, unemployed youth, as well as a significant section of the potentially productive labour force teetering around the poverty line (where such an indicator has been established). Their numbers fluctuate and are not precisely known. They are probably not the majority but they may sometimes be close to two-fifths of the people. They are the marginals, excluded from influence on the course of events: they are not members of the strong and most influential trade unions and therefore cannot rely on the negotiating process; they have neither the majority of votes, nor can they promote or change governmental action through the electoral process.

One characteristic which distinguishes the present situation from earlier periods in industrial countries is that a majority is now either benefitting from the system or hoping to benefit from it in the near future. Under such conditions there is a very wide coalition of vested interests, within which adversary relations between various groups can be pursued sometimes ferociously, both within the context of labour negotiations and in political infighting, but without producing any improvement for the disadvantaged. To raise the income of the disadvantaged minority and to ensure its steady employment should be the highest priority of policy-makers. The wide publicity which has recently accompanied a scheme by Professor Thurrow of M.I.T. for combatting unemployment through subsidized wages indicates a new sensitivity remi-

niscent, to people of my generation, of the 1930s, about a
problem often forgotten in the context of continuing expansion
and uncontrolable inflation. Professor Thurrow's scheme would
naturally raise many problems, as he himself acknowledges, but,
just as the creation of liquidity for development purposes, it
is a device for protecting certain priority objectives from the
impact of retrenchment measures when these become unavoidable.

But the problem must also be approached from the side of supply.
The situation seems to come partly within the framework of the
analysis applied by Samir Amin to the Third World where he
shows convincingly that the underprivileged are not given a
chance to acquire the type of goods which they could afford. The
whole productive apparatus of the industrial world is geared to
meeting the needs of an affluent or near affluent majority and
with ever more bulky investments, the apparatus has no great
incentive to adapt for a new market of the poor. This skewed state
of affairs is causing serious harm not only to the deprived, but
to the system itself, as we have been able to witness during
those years of enduring recession. In spite of sometimes considerable liquidity in the majority of households, the consumers
did not behave as they were supposed to do. They refused to
boost final demand and thereby stimulate expansion because they
had already reached, as consumers, a degree of saturation of the
goods produced by the system, and preferred to retain their
income in the light of future uncertainties. Meanwhile, the deprived did not find on the market at acceptable prices the goods
which they badly needed. In this way, the cyclical phenomenon has
become closely linked to fundamental structural defects, particularly stubborn unemployment and the unequal distribution of
income.

These situations are part of the total context in which development policies must now be redefined. As was said in the report
of the Dag Hammarskjöld Foundation *What Now* at the time of the
Seventh Special Session of the General Assembly: "the situation
cannot be understood, much less transformed, unless it is seen
as a whole". In fact, in the conjunction of massive poverty in
the South with deprivation in the North, there is perhaps an
element which could usefully be highlighted and analyzed in the
shaping of a new order, particularly in regard to trade and
industrial policies. A quarter century of almost uninterrupted
expansion had produced liberal attitudes with regard to trade.
In the North it had also opened the highly exciting vision of
a post-industrial society, which in turn would facilitate a new
international specialization within which the interests of the
industrial and developing countries would more easily converge.

Where is this vision today? Legitimate doubts about previous
policies need not generate the despondency and anxiety which we
now witness, inducing attitudes of retrenchment, or extreme

caution, which, in the case of trade, mean protectionism. These attitudes are now being rationalized in an attempt at gaining legitimacy. They are expressed in spurious euphemisms, such as "organized free trade", "orderly marketing agreements", "concerted regional autonomies", even "neo-mercantilism", as if from such language could ever emerge a scheme of international justice and rationality. The principle of trade adjustment for the sake of a new world-wide specialization and the advent of a post-industrial society in the North, inscribed in many legislations but nowhere implemented, should now be placed high on the agenda of a new "Grand Design" and become the main matter of trade negotiations.

Only with the continued expansion of trade can the North plan for a new type of industrial expansion and the South be given an outlet for its growing production of manufactures. The poor of the rich countries should be allowed to acquire the cheaper goods which the developing world will continue to produce for a long period under conditions of competitive advantage. In the present mood it is often said that export-led growth can only accomodate a small number of particularly well-positioned countries. But this again is the product of a static view underestimating or overlooking the constant shifting which is taking place and is the characteristic of the trade currents. It reflects an over pessimistic estimation of the expansion potentialities of Western society, a neglect of the rapidly growing trading capacity of socialist countries with their formidable numbers and expanding markets which could open up even under arrangements not implying full multilateralism.

Appropriate industrial plans for Northern countries should therefore encompass two types of policies: those designed to encourage and stimulate the shift towards the industries of the future, and those aiming at redirecting part of the production apparatus to produce the goods which are not internationally tradable at costs which would make them accessible to the poorest sections of their populations. The latter would involve mainly housing and related industries, transport and collective services, but also a range of other industries including food and pharmaceutical processing. Such policies, as part of a new "Grand Design" conceived to wage a real war against poverty wherever it is found, would seek to maximize the convergence of interests between various types of countries. They would give a larger significance to interdependence as well as to a New International Economic Order.

Restoring Lost Confidence

A United Nations "Grand Design" for the 1980s and beyond, if there is to be one, must aim above all at restoring the confidence which has been lost. This cannot be done by simply repeating old prescriptions, nor with a vision of the future as constricted as it is now. The new message should come out clearly for a reorder-

ing of objectives and a re-orientation of policies, taking
charge more forcefully than in previous exercises, of the full
dimension of human aspirations for social justice both within
and between nations.

One important instrument of action at the disposal of the United
Nations system is to be found in its operational programmes.
They should be overhauled and directed towards a cooperative
exploration of the difficult problems of the choice of technologies and forms of social organization. It is invidious, even
shocking and not very practical, to seek, as some are suggesting,
to subordinate the provision of financial or technical assistance
to criteria of good social behaviour. For who is going to judge?
But it is possible to assist those who wish to pursue a new
course towards equity and poverty eradication with the full facilities available to the United Nations system. It is often
thought that social innovation cannot be subject to laboratory
experimentation. This is not at all certain. The United States
has for some time been conducting and evaluating certain pilot
programmes to test the applicability of a guaranteed income, or
a negative income tax. There are, all over the Third World, spot-
actions which embody some of the concepts which must now be
introduced in the development syndrome. With the assistance of the
international system they could be used for demonstration effects,
and gradually be widened to encompass national policies. Thus,
the programmes of the United Nations system could develop a more
specific value than they now assume and become pioneering instruments for a new deal in global cooperation.

Can We Reach a "Global Compact"? *

Barbara Ward

A New Economic Order Takes Shape

There are a number of ways of thinking about a "New International
Economic Order". For instance, it would be quite rational to
decide that no issue is so new or so important in the world
economy as our sudden perception, in the Seventies, that there
may be limits to the world's supplies of raw materials,
thresholds to the amount of pollution the world's ecosystems
can bear and wholly unforeseen physical interdependences - of
soil, of water, of winds and climates - which, unsuspected even
a decade ago, could do permanent planetary damage to rich and
poor nations alike. But in fact the phrase, a "New International
Economic Order" today means something much more political,
specific and precise. Its roots lie in the developing nations'
fundamental aspiration to follow the political ending of colonization by a comparable economic and social emancipation.

The idea is clear. But given the interweaving of world economic
interests, the complexity of the thousands upon thousands of
transactions in planetary commerce and, above all, the degree of
economic dependence which grew up during the colonial years,
the task is proving more complicated than the political termina-
tions of empire. With the few tragic exceptions (among them South
East Asia or Algeria), the whole process - celebrating the first
formal Independence Day, running down the flag, signing up the
new constitution and taking one's seat in the United Nations -
all proved straight forward enough compared with trying to
unweave and reweave the patterns created in several centuries
of deepening trade relations in a world market. It is to this
infinitely more complicated task that the developing nations
are dedicated in their search for a "new economic order".

In formal terms, it can be said to have come to birth in May
1974 at the Sixth Special Session of the United Nations General
Assembly. A long resolution, carried by consensus - but significantly, with strong reservations on the part of the United
States, Britain, Japan and West Germany - laid down a number of
basic principles:

● that nations should enjoy sovereignty over their own resources,
including the right to nationalize them;

● that these resources should be developed by processes of
industrialization and by the adoption or invention of appropriate
technologies under local control;

---

* This paper also appeared in the Encyclopaedia Brittannica
Yearbook 1978.

• that the conduct of world trade should neither set special obstacles in the way of nations' access to other national markets nor work against some sort of more equitable balance between the higher export earnings derived from manufactured goods on the one hand and the lower prices for most raw materials and semi-manufactures on the other;

• that more concessionary funds should be made available to the poorer nations by the already industrialized and hence wealthy states.

It is perhaps significant that nothing was said about the need for institutional change *within* developing states in order to make them more able to benefit by changes at the international level. Clearly no amount of aid or trade will transform a feudal economy with ninety percent of the land owned by ten percent of the people or achieve the modernization of a military dictatorship bent on spending every available cent on arms or prestige. But the General Assembly is an *international* forum and to insist on internal reform is not its specific function.

Where the assembled nations did go into greater detail was in the reordering required in international trade. There was reference to the need for some kind of special fund to underpin the financing of buffer stocks in order to achieve greater price stability for a range of vulnerable commodities - coffee, sugar, tea, sisal, a number of minerals. Compensatory finance to offset sudden falls in export incomes was also brought up. The issue was raised whether primary exports supplied by poor nations might not in some way be "indexed" so that their price would automatically rise if the manufactures they import from industrialized countries continued to reflect an upward movement of inflation. Such, in broad outlines, was the first statement of the new economic order. But naturally it has a very long history behind it and some very vivid consequences flowing from it. Both must be examined if its full meaning is to be understood.

Colonial Ventures

The starting point is the very end of the fifteenth century and the fleet of little cockleshell boats of the merchant adventurers going out from Western Europe to trade for all the goods and luxuries of the East. Between the sixteenth and the nineteenth century, these men and their successors established a world market. They were not particularly interested in founding empires. They simply wanted to trade. They obeyed all the restrictive ground rules for commerce laid down by the great Khan Akbar, and his successors in India until the dynasty collapsed into local rivalries and wars. As late as the 1820s, British trade with China was confined to Canton and British merchants were not even allowed to take boat trips on the river. The experience was clear. Wherever strong local rule prevailed, the Europeans had no

choice - or even perhaps desire - but to remain traders. Some of
their governments at home were not sure that they even wanted
trade. It is ironic to remember that in mid-eighteenth century
Britain, when fears for the balance of payments were disturbing
the government, a semi-official outcry occurred against the
habit of new middle classes to buy foreign textiles (damasks
from Damascus, calico from Calicut, muslins from Muslim Bengal)
and put Britain into debt to foreign governments, including the
Indians.

But wherever local authority was weak, disorganized or tribal,
the traders moved in. Their reasons were various enough to
demonstrate how little the takeovers were acts of institutional
imperialism. Some wanted to protect their trade against local
disorder, some simply went in for loot. Sometimes the genuinely
imperial ambitions of a local proconsul, a Clive or a Wellesley,
played a key role. But, above all, the British, the French, the
Dutch, the Spaniards and the Portuguese were usually conspiring,
supporting local rivals and finally moving in largely to keep
the others out. The outcome of four centuries of confused local
resistances, collapses, revivals and interventions was a world
system controlled from Europe either by settlement as in the
Americas or by colonial rule almost everywhere else. All in all,
the system was still broadly intact as late as 1945. And one of
the fundamental purposes of its rulers was to trade and invest
in a worldwide market with the least possible interference from
anyone else.

At this point it is necessary to look at one or two of the
basic characteristics of a market, not simply a world market but
any market. In spite of its vast advantage as a decentralized,
objective, unregimented means of satisfying the infinite variety
and number of goods and services people usually desire, it has
certain characteristics which affect its usefulness and acceptability both at the local and the planetary level. Any market
is determined to a considerable degree by power. The early
theorists of the market - Adam Smith, Ricardo - on the whole
assume a rough equality in the bargain between buyers and sellers.
In this case, the market is indeed an indispensible tool. But
suppose the power is totally unequal? In the early nineteenth
century, the mass of the workers had nothing to offer but their
labour. They could not bargain at all and by what was called
"the iron law of wages", their reward for factory work would
fail to equal the bare basic cost of keeping them alive. This
level of "reward", as Engels and Marx pointed out, would hardly
provide purchasing power to match the increasing productivity
and output of the new machines. So, they said, the system would
collapse under crises of "over-production" which were really
ones of under-consumption.

However, by the end of the nineteenth century, the scarcity of

workers in North America, the increase in their skills and
education in Western Europe, the action of reformers, the beginnings of trade unionism with collective bargaining and, above
all, adult suffrage started a change in the *power* relationships
of industrialized markets. Then, after World War II, the
Keynesian idea that the maintenance of effective demand - in
other words, consumption - would be the key to economic growth
helped to produce a twenty-five year boom. True, in the Seventies, the question whether this power of ever-rising consumption,
intensified by high corporate rewards and by union strength, may
not be surpassing the economy's capacity to satisfy it without
inflation is a critical factor in the developed world's reaction
to the workings of the market, at home or abroad. But the important point here is to underline the element of power in determining the general functioning of any market system.

Another aspect of this power lies, of course, in monopoly.
Anyone who can corner or control the market in a certain essential resource has virtually absolute power, at least for a time.
The Arab nations with vast oil reserves and small populations
are in this position. North America's monopoly of surplus grain
is as great. Australia, North America and South Africa are not
far short of a monopoly in uranium. Then again nations with
obviously superior military power can monopolize the market. It
is often said, for instance, that the root of the weakness of
developing nations in trade is their enforced concentration on
raw materials. But the Soviet Union can fix the prices for its
exports of raw materials to Eastern Europe and buy back their
industrial goods with the same advantage. And, in the light of
history, we have to realize that one of the most effective
means of securing very great and even monopoly power is quite
simply by colonial control. Throughout its four centuries of
existence, the world market has been, broadly speaking, subject
to the power and regulation of the peoples of Europe and
latterly of their settler descendants in the United States.

Industry Takes the Lead
This colonial control was partly both caused and reinforced by
another factor - the industrial revolution. After about 1750,
first Britain, then Western Europe and America's North-Eastern
seaboard moved into wholly new types of mass production of
goods for people's daily needs and the production of machines
to make these goods. Local handicraft producers were all but
wiped out and moved into the factories along with the dispossess-
ed, landless workers. But in places like Bengal, new Lancashire
textiles wiped out the spinners and weavers and they had
nowhere to go. The muslims came from Manchester now, not Dacca.
As the nineteenth century developed, the old trading patterns
were simply reversed. Europe no longer sought Asian manufactures.
They opened up mines and plantations to provide their own
factories with basic materials. Africa, partly by direct invest-

ment, partly by way of the detestable export of slaves, had long been drawn into the system since slave labour helped to produce the cotton and sugar and tobacco in much of the New World. The small elites of feudal rulers in Latin America also joined in the trade, selling sugar, coffee, grain and meat in return for Western industrial goods. Without anyone in particular planning it, a world market was set up in which the power of the newly industrialized nations was the determining factor - although it was called "comparative advantage". The colonial rulers, the developed industrial firms, the traditional local leaders were in control of a system whereby raw materials flowed out of the "South" - Latin America, black Africa and Asia - to the North Atlantic core, there to be transformed into manufactured goods and sold in local markets and back to the primary producers.

In the process, all the services - shipping, banking, insurance, research for new products - remained with the Atlantic powers. All the "value added" which comes from, say, turning a cocoa bean into dessert chocolate was equally engrossed by the industrialized states. As late as the 1970s, the export of the twelve major raw materials (if we exclude oil) from the poorer nations earned $30 billions a year for the producers. But they cost purchasers $200 billion before they reached the final consumer. The $170 billion balance represents the whole "value added" of the industrial process, almost entirely absorbed by the industrialized nations.

The distinguished Dominican economist, Père Lebret, had a word for this basic world exchange. He called it *l'economie de traite*, the "milchcow economy", in which everything is sucked out of the "South" and sent North with just enough sent back to keep the system functioning. All the local services, all the means of communication, all the developed sectors served this pattern. The roads and railways led to the coast. Virtually all the big cities - from Shanghai to Valparaiso - were ports and acted as entrepot centres for an essentially external system. Latin America's coastal cities gave the continent a higher degree of urbanization in the early twentieth century - with not even five percent of the people in industry - than was the case in Western Europe with at least twenty percent in manufacturing jobs. Thus there grew up a subservient urbanism, attached not to the local hinterland but to the external Atlantic system. This, incidentally, is a basic root of the huge, unbalanced metropolises of the developing world today.

Into the Seventies

Such, broadly speaking, was the economic background, in part still hidden and misunderstood, of the world which emerged in 1945. The industrialized nations, made up of mixed and planned economies, contained about 35 percent of the world's peoples, enjoyed 75-80 percent of the world's wealth, 85 percent of its trade, 90 percent of its services, well over 90 percent of its industry and nearly 100 percent of its research - percentages which have since remained virutally unchanged (save that the percentage of world population living in the rich nations has fallen still further). The 70 percent of the world's peoples living in the developing world, or "the South" as it has come to be called, suffered - and still suffer - the corresponding opposite percentages and hence lack of power. A world market exists but wholly biased towards the needs of the industrialized giants. The question after 1945 has been not so much whether such a system could endure but how soon its inequities and instabilities would begin to emerge into the political arena.

The Fifties and Sixties marked a number of vital preliminary changes. The first was the ending of direct colonial control by Western market economies and the establishment, through the United Nations and its agencies, of at least the concept of a world-wide system of cooperation which transcended both power relations and purely economic interests. The second was a modest acceptance by the developed market societies (the Socialist states played only a very small part here) of the fact that ordinary commercial methods were not enough to secure world growth and that aid-giving and concessionary lending - the equivalent of nineteenth century philanthropy? - would be needed to give the new nations an extra shove towards evolving their own productive base and then, by following traditional "stages of growth", reach at last the felicity of the industrialized consumer society. The third change was the phenomenal growth of large multinational corporations, based in the main in North America (with a few in Europe), whose leaders felt quite able to conduct world trade without the backing of colonial control and indeed saw themselves - however inappropriate their highly capital intensive technologies in labour rich economies - as main tools of modernization in "Southern" markets. Nor was their attitude wholly irrational since the developing governments often encouraged them by every kind of concession to enter the local economy, usually to hasten by all means the process of industrialization which had been the neglected Cinderella of colonial times. The fourth development was the uneasy sense, which began as early as the mid-Fifties, that this combination of a formal ending of political colonization together with the rapid expansion of Western-based (and usually Western-owned) local industrialization might in fact be leaving the old relations of dependence intact. Nominally the world was free. Actually the pattern of its economy was still colonial.

This was the fundamental uneasiness which began to express itself in a series of Third World Conferences. The Afro-Asian Conference at Bandung was the first in 1953. Then came the series of "Non-Aligned Nations" Conferences - Belgrade in 1961, Cairo in 1964, Lusaka in 1970, Algiers in 1973, Colombo in 1976.

At the same time, the developing nations began to wonder
whether their fundamental inherited role as suppliers of raw
materials would be much changed by such new international
agencies as the General Agreement on Tariffs and Trade (GATT) or
the International Monetary Fund (IMF). They noted that over 80
percent of their trade was still in primary produce. They had
barely 7 percent of the world's industry and although the Fifties
and Sixties were years of rapid and even unprecedented growth -
the average annual growth rate was of the order of 5 percent -
they seemed to remain on the lower steps of a moving staircase
for, as they went up, the rich went up ahead. The old dependence remained. Indeed, it was becoming reinforced by the new
debts incurred for modernization. With these pre-occupations,
they persuaded "the North" to join with them in establishing a
new trade organization - the U.N. Conference on Trade and
Development (UNCTAD) - to give more weight both to their decisions and to their difficulties. Then, at UNCTAD's 1964 Conference, they set up the Third World "Group of 77" (it now has
114 members) to be an instrument of greater influence, in other
words, of power in world trade negotiations.

Such was the position in 1973 - the Northern states feeling they
had behaved with reasonable openness and generosity, abandoning
colonial control, transferring about $12 billion a year in aid,
giving some openings to Third World trade through a careful
list of General Preferences and joining in endless discussions
with their Southern partners, all designed to disentangle difficulties and grievances. But these seemed relatively small
advantages compared with the massively unchanged relationships
of power and wealth. Apart from a few developing states - South
Korea, Taiwan, Brasil - few had lessened their dependence on
primary exports. It was in this scene of deepfelt disadvantage
that the decision of the oil producers and exporters (OPEC) to
increase oil prices five-fold in 1973 produced its revolutionary
effect.

It was not a simple or uniform effect. Indeed, for non-oil producers such as the Indian sub-continent, the increased costs in
fuel and fertilizer were catastrophic. Some others - highly
populated oil-producing states like Nigeria or Indonesia, for
instance - felt the increase chiefly as a partial relief from
insurmountable economic difficulties. The chief shock was in the
North. France, West Germany and Japan had become largely dependent on imported oil. America's reserves were declining. Above
all, after a twenty-five year "binge" in growing use of oil at
under two dollars a barrel (up to 15 percent a year in Japan,
for instance), the developed market economies suddenly found
themselves sharing something of the traditional position of the
Southerners - to be no longer in control of one of their most
crucial economic decisions. "The New Economic Order" came to be
generally seen - as, in the eyes of the South, it always had

been seen - as a question of change in the balance of power in the market, the power without which economic bargains are invariably biased towards the heavyweights.

The new strength of OPEC was enough at least to open in very short order new and more serious negotiations between North and South on the best means of regulating their economic relations with each other - once again, the planned economies have played virtually no part. The two chief forums of negotiation have been UNCTAD and the so-called Conference on International Economic Cooperation (CIEC) in Paris, an *ad hoc* body of 27 nations - 8 from the North and 19 from the South, of which 8 are members from OPEC. On the agenda of both groups are the main points of the Sixth Special Assembly Resolution.

It must at once be admitted that, after two years of discussion, there is not too much progress to report. The reason lies in the very disturbance and disarray of the world economy. The OPEC price rise coincided with an almost universal boom in the industrialized nations and by a harvest failure so great in the Soviet Union that it quietly bought up virtually the entire North American grain reserve in 1972/3. The result was a tripling of world food prices and all three together - boom, fuel (with fertilizer) and food - set in motion an inflationary spiral which even tough recessionary measures did not check. The phenomenon of "stagflation", of falling jobs and rising prices, dragged on in the North and there could hardly have been a less favourable background for the consideration of the South's main demands.

To transfer more concessional aid to the South when internal unemployment was above 6 and 7 percent (and among young workers up to 25 percent) was felt in domestic terms to be politically impossible. To give greater access to Third World manufactures - say, of shirts and shoes - would knock out yet more labour-intensive industries in the unemployed sectors of the North. To link raw material prices to the cost of manufactures by a form of indexing could be seen as a method of institutionalizing inflation. Even the concept of greater stability of prices achieved through a Common Fund purchasing a variety of buffer stocks in time of high supply or low demand and releasing them to offset incipient scarcities seemed too like consessionary aid for easy acceptance. In any case, the North could not be sure that the one commodity whose price they would wish to see stabilized - oil - would ever figure in the programme. The result of these direct and biting conflicts of interest has at least not been break-down. But so far a constant postponement of decisions until the next meeting has proved the chief means of evading deadlock.

The Grounds for Hope

Yet there are four reasons for modest optimism. The first is simply based upon moral experience. The rich have learnt, especially under pressure, to be more just and understanding with the poor. The world economy has its reformers just as had Victorian Britain. The pattern is not lost.

The proof lies in the second reason. The wealthy industrialized powers have not, in fact, shown themselves entirely obdurate or lacking in all readiness to abandon their relative positions of power. For instance, in 1974 the IMF set up a "special facility" of $3 billions to help the poorest nations to meet new fuel costs and raised it to $10 billions in 1977. In February 1975, at Lomé, capital of Togo in Africa, the members of the European Economic Community met with a wide range of associated states from Africa, the Pacific and the Caribbean - incidentally, among the poorest of all the world's communities. Some important - and possibly exemplary - agreements were reached on the issues most close to the developing nations' concerns. Duty-free access to the EEC market without any reciprocity of concessions was arranged for most of the poor countries' industrial products and - with certain restrictions - for their agricultural exports. A fund of $450 million was established to be used (over five years) to offset price fluctuations in important primary products - the so-called Stabex scheme. In addition, a general aid figure of $3.55 billions was negotiated, also for the next five years.

This sense of rather greater responsiveness was apparent again at the Seventh Special Session of the General Assembly later in 1975 where, although without specific agreements, a certain readiness emerged to recognize the fact of the South's long-standing grievances of trade discrimination and - a new opening - to express some signs of a new understanding that there could be a genuine interdependence of interests between North and South.

And this is the third reason for moderate optimism. Although the negotiations since 1976 both in UNCTAD and in the Paris talks have ended in postponement, there has been some progress towards policies of greater stability in world prices for primary products, in part because of the need to offset persistent inflation, in part because such a policy might conceivably include an agreement on stable prices for oil. In other words, the changed power relationships are bringing firmer *Northern* interests into play and here it is possible to discern common ground. Indeed, the United States Ambassador to the United Nations went so far as to say: "....there must be consensus, first and foremost on the principle that our common development goals can be achieved only by cooperation, not by the politics of confrontation. There must be consensus that acknowledges our respective concerns and our mutual responsibilities. The consensus must embrace the broadest possible participation in international decisions. The developing countries must have a role and voice in the international system, especially in decisions that affect them".

This need not be entirely dismissed as rhetoric.

"Stagflation" in the North cannot be broken without an end to the pressure on prices. Equally, in the short run, as they build up their economies, the Southern states need a reasonably prosperous North to provide capital and markets. The combination of pressure from the "under-privileged" and enlightened self-interest on the part of the fortunate may, as in Victorian England, be beginning to work.

The fourth reason for moderate optimism lies not in the present specific stage of the negotiations for the new economic order but in the wider experience of the world economy in the twentieth century. Between 1927 and 1929, it was the collapse of purchasing power among primary producers, ending with the American farmers, that started the crisis of 1929. Then the increased protectionism of the industrialized nations turned it into the universal crash of 1931. Nothing was done and the drift to war began. In 1947, once again, purchasing power was totally enfeebled, this time, in Europe and throughout its colonies, by six years of battle. This time, however, the challenge met a remarkable response. The United States, with half its present standards of prosperity, gave away with the Marshall Plan some 2.5 percent of its Gross National Product - ten times the present percentage of its aid - for four or five years to restore Europe and revive the trade of the whole world. It is surely not pollyanna optimism to hope that it will occur to the statesmen of the North that the place where purchasing power today is non-existent but resources are waiting to be developed is in the quarter of the world that subsists on an average per capita income of little more than $150 a year. A Ten Year "Marshall Plan", financed by the North and OPEC, to build up the South's agriculture and industry, to enfranchise the mass of poor consumers, make them productive and give them steady work and just rewards, would create new resources and new markets for both North and South and allow the rhetoric of interdependence to be turned into a genuine alliance of productive interest.

In the twentieth century, we have contrived both to fail and to succeed. It is hard to believe that, with such immediate historical experience of the way up and the way down, we shall choose the path of disaster. By the next meeting - in Paris or in UNCTAD - perhaps the genuine "global compact" of the Eighties will begin to take shape. Perhaps the world can move from the hope and the dream to the substance of reality. To use, not inappropriately, a Moslem metaphor, we can pass from "the Gates of Ivory to the Gates of Horn".

Part II: The New International Order: Special Problems

"The complaint of the poor nations against
the present system is not only that we are poor
both in absolute terms and in comparison with
the rich nations. It is also that within the
existing structure of economic interaction we
must remain poor, and get relatively poorer,
whatever we do. . . . The demands for a New
International Economic Order is a way of
saying that the poor nations must be enabled
to develop themselves according to their own
interests, and to benefit from the efforts
which they make."

Julius K. Nyerere

Employment Problems and Policies in Less Developed Countries

Sukhamoy Chakravarty

Introduction

The employment problem in less developed countries is currently
very much at the centre of discussion for reasons both of equity
and of productive efficiency. While the ILO through its World
Employment Programme has done a great deal to heighten our
awareness of the problem as well as deepen some of our perceptions, various proposals aimed at restructuring the world economy
have placed considerable emphasis on the creation of sufficient
employment opportunities as part of the overall package of
policies involving trade, capital flows and the transfer of
technology.

The present preoccupation does not imply that discussion of the
problem has to start from a state of virtual ignorance. To be
precise, it marks a shift in emphasis which, if accepted, would
suggest different types of remedial action from the ones
contemplated in earlier discussions. Earlier literature on the
employment problem rested on three basic premises: (i) unemployment in less developed countries had little to do with the
Keynesian type of unemployment; (ii) secondly, the unemployment
problem was essentially a surface problem. The real and,
dimensionally speaking, massive problem was one of underemployment, sometimes misleadingly referred to as disguised unemployment; (iii) and finally, the generation of productive employment
opportunities was intrinsically linked with large-scale
accumulation of capital and know-how.

The current view differs from the position stated above in at
least three respects: (i) it considers urban unemployment to be
sufficiently serious in its own right as distinguished from
*under*employment; (ii) it does not view the rural labour reserve
as a pool which can be used productively in non-rural uses, as
some models of development had assumed; (iii) it does not view
rapid accumulation of capital to be the principal instrument for
eliminating unemployment or underemployment.

In contrast, it places much greater emphasis on the scope for
technological variability in production, even though the observed
data may not always show it because of somewhat artificial price
structures often erected by the governments of the developing
countries.

This brief summary cannot do full justice to all the nuances of
the arguments, old and new. But it tries to draw attention to the
main emphases pertaining to the current phase of thinking in
contrast with the past.

What is missing, however, from both these arguments is that the employment problem in less developed countries cannot be fully grasped unless one has tried to relate institutional factors to the unbalanced composition of resources, which typically distinguishes a developing economy.

What one needs is not merely a catalogue of institutions existing in urban and rural sectors, but the precise manner in which institutional mediations take place, which do two things at the same time: (i) it allows more people to subsist in a given natural environment than would appear possible on the basis of casual thinking; (ii) it also inhibits the finding of a proper solution by making the persistence of low productivity features a structural necessity of certain specific modes of adaptation.

The problem is best seen by considering a closed peasant community where land and cooperating capital goods are scarce in relation to labour, but are assumed to be equally owned. Such a society, if techniques are primitive, will generate a small volume of net output per head. It need not, however, suffer from unemployment since each person will be involved in the production process and each will have an income, partly based on his labour and partly based on the property that he owns. Differences in income per family may arise because of the uneven character of land, different characteristics of individuals, etc. But with the above conditions imposed, these are not likely to be systematic or substantial. If such a society tends to breakdown, it will be due to factors which lead to the breakdown of conditions under which a positive surplus arises. This may happen because of sudden increases in population or soil erosion or the influx of immigrants, etc.

Now let us consider the same economy in terms of aggregate resources, but assume that some people own only unskilled labour, whereas others own land and/or capital. Furthermore, let us assume that this society is characterized by a regime of competition. Let us assume that competition is perfect. In this situation, a competitive equilibrium need not imply *full use* of available labour at a *positive* wage rate. It is even more unlikely that this wage rate will exceed a reasonable standard of living. If wages are fixed exogenously at a preconceived subsistence level, then equilibrium may involve substantial unemployment. As a matter of fact, it is not clear that we can call such an outcome an equilibrium one involving a *compatible* bundle of choices on the part of all economic agents.

If it is not an equilibrium, however, then we would expect a downward pressure on wage rates to develop. But supposing that there is a physical minimum below which wages cannot fall, if wages must provide the sole source of expenditure then the labour market does not get cleared. In a planned economy this problem can be taken care of by distinguishing between an "accounting wage", which can be very low, and a "subsistence" wage, which includes some share of the surplus of aggregate output over wage payments. But there is no such organization in a competitive market. On the other hand, we do find considerable unemployment with a wage rate, sometimes well above a subsistence wage. Obviously, something must give in to render the outcome a determinate one.

I believe that there is no general theory in this regard. Much depends on custom and tradition. One would therefore expect different societies to react differently. But it is virtually certain that the so-called labour market would not function competitively, markets for labour would get fragmented into several submarkets with very limited mobility, nonmarket modes of payment will arise, especially in agriculture and service sectors. In certain societies, specific types of transfer payment will arise based on caste, ethnic origin, etc. On the whole, if subsistence agriculture is important there is going to be less open unemployment, but more disguised unemployment. There will be a similar downward pressure on subsistence requirements and employers will try to maximise labour per unit of "wage", if certain conventions exist regarding what constitutes a subsistence wage.

Disguised or visible underemployment will imply that the extent of utilization of the labour resources available will fall considerably short of the maximum. Open unemployment will tend to be more concentrated in urban areas, firstly because the wage contract is more often binding there than in rural areas and, secondly, because transfer payments may be more developed there, as very often these reflect unemployment in specific age-groups such as the young, moderately educated, etc.

Conceptual and Methodological Issues

Once these basic facts are understood, it becomes quite clear why the measurement of unemployment in less developed economies presents such great problems. This is sometimes expressed by the statement that unemployment in less developed countries is best seen as a variable having several dimensions. Thus, it has been said that we need four criteria to determine whether a person may be called unemployed or underemployed: (i) the time criterion; (ii) the income criterion; (iii) the willingness criterion; and (iv) the productivity criterion. (1) A variant of this approach is given by Sen who talks about three distinct aspects of the problem: (i) the recognition aspect; (ii) the income aspect; and (iii) the production aspect. (2)

In earlier days, more emphasis was laid on the time and willingness criteria. The questions typically asked were of the following type: how many hours does a person work? Is he willing to do more work if he is offered some?

Estimates based on this criterion have invariably produced

unemployment figures which are on the low side. Given what is said above, this should not surprise us. However, the figures were mistakenly interpreted by some people as suggesting that un-employment was not much of a problem in less developed countries, especially in rural areas. It was, of course, recognised, even at that time, that productivity of labour was rather low, on which macro-economic models of growth relied heavily.

But this was also contested by several economists who thought that much depended on the type of change that was being postulated. Some economists, notably Schultz, went to the extent of fitting a production function to disprove the so-called surplus labour hypothesis. (3)

Faced with these difficulties and the inadequacy of the time criterion, the so-called *poverty* criterion, i.e., whether one has an income exceeding a minimum, has come into use. The idea here is that one should fix a level of real income as the "norm" and then find out what percentage of the labour force has an income falling below this norm. This approach was recommended by D. Turnham in his review of the employment problem to focus attention on what he felt to be the most important dimension of the employment problem. (4)

In my opinion, used exclusively, this represents an overreaction since employment represents a *specific* input into the production process, which cannot be ignored in an adequate conceptualization of the problem. While it is doubtless true that, from the welfare point of view, what matters most is whether the man-day performed by a person is being rewarded in a manner that gives him a "minimum income", it will amount to using an "output" measure of input, as it were quite apart from the fact that all such norms are likely to be arbitrary in character. As pointed out repeatedly, there is a considerable amount of *waste* involved in the use of human resources in many developing countries. It is not possible to throw much light on potential improvements in real income and its distribution that can be brought about through promoting fuller employment when the measure already includes an estimate of marginal valuation of employment itself.

Thus, if our major objective is removal of poverty, it becomes necessary to identify employment in units independent of what is paid for it. For this purpose, it becomes necessary in some basic sense to take note of *"time"*, measured in terms of expenditure of social labour. This is a point which leads us to consider the length of the working day or the number of days in which a labourer works a specified number of hours in agriculture as crucial factors in determining the labour-intensity of a production process. This is also a point which is unfortunately ignored in much conventional discussion of the production function, an omission to which Georgescu-Roegen has in particular drawn attention. (5)

To sum up, to understand the employment problem in less developed countries in all its aspects, there is no getting away from its basically multi-dimensional character. (6) This implies that for detailed implementation of employment policies, much care will have to be given to the problem of formulating employment targets. However, it is understandable that for certain macro-economic purposes one may find it necessary to get some estimates of "equivalent unemployment" which is expressed as a fraction of the labour force, however measured. But then one should be careful in not reading too much into these estimates. (7) They can be made to look large or small, depending on the assumptions as well as the method of enquiry used, although it may be the case that with reasonable definitions, one would get a relatively narrow range of figures for a particular country at a given point of time. It is in regard to intertemporal and, more particularly, interspatial variations that difficulties are likely to crop up.

Having said this much on the conceptual and methodological grounds, I would agree that, on the basis of studies that I have come across on the employment situation in different developing countries, one can possibly maintain the following set of propositions:

(i) that the "unemployment problem" is extremely serious in less developed countries;

(ii) that it is at present much more serious in the less developed countries than in the richer countries;

(iii) that one can work out estimates of "unemployment equivalents" if one dimensional magnitudes are insisted upon, that may include 20-25 per cent or so of the labour force in many less developed countries;

(iv) that there are sufficient qualitative indications that the unemployment situation has become more serious in some of the larger developing countries over the last two decades, although the precise magnitude of the deterioration may be subject to many questions;

(v) that on present indications, it is very likely to increase further unless counter influences appear;

(vi) that these counter influences involve both national as well as international action.

Employment Policies

I believe that we need not spend too much time elucidating the first three propositions. We need, however, to analyse proposition (iv) - (vi) as they imply both questions of diagnosis and prescriptions.

A widely accepted explanatory scheme of the unemployment problem, which finds an eloquent expression in the ILO mission to the Philippines, runs in terms of market imperfections, especially the ones created by government policy in regard to import sub-stituting industrialization and unregulated educational expansion. (8)

I do not wish to deny that these policies may have, for one reason
or another, been adopted by many developing countries. It is also
possible that in certain situations these policies may have
caused an accentuation of an otherwise difficult situation.
However, as I understand it, these policies are best seen as
symptoms of a difficult situation which a policy maker simply
cannot wish away.

On the question of markets, we have already seen that there are
many structural reasons why labour markets in the developing
countries tend to be imperfect. As a matter of fact, we have
seen that in situations of severe demographic pressure even a
competitive market is likely to end up with very low wages and
high returns to property. To guarantee workers a minimum standard
of living, minimum wages may be decreed which, if properly
implemented, would then lead to unemployment. There is here clear
evidence of a *dilemma*, which governments in the developing countries have so far been unable to resolve

A theoretical answer can be given by using "accounting prices"
for choosing labour-intensity of production while allowing
sufficient redistribution through *taxes and transfers*. It is
precisely at this stage that serious difficulties arise, even if
one were to grant that the scope for technological choice is very
large. To effectively implement transfer, sizeable revenues can
be generated only through the relatively heavy taxation of
property. One particular tax that commends itself especially to
economists is the direct taxation of land on a progressive basis.
It is not difficult to administer; the usual argument of
inadequacy of records is more often an alibi for inaction than an
insurmountable difficulty. In urban areas, progressive income
tax, even with suitable exemptions for savings, can be
administered, helping to raise revenue without adverse effects on
private savings. However, both these policies run into great
difficulties from the political side, especially the former.
The amount of transfer payment that any government can possibly
organize in this context is very limited, particularly if, at the
minimum, public investment in infrastructure is to be provided,
which is very often the case. Most governments under these
circumstances resort to borrowing directly from their banking
system, which has its usual inflationary consequences. The result
tends to reduce interest rates in real terms, thereby ecouraging
the use of more "capital intensive" methods of production and
possibly acts as a disincentive to saving as well.

The purpose of mentioning these points is to indicate that, in
the absence of countervailing action by the government to redirect
the flow of incomes, there is little theoretical justification
for assuming that the market mechanism can in such situations do
the job, even if we could assume it to be perfect for the sake of
argument and postulate a very high degree of substitutability
between "capital" and labour.

We now come to the question of import substitution. Its negative aspects have recently been widely discussed, especially after OECD studies showed that effective rates of protection were exceedingly high on most manufactured commodities in developing countries. While one may enter into nice theoretical arguments concerning the welfare significance of these measures in the presence of substitution on the input side, or discuss which measure is the most appropriate one in the presence of non-tradeable inputs, etc., there is little doubt that, in many cases, import substitution may have been indiscriminating and excessive. But it is not appropriate to stop only at this point. It is also necessary to point out that the export prospects for many developing countries, concentrating on primary commodities and simple manufactures, have been very difficult at times when their need to import has been especially great. Strict rationing of foreign exchange has been necessitated to allocate the relatively meagre foreign exchange earnings. Given the distribution of incomes, this has meant, in many cases, excessive profitability in the domestic production of certain types of commodities, not to speak of rents accruing to holders of licenses when they have served merely as intermediaries.

Here again, the main reasons have been twofold: (i) limited capacity to import often due to an unfavourable economic environment; and (ii) a very unequal distribution of income engendered by a very uneven distribution of nonhuman property.

I now come to the question of education. Here again, we find a great divergence between the private and social benefits of education, along with an uneven distribution of the costs of education. It is not easy to see how the market mechanism will do the job properly, even though I feel that the process of education expansion has been lopsided, with higher education often ending up as the largest beneficiary. The analysis sketched here suggests that there are fundamentally three sets of forces which have acted against employment creation:

(i) inability to siphon off a sufficient amount of economic surplus for productive investment;
(ii) limited flexibility in regard to the foreign sector, implying a low capacity to import;
(iii) inappropriate composition of products and techniques stemming in part from a skewed distribution of incomes and the adoption of an imitative technology, which has been partly encouraged by the practice of aid giving, especially aid tying and the policies adopted by multinationals in their purchase of machinery.

If the preceding analysis is correct, use of the price mechanism alone in the absence of government intervention is unlikely to help significantly in generating higher levels of employment at reasonable levels of productivity even assuming sufficient scope for technological substitution exists. A properly administered system of accounting prices may be more useful. But, unfortunately, while much has been written on the question how to *compute* shadow prices, given alternative specifications of preference functions and constraints, very little attention has been paid to the problem of *implementation*. By implementation, I mean bringing into being an effective configuration of economic behaviour where the two roles of prices, an allocating role and an income distributional role, will be decomposed into appropriate directions.

I now turn to the question of whether a switchover to export-promoting industrialization will generally prove more helpful to the less developed countries from the viewpoint of employment creation. The Hecksher-Ohlin-Samuelson model of trade would appear to suggest that it should. There are, however, a few reservations that we should keep in mind. First of all, the explanatory power of the model as originally formulated may not extend over the whole spectrum of commodities which are traded. Secondly, even where the argument applies, it may be essential to carry out suitable adjustment policies in the developed countries, where protectionist policies are especially strong precisely in regard to these commodities, e.g., textiles. Thirdly, one may need to look more carefully at "processes" rather than at whole "commodities". Fourthly, the capacity of less developed countries to import may need to be raised so as to obviate the need to impose otherwise unavoidable quantitative restrictions on imports. Finally, one should bear in mind that the beneficial effect to the economy will also depend, at least in part, on whether this growth takes place through the agency of vertically integrated international organizations engaged in the worldwide "sourcing" of labour or through efforts aimed at domestic export diversifications.

If international action can be initiated on a significant scale on some of the issues raised above, there are reasons to believe that an orientation in favour of exports will help a substantial number of developing countries on the employment side. The effect will be more pronounced if parallel domestic action is undertaken by less developed countries in the area of education and skill formation.

Additional Possibilities
What I have said so far may not sound particularly optimistic. In a sense, this may be true. But there are a few other possibilities which need to be taken into account before forming an overall judgement.

Foremost in my mind is the role that agricultural development can play in promoting employment expansion. But it is critical to the whole success of the agriculture-based strategy that technological change is directed into land-augmenting directions which lead to fuller and more productive use of labour. The so-called "Green Revolution" has theoretically suggested that such a policy may be empirically relevant but, in practice, it has not had the desired effect so far. I believe that this is due to the absence of an appropriate policy framework. Thus, we have seen that a technological innovation which has been described as scale neutral has conferred maximum benefits not merely absolutely but also relatively on the most affluent sections of rural society. To reverse this, institutional innovations will be called for along with wider availability of such critical inputs as fertilizer, pesticides, power, etc. The latter involve large-scale investment if they are to be produced at home, as they have to be in the case of power or transport, or through imports where they constitute tradeable inputs. In the latter case, large demands for foreign exchange will arise which will need to be met by national and international action. In any case, substantial efforts at resource mobilization will be called for.

A second possible area which can work effectively only in *conjunction* with the first is the use of rural public works. But this policy is unlikely to work out successfully unless certain criteria are properly formulated and strictly adhered to in regard to the distribution of benefits and costs associated with the execution of these programmes. I think that the questions here are not merely administrative, but also basically economic in character. (9)

A third line of attack will be to change the product mix in favour of labour-intensive commodities along with the use of more labour-intensive processes. The first part of the policy cannot work, however, unless the distribution of incomes is altered or, as a weaker alternative, the policy of massive taxation of luxury commodities is implemented. It may also involve *ex ante* weeding out of investment proposals in these areas so that additional capacity is not allowed to be built up. It has sometimes been mentioned that the redistribution of incomes cannot help much in promoting employment since the direct and indirect amount of labour needed to produce the typical rich man's consumption basket is greater or at least as great as that of a representative poor man. I think that the conclusion is crucially dependent on the labour-intensity of agriculture and of certain mass consumption goods such as textiles. If these sectors are allowed to develop in an employment intensive manner, redistribution is likely to promote employment in many situations.

As regards labour-capital substitution possibilities, I do not think that estimates of substitution elasticities based on an aggregate production function can be taken very literally. Furthermore, even if they are considered to be statistically reliable, it is not clear that one can infer much regarding substitution possibilities in the micro-economic context from these estimates. Recommendations on wage policy based on the estimated value of this parameter could be misleading as these are often based on the assumption that the real wage rate is an exogenous variable.

Wage policy is, however, a critical part of an overall incomes policy. Here, I believe that what classical economists have had to say is still of considerable importance. Unfortunately, the question of wage policy is quite often dealt with in isolation, thus leading to outright rejection. It is only the oligopolistic sectors which tend to go along with demand for wage increases, because they can pass it on to the consumer.

Finally, I come to the area of research on technology aimed at altering the bias of technological change. While I am all for further work in this area, I doubt that we can expect very significant results in this area within the next decade or so. I am also of the opinion that the usual treatment of bias in technological change leaves a lot to be desired. Truly speaking, this is an area where our knowledge is still very incomplete. It is not even quite clear that we have even hit on the right way of approaching the problem. Meanwhile, I believe that the problem of adaptation has a more important role to play. This may involve, among other things, the development of an indigenous "capital goods industry" in the Third World countries, especially the bigger ones.

Summary

To sum up, it is not possible to state that there is one simple answer to this extremely important problem. There are basically two types of answers which deal with somewhat different sets of issues. One class of issues has to deal with the choice of products and processes aimed at generating a desired profile of employment over time. The other has to deal with the question of institutions. There are some areas where both considerations point in the same direction. They would obviously deserve the greatest amount of attention. Agriculture is the leading example in this regard, but most countries will need to ensure that premature and indiscrimi-nate mechanization does not rob this sector of its employment potential. Furthermore, it is also necessary to ensure that infra-structural arrangements are created which help small and middle farmers to adopt practices such as multiple cropping, thereby combining increased labour use with higher productivity of land. The role of public irrigation facilities cannot be over-emphasized in this context along with the suitable provision of credit. For those who do not own land, the question of security of tenancy is very important. All these proposals involve the significant restructuring of agrarian institutions along with an adequate productive outlay on public and private account.

Secondly, the choice of cropping pattern within agriculture is also of importance since the labour-intensity of different crops varies considerably. Thirdly, while the export of labour-intensive manufactures, wherever economic, may be deemed an advantage in the short term, in the long term it is obviously necessary to carry out industrialization in greater depth. Regional economic integration may prove helpful, especially the idea of collective self-reliance. Concrete proposals ought to be worked out on an area-specific basis.

Fourthly, a vast amount of work needs to be done in the area of technological change. If existing biases are to be corrected, governmental intervention is called for; this may often require organized international action since no country may be able to carry out the required job. In the short run, a great deal of attention has to be paid to the question of the adaptation of existing technological practices. In particular, the question of the appropriate scale of an "activity" needs to be worked out very carefully. The Japanese experience may be useful in this regard.

Finally, institutional adaptations are necessary in regard to the generation of a sufficient investible surplus and its proper deployment. It has been rightly pointed out that, in many situations, inequality does not necessarily promote savings, let alone the right type of savings. While this takes away one of the classical arguments in favour of inequality, it does not solve the problem of how best to promote savings, especially public savings. While well-designed fiscal and monetary policies are essential, and this requires significant structural changes domestically, the creation of an appropriate international environment can also be a very important contributory factor.

Notes and References

1. See R. Krishna: *Unemployment in India*, EPW, Bombay, March 3, 1973, p.475.
2. See A.K. Sen: *Employment, Technology and Development*, Oxford University Press, 1975.
3. See T. Schultz: *Transforming Traditional Agriculture*, Yale University Press, 1964.
4. See D. Turnham: *The Employment Problem in Less Developed Countries*, OECD, Paris, 1970.
5. See N. Georgescu-Roegen: *The Entropy Law and the Economic Process*, Harvard, 1971.
6. For developing countries, extending planning models along the employment dimension have run into difficulties precisely because of this inherent multi-dimensionality of the employment-output relationship.
7. It would be somewhat ironical if at a time when scalar measures of productive performance of an economy are being very much questioned, we come up with estimates of "equivalent unemployment" as if they constituted more robust constructs. Just as in the case of GNP, supplementary measures are increasingly felt to be necessary so as to highlight different aspects of the policy-making process, it is necessary that in the case of employment we do the same.
8. See G. Ranis: *Unemployment and Factor Price Distortions*, in 'Third World Employment', (edited by R. Jolty et al.), Penguin Books, 1973, pp.144-158.
9. See S. Chakravarty: *Mahalanobis and Contemporary Issues in Development Planning*, Sankhya, 1975.

Growth for Whom?[*]

Harlan Cleveland

The Dimensions of World Poverty

In recent years the call for meeting basic human needs, especially
in the world's less-developed "South", has become a code word for
economic justice - for fairness - for equity in the distribution
of the benefits of growth, not just among nations but among people
within nations. It is a way of saying that something must be done
about the scandal that too much of the economic growth produced by
"development" has siphoned up to the rich rather than trickled
down to the poor.

"Basic human needs" are usually defined as "enough" food, shelter,
clothing, health, education, employment and security of the person
for everyone everywhere. Three related ideas are spreading fast:

● that people are entitled to a minimum level of life and literacy
by virtue of being people,

● that this "poverty line" is properly a matter for international
as well as "domestic" politics, and

● that the meeting of basic needs should be regarded as a first
charge on world resources.

The dimensions of world poverty are all too familiar. But they
cannot be understood if they are measured only in money terms -
which would inform us that the standard of living in Abu Dhabi
and Qatar are higher than in Sweden and Switzerland. Moreover, per
capita averages for income or GNP miss the crucial fact that the
poorest people are almost by definiton least plugged into the
money system and most dependent on barter, in-kind compensation,
and their own skills to grow their own food, build their own
shelter, make their own clothing, fashion their own tools, fix
their own machinery, maintain their own health, educate their own
children, and protect their own persons. This could mean that
very low "income" figures might exaggerate the desperation of
their circumstances. But if other indicators are examined as well,
it quickly becomes clear that poverty is the prevailing condition
for one-eighth to three-eighths of the human race:

---

[*] This essay is part of a longer discussion of growth policy in
global perspective, *Growth for Whom? Growth for What?* by Harlan
Cleveland and Thomas W. Wilson, Jr. (Aspen Institute for Humanistic Studies, New York, 1978).

In Total World Population of 4 Billion	
Undernourished (i.e. Below Suggested Calorie/Protein Levels)	570 Million
Adults Illiterate	800 Million
Children Not Enrolled in School	250 Million
With No Access to Effective Medical Care	1,500 Million
With Less than $ 90.00 Income Per Year	1,300 Million
With Life Expectancy Below 60 Years	1,700 Million
With Inadequate Housing	1,030 Million

Source: John and Magda McHale, *Basic Human Needs: A Framework for Action*. A report prepared for the U.N. Environment Programme. (New Brunswick, N.J.; Transaction Press, 1977.)

Economic Growth and the Rich-Poor Gap

During the decades of the '50s and '60s the world's developing countries as a group - Africa, Latin America, and Non-Soviet Asia - achieved an average growth of 5% per year in their GNP. That is an impressive rate of "progress"; the United States has not managed so ambitious a growth rate for several years now. Yet in the '70s, compared to the '40s, more people than ever seem to be "poor" - whether poverty is measured by malnutrition, mortality, illiteracy, the lack of remunerative work and disposable income, or the absence of critical social services. About half of this disappointing result can be traced to "modern death rates combined with medieval birth rates". The same countries, over the same two decades, increased their population by about 2,5%. The other half of that impressive 5% growth seems to have gone mostly to the more affluent "middle class" countries in the group, and to the upper and middle income classes inside the poorest countries.

World Bank President Robert McNamara said it to his Board of Governors in 1976, and repeated it in 1977: "....growth is absolutely essential to development. But growth, no matter what its magnitude, cannot assist the hundreds of millions of absolute poor unless it reaches them. It is not reaching them adequately today".

The favored development model which produced this scandal came out of the West. For several decades it was taken for granted that the modernization of pre-industrial societies would follow the general pattern established by the people that pioneered the Industrial Revolution in Europe and, stimulated by Europeans, carried it further in North America, Japan and the Soviet Union. The essence of the Western model - developed through three centuries of scientific discovery, technological invention, industrial innovation, business entrepreneurship, free enterprise economics, and learnings about the management of large complex systems - was that the key to military strength, national prestige, stable money and rising standards of life was to put more and more energy and machinery at the disposal of each worker and each consumer.

The comparatively egalitarian consequences of this policy, over the long run, blurred the memory (in the West) of the suffering and unfairness at the earlier "stages of growth". The historical record is clear enough: in the early periods of industrial growth, the few got richer and the bulk of population, treated as means and not as ends, got relatively poorer.

Mass production, mass marketing, mass organization of labor and mass politics eventually began to spread the benefits of industrial progress through better wages, lower prices and more public responsibility for individual equity and the general welfare - still with major exceptions for those bypassed or excluded from the benefits of prosperity. It nevertheless came to be widely believed that there was something inevitable about the widening of the gap between rich and poor in the early stages of development. If the rich did not get rich fast, it was said, a "capital shortage" would slow down the putting of more and more energy/equipment behind each worker.

The prevailing mental image could be represented this way:

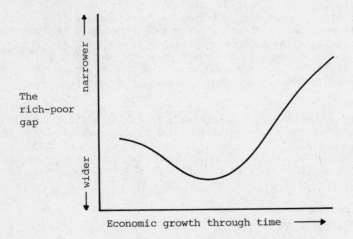

At a meeting in Persepolis, in 1975, a young American trained Iranian economist was asked by foreign visitors about how Iran intended to build equity into its plans for rapid industrialization. "We have all studied the same economic history at the same graduate schools," he replied, "so we all know the rich-poor gap has to get worse before it gets better. Ours is still getting worse, so we figure we're right on the curve".

Growth for Whom?

As the global fairness revolution gained momentum in the 1970s, the prevailing economic theories of modernization were increasingly called into question. For one thing, they did not seem to be working very well in the industrial nations which had served as the models, and from whose earlier experience the theories were derived. Contrary to the teachings of Lord Keynes, the coexistence of inflation and sluggish growth rates came to be the norm, and forecasts based on earlier business-cycle models were often awry.

The societies with the most advanced technologies also seemed awash in social problems, including persistent unemployment and youthful crime, addiction and alienation. Mass production and mass consumption were conspicuously failing to induce mass happiness or even mass welfare. The very premises of modernization were under attack from inside the citadels of modernity. The detrimental side-effects of indiscriminate growth became too evident to ignore.

Outside the industrial world, among leaders and thinkers of the developing "Third World", the older models also seemed tarnished by their impact on local economies and cultures. Industrial production and urban in-migration seemed to bring along with them skewed patterns of consumption, new modes of living, and alien personal and social mores, often seen by newly sensitive and self-confident leaders as a threat to traditional values and established institutions. If the net results of transferring the "industrial model" to developing countries were to be growing inequalities between rich and poor and between city and country, and a tendency toward cultural homogenization in the modern sector, then perhaps there were better ways to pursue "development".

In a complex world of a hundred different real "development models", it is perilous to generalize. Even the easy historical judgment that the "Western model" has been bad for the environment should have in memory that Buddhist cremation practices, the demand for charcoal for brush inks, and the building of wooden temples have in pre-industrial centuries been blamed for deforestation in East Asia. The Fertile Crescent and the North African littoral were not turned into deserts by industrial "growth-mania".

Reservations about the "Western model" can similarly be balanced, out there in the real world, by the record of societies which have embraced industrialization and "taken off" more or less the way the theorists said they would: Taiwan, South Korea, Hong Kong, Singapore, Israel, and the modern sectors of Brazil and Mexico are obvious examples, each with its own unique history and resources and circumstances, and attitudes toward education and governance, to help explain what happened. Any necessary correlation between slow growth and failure to meet human needs is contradicted by the record of Sri Lanka, which scores so high on indices of social welfare and longevity even though it ranks among the "poorest of the poor" in per capita GNP. And most generalizations about development need to record a large if ambiguous exception for China, which has combined pockets of high technology and a broken-down educational system with a spectacularly effective mobilization of the world's largest national population to produce and distribute the physical necessities of life.

And yet there *is* something new under the Southern sun. It is a growing awareness that the end-purpose of the whole development enterprise is, after all, to meet human needs, - in other words, that the key question to ask about development is "Growth for whom?"

Putting Basic Human Needs First
One of the early Declarations about a New International Economic Order issued from a meeting of governmental and non-governmental leaders and experts, held at Cocoyoc in Mexico in October 1974. The essence of the reappraisal was captured in this key paragraph of the Cocoyoc Declaration:

"Our first concern is to define the whole purpose of development. This should not be to develop things but to develop man. Human beings have basic needs: food, shelter, clothing, health, education. Any process of growth that does not lead to their fulfillment - or even worse disrupts them - is a travesty of the idea of development".

Most of the early rhetoric in the "North-South dialogue" about a New International Economic Order dealt with fairness *among* nations. But the scandal of unfairness *within* nations - expressed in the widespread endorsement of "basic needs strategies" - has now quite suddenly come to be central to plans for international economic cooperation and development assistance.

Some established elites see the new code word as a threat to existing patterns of wealth and power; "basic needs" have never-theless crowded their way into the vocabulary of development planners and policymakers. The World Bank Group has overcome an earlier reluctance to support rural reforms, health, education

and family planning. The U.N. Environment Programme, declaring
poverty to be the ultimate pollution, now sees a basic needs
strategy as part of the answer to environmental degradation.
The International Labour Organization has called on governments
and international organizations to place basic needs at the
center of world development. The World Health Organization has
done an about-face to focus on health services for the very
poor. The Food and Agriculture Organization is reorganizing to
reflect the new priorities. The U.N. Children's Fund (UNICEF) is
expanding its concept of "basic services for those least served".
The U.S. Congress has revised the mission of the Agency for
International Development (AID) to place its main emphasis on
projects for relief of the worst poverty. President Carter has
promised the United Nations that "... the U.S. will be advancing
proposals aimed at meeting ... basic human needs..." Even those
practitioners of development aid that are not doing anything new
feel the need to claim that what they were already doing was part
of an unarticulated "basic needs" strategy.

In short, "basic human needs" have been promoted from an aspiration to an entitlement, as an important part of the answer to
"Growth for whom?" in those societies where basic needs are not
already guaranteed by welfare systems, unemployment insurance and
"poverty lines". How far this theme has penetrated the thinking
of both industrial and pre-industrial worlds was shown by another,
more recent Declaration about the New International Economic
Order, this one from an International Conference on Human Needs
in one of the world's most affluent cities. The "Houston Declaration" of June 1977, citing the fact that economic growth had
"tended to help the relatively affluent while leaving the poor
where they are", prescribed a basic-needs strategy as the remedy:

"(3) The first thing to do about reshaping the international
economic system is to get our priorities straight. The satisfaction of basic human needs - the food, health, shelter, clothing,
education and employment which are prerequisite to human dignity
- should be treated by each nation, and by the international
community, as a first charge on the world's resources.

(4) The satisfaction of human needs is indeed the whole purpose
of growth, trade and investment, development assistance, the
world food system, population policy, energy planning, commodity
stabilization, ocean management, environment protection, monetary
reform, and of arms control.

(5) Meeting human needs thus emerges as a new, compelling focal
point for a new international economic order. Reshaping the international economic system, to achieve more fairness and wider
participation, can both facilitate the meeting of basic needs
inside nations, and attract greater resources to the task. Wide

acceptance of responsibility for meeting "human needs" will
enable industrial and developing nations to get beyond 'dialogue'
to a practical start on a new international economic order."

Basic Needs Strategy and External Assistance

The art and science of "development" is a story of the search for
magic "keys" to growth that would shortcut the modernization
process and close the gap between the developing and industrial
worlds. Each expert enthusiasm left its mark by accretion on the
doctrine of development assistance - relief and rehabilitation,
recovery by outside investment, technical assistance, central
economic planning, training institutes, "institution-building",
public administration, social development, community development,
rural clinics, barefoot doctors, family planning, and "appropriate
technology". It would be a sad turn of events if the current
re-awakening to the end-purposes of development were to become
another fashionable fad in the shaping and operation of development assistance programs.

A basic-needs strategy may not call for focusing *external* aid on
those sectors of a developing economy that most directly touch
the "poorest of the poor". The main factors in a basic-needs
strategy will always be internal policies, programs, and projects
for social change - including land reform, tax policy, and
educational entitlements. If a nation's development is set on a
course that gives priority to basic human needs, the input from
outside aid can go in almost anywhere that fits that emerging
strategy.

A World Bank staff paper summed things up this way:

"Economic growth appears to have done very little for the poorer
of the Third World's rapidly growing populations....The economic
emphasis has tended to lose sight of the ultimate purpose of the
policies....The demand now is to put man and his needs at the
center of development".

That is, in fact, the general shape of the transition in growth
policy now under way in the developing world: people and their
most pressing needs are being moved - not without resistance -
toward the center of the picture. It's about time.

Restructuring Industrialized Countries and the New International Order

Louis Emmerij*

Introduction

This paper is concerned with the interdependence between changes in the economic structure of industrialized countries and the industrialization efforts of developing countries. Traditionally, industrialized countries have reacted rather passively to those efforts, either by increasing tariffs on the imports of certain products or by letting competitive goods enter and thus creating trouble in the local industry producing these goods.

Another, more active, way of dealing with this interdependency is possible. Such an approach, advocated by the Dutch government in 1974-75, would consist in anticipating changes in industrialization patterns of Third World countries and identifying those firms in the industrialized countries which would have a low chance of surviving the increased competition from developing nations. Instead of building higher protective walls or extending subsidies - at the expense of the consumers who would have to pay higher prices - the government would stimulate both employers and workers to switch to lines of production in which industrialized countries maintain their comparative advantage. This approach has run into trouble because of the economic and employment problems which have faced those countries since 1972-73.

Quite a few individual firms have adopted their own active and anticipatory policies in the light of changes in the world economy. They have switched part of their production to low wage countries and have thus increased their competitiveness. This fact troubles the discussion on an equitable international division of labour. Trade unions in the industrialized countries rightly protest against such practices which endanger the employment situation of their members without necessarily contributing to the economic development of the receiving (developing) countries.

It is interesting to observe that the world economic model that has functioned until quite recently was largely based on complementary development patterns in both industrialized and developing countries. Indeed, the overwhelming majority of developing countries adopted economic development strategies which put very heavy emphasis on the so-called modern sector of the economy, including the extraction of raw materials and the production of cash crops for export purposes.

This development approach was based on the belief that the modern sector constitutes the sole locomotive of growth, fuelled by

---

* In close cooperation with Joan Verloren van Themaat

cheap labour migrating from the traditional sector. It was necessary to expand the modern sector as fast as possible so that this
locomotive could pull the wagons of the traditional sector up to
such a cruising speed that the terminal station of sustained and
balanced economic growth at high levels would be reached within
an acceptable - in terms of duration - transition period.

In this set-up, the industrialized countries were able to export
expensive machinery, embodying capital-intensive and sophisticated
technology, to the developing countries. This was perfectly consistent with the development model adopted by the developing
countries because, once again, the emphasis was on the modern
sector, on capital-intensive technology, and increasing the rates
of productivity in that sector as fast as possible. The know-how,
the technology, the organizational skills of industrialized countries were seen as positive contributions to this developmental
effort.

However, ever since the end of the 1960s and even more forcefully
since the beginning of the 1970s, it has been observed empirically
and more and more frequently that although the economic and social
development strategies adopted by developing countries did indeed
produce high overall rates of economic growth (in order of 5 per
cent per annum during the decade of the 1960s), the fruits were
very unevenly distributed between regions within a country as well
as between groups within the population. What had happened? The
modern sector had expanded as was the intention, but because of
the high capital intensity of the production techniques used and
therefore also of the high labour productivity, the number of
jobs created in that modern sector was lower than anticipated and
needed. On the other hand, however, the demographic expansion of
most developing countries had been such that in the early 1960s
people rightly started to talk about a population explosion. Thus
more people presented themselves on the labour market in search
of employment opportunities than had been anticipated in the
theoretical growth models.

If one puts these two sides of the equation together, i.e. fewer
jobs created and more people in search of jobs than anticipated,
one has in a nutshell the explanation of why high rates of economic growth were not accompanied by sufficiently high rates of
employment creation and why the income distribution in many
developing countries could become even more unequal. It is also
the explanation for the very fast expansion of the so-called
urban-informal sector. Many people in the rural traditional areas
were hypnotized by the steel and glass urban modern sector, by
the high income possibilities, and they therefore started to move
towards the sparkling lights of the city. Obviously, the majority
of these migrants did not find the lottery ticket consisting of a
high-income urban job. Rather than return to the rural areas,
however, they settled at the margins of the modern sector, both
in the geographical and the economic sense.

It was in this situation of emerging and growing unease about the realistic possibilities of the adopted growth strategies to deliver the goods within an acceptable period of time that the search started for alternative development strategies, or at least for important modifications to the existing strategies.

The developing countries called for a New International Economic Order and increased self-reliance, and tension emerged with respect to the "old" economic objectives and instruments of the First World. Activities of multinational enterprises needed to be controlled and curbed; trade barriers were erected by developing countries; exports of primary products needed to be cartelized, etc. What was good for the rich countries did not always appear to be good for the developing countries.

More recently, another set of criticisms, this time from the rich countries, has been levelled at the international economic system. The energy crisis, the call for new lifestyles, environmental problems, the increase in unemployment, focused attention on certain aspects of the international economic system which seemed favourable to certain developing countries and less so to the rich countries. This time, the industrialized countries are calling for new international strategies: protectionism, regulated trade, differentiation are the new names under which the rich are confronting the poor.

Is there a danger of a widening gap in the objectives pursued by the rich and the developing countries, and what conditions must be fulfilled to establish a new complementarity that will serve the world as a whole better than the old international order?

Against this background we shall discuss the following subjects:
(i) aspirations of developing countries with respect to North-South trade and the industrial structures of the rich countries;
(ii) the relation between trade movements and emerging development strategies of the developing countries;
(iii) changes in industrial societies as a *result* of the development of the Third World; and
(iv) the effect of recent changes in the industrial structures of developed countries on the Third World.

Aspirations of Developing Countries

At international discussions developing countries have always emphasized the necessity to increase their exports to the industrialized world. Obviously, an increase in export earnings has never been an objective *per se*, but served in the first instance as a means to generate foreign exchange to buy Western products. The complementarity in the world economy was such that an ever-increasing procurement of capital goods from the rich countries was considered by most developing countries an absolute necessity for sustained optimum development.

Hence, developing countries claimed that industrialized countries

should: (i) reduce trade barriers for manufactured and agricultural products; and (ii) adjust their industrial structures
accordingly. In addition, claims were made in favour of the transfer of capital and technology from the rich to the poor countries
in order to assist in the industrialization and export efforts of
Third World countries.

The figures given in Table 1 clearly show why developing countries
have insisted on these measures. Exports to the industrialized
West have been by far their most important source of foreign
exchange, and are likely to continue to be so in the future.
Developing countries depend for over two-thirds of their exports
on the markets of the industrialized West, and trade only one-
quarter among themselves. This dependence of developing countries
with respect to both exports and imports is considered by many to
be a matter of course.

Table 1: *Destination of developing countries' exports in 1976 in
mln. $ (excl. OPEC)*

Industrial market economies	$ 80,000	68%
Developing economies	$ 29,000	25%
Centrally planned economies	$ 8,000	7%
Total	$ 117,000	100%

Source: GATT: *International Trade 1976-77*, Geneva, 1977.

In this respect it is interesting to note the behaviour of the
centrally planned economies which are standing on the sideline
and which have a relatively much smaller volume of trade with the
Western developed countries. Although they are interested in
improving their trade with the West, they adopt a much more
selective and cautious approach. The main reason for this state
of affairs cannot be traced to their low level of development
compared to the West, as seems to be suggested by the RIO
Report. (1) The difference in volume between East-West trade and
South-West trade is too important to be explained in that manner.

Table 2: *World trade of industrialized market economies*

with	per cent trade	per cent of world population
Centrally planned economies	5.8	31
Developing countries	26.5	48

Source: Tinbergen et al: *Reshaping the International Order (RIO
Report)*, 1976.

A major explanation, on the contrary, can be found in the fear of
too great a dependence created by trade relationships. It is felt

by the centrally planned economies that such a dependence constitutes an important "cost" connected with trade - a "cost" which
is not offset by the advantages of a more elaborate international
division of labour. Their attitude towards international trade is
thus partly an outcome of their version of self-reliance.

In closing this short section we wish to draw attention to the
fact that a comparison of Tables 1 and 2 will reveal that while
developing countries depend for two-thirds on the industrialized
countries and for one-quarter on themselves as far as exports are
concerned, the situation is reversed when it comes to the trade
patterns of the industrialized countries: i.e. for just over one-
quarter on the markets of developing countries and for over two-
thirds on each other.

North-South Trade and Emerging Development Strategies

There are potential contradictions between the aspirations of
developing countries to promote their exports to industrialized
nations on the one hand, and alternative development strategies
which are considered desirable on the other. (2) The development
strategies which are mentioned most frequently are those related
to "basic needs" and to the concept of "self-reliance". These
show a clear relationship to which we shall return later. First,
we shall illustrate the tendency for North-South trade to favour
the richer developing countries at the expense of the poorer.

The potential rate of increase of export earnings from agricultural products is low. Demand by developed countries does not
show a high growth rate and much is produced in the rich countries,
either directly or via substitutes. Expansion of trade in these
products must come from exchanges between developing countries
- if they manage to increase the rate of growth of their agricultural products which stood at only 2.1 per cent per annum
between 1971 and 1975.

On the other hand, industrial production in developing countries
as a whole increased at an annual rate of 7 per cent during the
same five-year period (3), and it is in this sector that those
countries are hoping to make their export breakthrough. Indeed,
we have watched a most important shift in the composition of the
export package of developing countries over the last 15 years or
so - a shift which until recently has received only limited public
attention. Although this has been considerable, however, it has
not been an even development because only a few developing countries have been responsible and have benefited from it, as is
illustrated in Tables 4 and 5.

Clearly, the low income countries of the Third World, especially
those of Africa and South Asia, have profited least from the
expansion of international trade. Within those countries which do
benefit, the advantages often do not reach the groups outside
the modern sector (see our Introduction). If national development

strategies continue as they are, it is not likely that these
groups will benefit to any greater extent from trade in the
future.

Table 3: *Composition of exports from developing countries (excl.
oil): 1960-1974 (in %)*

	1960	1970	1974
Agricultural products	42	35	31
Raw materials	37	26	25
Manufactured products	19	37	44

Source: Committee for Development Planning, Projections and
Policies, in *Rijksbegroting 1978*.

Table 4: *Indices of purchasing power of exports, 1976 (1970 = 100)*

All developing countries	199
OPEC	368
Fast growing manufacturing exporters	178
Developing countries with GNP/cap. of +$ 250	113
Developing countries with GNP/cap. of -$ 250	84
Least developed	82

Source: as Table 3.

Table 5: *Origin of manufactured exports of developing countries,
1975 (in mln. $)*

East Asia	17,700
Latin America	6,500
South Asia	3,000
Sub-Sahara Africa	700
Other	5,000

Source: World Bank: *Trade Liberalization and Export Promotion,*
June, 1977.

An important aspect of an enlarged trade volume with developed
countries is the dependence that often results from it: dependence in an economic, political, social and cultural sense. Most
developing countries that have successfully followed an export-
led development strategy illustrate this point: Gabon, Ivory
Coast, Singapore, South Korea and Taiwan are examples. The
"unequal exchange" between the developed and developing countries
is more than just an economic phenomenon. It usually also means
a large influx of foreign capital, expatriates, foreign ownership
of large sectors of the economy, a foreign influence on the way
in which different economic sectors are expanded, etc. The Ivory
Coast and Gabon are well-known examples in Africa. Several OPEC
countries have followed suit. Governments are tempted to become
outward- (i.e. North-ward) looking, rather than devote their

attention to domestic problems. It must have been this kind of
argumentation that led Galtung to the following formulation: The
point is not to cut out trade but to redirect it and recompose it
by giving preference to cooperation with those in the same
position, preferring the neighbour to the more distant possibility, cooperation to exchange, and intra-sector to inter-sector
trade. (4)

Thus, policies in favour of a strong export promotion to the
industrialized world may threaten the objective of self-reliance.
On the other hand, if developing countries "de-link" from the
North, havoc may be created in the South. A basic needs strategy,
because of its emphasis on the production of basic goods and
services, will enhance trade between developing countries and
thus reduce their dependence on the industrialized world. It is a
step in the right direction without going too far. The question
in how far the semi-industrialized Third World countries may take
over the role now performed by the First World and in this manner
create a new dependency is a question for the 1980s ...

Policy Measures in Industrialized Countries
We have discussed in Section 1 the claim made by developing countries that their products are prevented from penetrating the
markets of the rich countries not only by trade barriers, but
also by the industrial structures of those countries. An active
policy of restructuring is needed. The governments of the rich
countries should restrict those industries (i) for which developing countries have a "comparative advantage"; and (ii) whose
products have to be produced in the Third World in order to reach
the objectives of the Lima Declaration.

This is a complex matter which is influenced by a whole series of
factors such as the decision-making structure within the economy,
educational policies, labour market policies, regional policies,
research and development, etc. The influence of these measures on
the industrial structures of developed countries is considerable
and should not be underestimated merely because of their indirect
relation with the import level.

Besides these indirect measures which have a bearing on the
direction of industrial restructuralization, governments can
introduce measures which directly influence those industries which
compete with imports from developing countries. Two categories
can be distinguished:
(i) Stimulating investments in industries which *do not* compete
with products from the Third World, thus, by the same token,
reducing production activities which *do* compete with those of
developing countries. This is the approach adopted by The Netherlands with respect to developing countries.
(ii) Regulating investments by means of licensing. Investments in
industries that compete with developing countries (e.g. producing

clothing products below a certain price level or of a certain type) could be forbidden. Such regulations have existed for some time in the fields of health, environment, spatial planning, etc.

Dutch experience with the measures mentioned under (i) above shows that considerable difficulties are encountered when it comes to their implementation.

Firstly, whatever financial incentives the government is prepared to give, their actual realization depends on the discretion of the enterprises in question - at least as long as we are concerned with a mixed economy. Doubts can be expressed as to whether financial incentives indeed promote investments and whether, in general, they have any real influence on the decision-making process in business. The present discussion in The Netherlands on the extent to which profits are (or can be) translated into employment-intensive investments reflects the same problem. Financial incentives might in fact increase the profitability of an enterprise without leading to additional investment.

Secondly, and related to the above argument, is the fact that when employers do not want or do not plan any restructuring, there is little that governments can do about it within the present, quite restricted, philosophy about government intervention in business. We should add that it is often quite difficult to identify *new* production activities for enterprises which are faced with competition from developing countries.

Thirdly, most enterprises find it difficult to forecast cost-earnings ratios other than on the basis of the present situation and past trends. They have a particular problem in assessing the rate of technological innovation or the activities of competing firms. Hence, a frequently heard complaint by employers that it is next to impossible to anticipate which lines of production should be phased out because of the comparative advantage of developing countries. Anticipatory adjustment policies will therefore not be very popular.

Finally, trade unions will also tend to take a dim view of such measures as anticipatory adjustment and restructuring policies if they come at a moment of growing unemployment in the rich countries.

The two broad types of policy measures indicated earlier can be used in a variety of ways to stimulate or to hinder the development strategies mentioned in Section Two. In what might be called the pure *international division of labour strategy* it is assumed that the world economy at large benefits from smooth adjustments of those industries which are producing at lower costs in developing countries. The free movement of capital and goods will ensure that there will be replacement by industries in which the rich countries have a comparative advantage. Political factors are

ignored. The aim, therefore, is an unqualified abolition of trade
barriers. The role of the government is to facilitate the
industrial restructuring process. This classical approach could be
"refined" by taking social costs into account, such as pollution
and other environmental factors. This could lead to suggestions
that capital-intensive but polluting industries be located in
sparsely populated regions of the developing countries, and
labour-intensive but non-polluting industries in densely populated
countries like The Netherlands. In this context, it is sometimes
advocated to keep such industries as the clothing industry in Holland or Belgium! (5)

What could industrialized countries do in order to stimulate a
basic needs strategy - assuming that developing countries would
like to adopt such an approach? Clearly, the rich countries would
or should adopt selective and differentiated trade and adjustment
policies, for example along the following lines.

First, products mainly produced in the poorest developing countries should be subject to decisively lower trade barriers than
products from other developing countries. Restructuring of these
industries should receive priority.

Second, products for which it has been demonstrated that they are
generally produced by relatively poor sections of the population
should receive trade preferences.

Third, products which are produced in countries with regimes
which have effective income redistribution policies should receive
trade preferences. It will be difficult to apply this differentiation in restructuring policies since these products are also
produced in other countries.

Fourth, agreements could be concluded with certain developing
countries in which both aid and trade would be regulated. The
export of those products which would fit the basic needs strategy
could get preferential treatment.

Fifth, the basic need "human rights" should get special mention.
A negative criterion could be that trade preferences will be with-
held from governments which violate basic human rights.

If developing countries were to move in the direction of *self-
reliance*, industrialized countries would be forced, almost by
definition, to invent their own version of self-reliance. From
Tables 1 and 2 it would appear that the industrialized market
economies as well as the socialist countries are already more
"self-reliant" than the Third World.

Some authors, such as Galtung, and also the resolutions of a
number of important conferences, such as the 1976 Colombo Conference of Non-Aligned countries, claim that trade movements between

the North and the South should be drastically reduced in favour
of enlarged trade among "equals", i.e. the developing countries.
In a strategy of collective self-reliance the complete abolition
of trade barriers on the part of the rich countries, or the
promotion of certain exports, would not be desirable. The benefits, but also the costs, of world-wide trade will tend to be
minimized. This leads us into the final section.

Problems of Rich Countries

The industrialized countries have entered the longest period of
high unemployment since World War II. It looks as if the days of
full employment, as defined today, are over, and this for two
reasons. Firstly, because the rate of economic growth in future
will be lower than was the case during the 20 to 25 years following World War II. Secondly, because the active population will
continue to increase. The future rate of economic growth is likely to be lower than in the past because of series of factors.
There is first of all the fact that the manufacturing base, the
engine of our growth, is becoming smaller in favour of the
tertiary sector. On top of that, there is the energy and raw
materials constraint and the growing web of environmental laws.
Finally, there is a vocal group who favours zero growth, i.e. a
voluntary reduction of economic growth even if it were possible
to grow at a faster rate.

The active population will continue to grow not so much because
of demographic trends, but because the female labour force
participation rates will continue to increase. Thus, the future
growth path will have increasing difficulty in getting back to
full employment as we now understand it. There are several ways
in which the industrialized countries could possibly react in the
face of such a long term structural situation. We shall examine
them inasfar as they reflect on the developing countries.

Protectionism. Most studies on the subject indicate quite clearly
that imports from developing countries are responsible for only a
small proportion of the total volume of unemployment in the
industrialized world. (6) However, it is also true that the effects
of such imports hit hardest at certain industrial branches, very
often located in specific regions and employing relatively many
unskilled workers, for whom it is often difficult to find alternative employment opportunities. Hence, the pressure is on for a
political choice to introduce protectionist measures that will
favour these industrial branches. In fact, this is precisely what
is happening at the time of writing in the Brussels negotiations
regarding the extension of the Multi-Fibre Agreement. This is a
typical trade-off problem between long term and short term considerations. Although exports from rich to poor countries will be
hampered in the long run, protectionism looks like a perfectly
rational policy in the short term, if immediate problems must be
tackled.

However, since the largest single cause of labour displacement is changes in labour productivity, (7) it is difficult to conceive how a protectionist strategy can have an important impact on the employment situation in general. Protectionism fits into a collective self-reliance approach of the *industrialized* countries under which they cling to labour-intensive industries and restrict technological progress, partly to get back to the traditional concept of full employment.

Expansionism. The protectionist approach amounts to a more employment-intensive development strategy for the West. An alternative would be to stimulate demand in order to break through the growth rate bottleneck. Thus far, attempts to stimulate internal demand appear to result in rising inflation rates.

The idea has been put forward (for example by Chancellor Kreisky and EEC top man Cheysson) to initiate a sizable transfer of capital to the developing countries. This would be good for the Third World and for tackling the stagflation and unemployment problems of the industrialized countries. Would the implications of such a move for the industrialized countries be any different as compared to a domestic increase of government expenditures? Apart from the political gesture involved, the economic difference could lie in the demand structure of developing countries, which tends to be quite unlike that of industrialized countries. The governments of the latter are limited in the way they can spend additional money domestically. Well-directed expenditures in developing countries might have a greater multiplier effect than the same amounts of money spent at home. *If* this is the case, it would be tempting for the rich countries to stimulate capital transfers to those developing countries with the greatest multiplier effects for their own economies. It remains then to be seen in how far such an approach coincides with the development strategies (basic needs, self-reliance) mentioned in Section Two above ... A comparison with the effects of the Marshall Aid for the United States of America would perhaps be in order here.

Redistribution of employment opportunities. The one big difference between the economic crisis of the 1930s and the present situation is that national income now continues to increase, albeit at a slower pace than before, but that unemployment levels continue to be high. In the 1930s everything went down: employment levels, production, income, etc. We witness at present in many industrialized countries a second structural shift (next to the economic one mentioned earlier), and that is the shift in the ratio between the active and non-active population. Unemployment figures conceal several important changes which are closely related to the deteriorating employment situation. For example, the number of people, particularly those in the 55-64 age bracket, who are being put in the category "unfit for work", is related more to the unemployment rate than to their physical situation! In The Netherlands this category is about twice as large as the unemployment figure. It is forecast that the number of people in the "unfit for work" group will increase to close on half a million in 1980 or about 10 per cent of the active population. (8) If we add up the three categories "unemployed", "unfit for work", and absence due to "sickness" in The Netherlands today, we come to the stunning result that out of an active population of about five million, almost one million people are being supported by social welfare regulations of one type or another.

On top of all this we must face the fact that attitudes towards certain types of work are changing fundamentally. For example, a recent study made by the Institute of Development Research demonstrates that even in the rapidly declining clothing industry, which experiences widespread unemployment, employers are confronted with serious problems in the recruitment of certain types of workers. (9)

A possible way of dealing with this complex set of interwoven economic, social and psychological factors is to act simultaneously on the demand side by stimulating employment opportunities, and on the supply side by influencing the number of people who present themselves on the labour market.

Taking the demand for labour first, it would be a very selfish and indeed self-defeating attitude to cling to labour-intensive industries behind tariff walls. This would be bad for the developing countries, bad for the incomes of the workers in the industrialized countries, and bad for the consumers who must pay higher prices for their goods.

Instead, industrialized countries should move without hesitation into the direction of stimulating those industries in which they have a comparative advantage on the international market - industries which on the whole will be highly capital- and skill-intensive. In this "integrated sector" (integrated in the world market), incomes and profits should be the criteria rather than employment. This is in line with the recommendations of a recent and important report of the Netherlands Scientific Council for Government Policy. (10) Overall, the capital intensity and hence the labour productivity of the integrated sector will increase and, given the assumed constraint on the future rate of economic growth, employment opportunities in this sector will tend to decline. Seemingly, therefore, the situation will worsen. However, the possibilities for public expenditure will improve because of larger incomes and profits of the integrated sector.

Thus, employment opportunities could be created in the local sector (i.e. the sector which is not integrated in the world economy but is nationally and locally-oriented) and more particularly in what has come to be called the "quaternary" sector, by which is meant the non-commercial part of the tertiary sector.

This local sector is almost by definition more labour-intensive.

As it does not compete on the international market, however, it does not stand in the way of the industrialization efforts of the developing countries. Additional employment opportunities could therefore be created in education, health, restoration of city centres, construction of parks, etc. It is indeed not a question of insufficient work, but rather of means having to be found to create a demand in those sectors where the automatic functioning of market forces does not necessarily create such a demand. In this context we have introduced in The Netherlands the term "socialization of demand".

But this is most probably not sufficient to satisfy the increasing numbers of people who are in search of jobs. Therefore, action must also be undertaken on the supply side. Discussions abound about possible ways of redistributing the existing amount of employment by such measures as incresing compulsory schoolleaving age, advancing the age of retirement, longer holidays, working half an hour less per day, shortening the work-week, putting two people in the same job, etc., etc. Without necessarily rejecting this approach, we would like to advocate a more comprehensive approach which would amount to people spending less time over their entire lifespan on the labour market, by introducing the idea of recurring periods of education, work and retirement.

Instead of influencing the number of people on the labour market by expelling them through unemployment and declaring them "unfit for work", it would surely be much more advantageous, both economically and psychologically, if the individual could himself take the initiative to withdraw from the labour market from time to time in order to improve his knowledge by going back to school or university. He should also be entitled to decide for himself whether he will take part of his retirement benefits at an earlier age in order to undertake those things which motivate him at a certain point in time.

Thus, instead of spending a fortune on maintaining close to one million people who all feel rejected, the same amount of money could be spent in a much more productive and psychologically advantageous manner.

This scheme implies a different definition of "full employment" and a substantial change in post-compulsory education and in social welfare, including pension regulations.

But it could be done, provided we do not listen to the sirens of protectionism and of selfishness. It would also be beneficial to the developing countries provided they do not listen to prophets who preach "de-linking" from the industrialized countries.

Notes and Références
(1) J. Tinbergen et al: *Reshaping the International Order*, Dutton,

New York, 1976, p.17.

(2) See, for example, J. Somavia in RIO Report, p.325.

(3) Committee for Development Planning: Report on the 13th Session, in *Rijksbegroting 1978, Memorie van Toelichting*, Government Budget 1978, The Hague, 1977, ch. 5.

(4) Trade or Development - Some reflections on Self-Reliance, *Economic and Political Weekly*, February, 1977.

(5) See, for instance, *Sector Analyse* (Bijlage bij de Memorie van Toelichting van de Rijksbegroting 1978), chapter on Economic Affairs.

(6) F. Wolter: *Adjustment to Imports from Developing Countries*, Kiel, 1976; and H. Lydall: *Trade and Employment*, ILO, Geneva, 1975.

(7) See F. Wolter: *Adjustment to Imports*.

(8) See Ministry of Economic Affairs: *Economische Structuur Nota*, The Hague, 1976.

(9) Instituut voor Ontwikkelingsonderzoek: *Een Toekomst voor de Nederlandse Confectie-Onderneming* (A Future for the Dutch Clothing Industry), Tilburg, 1977.

(10) Wetenschappelijke Raad voor het Regeringsbeleid: *Maken wij er werk van?*, The Hague, 1977.

Targeting Progress in Meeting Basic Needs

James P. Grant

Introduction

Jan Tinbergen is that rare economist whose work is characterized
by concern both for advancing equity and justice along with
development and for increasing national output. It was not surprising, therefore, when the "Reshaping the International Order"
(RIO) (1) project, which was coordinated by Jan Tinbergen, gave
major attention in its discussions and conclusions to the
reduction of absolute poverty as well as to measures for accelerating growth in the developing countries. The RIO Report called
for the development of indicators of poverty that would be internationally accepted and that would encompass a strong social
component as well as per capita income.

This paper proposes that a new standard for measuring progress in
meeting basic needs be given international consideration. It
proposes that progress be measured in terms of the *rate* at which
the gap in social conditions in the most advanced and in the
developing countries is being narrowed. One measure of social conditions is the Physical Quality of Life Index (PQLI), which is a
composite index of three sets of descriptive statistics - those
for infant mortality, life expectancy at age one, and literacy,
each indexed from a low of one (assigned to the world's worst
performer in 1950) to a high of 100. (2)

In retrospect, the targets of Development Decade II probably
should have included an equivalent reduction in the international
disparities in social indicators in addition to the recommended
3.5 per cent annual increase in per capita income. The advantage
of indexing social indicators is that annual percentage targets
can be set in accordance with some long range development goal.
For example, a 3.5 per cent annual improvement in each of the
components of the PQLI for any particular developing country
would halve the present disparity between that country and the
most advanced countries and would boost a current PQLI of 50 to
approximately 75 by the end of the century.

As the concept of overcoming the worst aspects of absolute poverty
within a given timeframe (for example, by the year 2000) gains
support in both numbers and intensity, it is becoming increasingly
evident that some readily usable measure of progress in meeting
basic needs is required. Like most great ideas, the concept of
eliminating at least the worst aspects of poverty within a
relatively short time is being nourished from many sources. One
such source was effectively identified by the late Senator Hubert
H. Humphrey in 1973 when he spoke of: " ... the veritable intellectual revolt among scholars of development who are turning
against the long held view that growth alone is the answer that

will trickle benefits to the poorest majority ..." His comments
paralleled thinking emerging in many developing countries, the
World Bank, and key United Nations agencies.

Another source of support for this concept is the association that
is made between basic needs and the new emphasis on human rights.
Basic (physical) needs and human (political and social) rights are
increasingly being seen as parallel and interconnected.

The concept of seeking to address basic human needs problems in a
quantifiable way within a given timeframe emerged with major force
in the summer and fall of 1976. (3) It first came to widespread
public attention with the issuance of *Employment, Growth and Basic
Needs: A One World Problem*, the Report of the ILO Director General
prepared for the June 1976 World Employment Conference. (4) This
report not only presented the most thorough discussion to date of
basic needs and how these might be more effectively addressed
through international cooperation, but also made the far-reaching
proposal that steps be taken to achieve satisfaction of the most
basic needs within a given timeframe - by the year 2000. The end-
of-the-century timeframe proposal proved too innovative to be
accepted at the World Employment Conference; however, in the
intervening months, the proposal has received a growing number of
endorsements from around the world.

By the end of 1976, both World Bank President Robert McNamara and
the RIO Report, based on work begun long before, had come to the
same conclusion. McNamara gave explicit endorsement to the idea
that goals be set for a given timeframe in his address to the Board
of Governors of the World Bank on October 4, 1976. He called for
"a basic understanding" and a kind of "global compact" that would
have as a major objective "the meeting of the basic human needs of
the absolute poor in both the poor and middle income countries
within a reasonable period of time, say by the end of this
century". Later in the same month, the Tinbergen-led group of 21
international experts issued the RIO Report that called for a
"global compact on poverty" between rich and poor nations, with
the goal of overcoming the worst aspects of absolute poverty within
countries by the year 2000.

The Measurement of Physical Well-Being
The plethora of public attention to the concept of meeting basic
needs within a definite timeframe presents at least two operational
problems: how to measure progress in meeting basic needs and how
to access whether the worst aspects of global poverty have indeed
been overcome by a given date. Traditionally, the answer to such
questions has been sought in the various forms of measuring
income. For example, the World Bank has made estimates of the
numbers of persons having per capita incomes of less than U.S.
$ 50 and U.S. $ 75. But such measures can be almost meaningless
for low-income societies. Per capita income statistics do not take
into account many of the productive activities - for example,
gathering food, firewood, building houses made with indigenous

materials, or producing vegetables on family plots - associated
with subsistence farming.

Any given income can represent completely different qualities of
life for rural people with land than for city dwellers. Moreover,
different currencies can have vastly different purchasing power;
foreign exchange rates frequently grossly distort the relative
purchasing power of different currencies. In addition, purchasing
power varies between low- and high-income countries and between
geographic regions. (5) Use of income data which is often not
deflated is further complicated today by global inflation. A 1978
dollar is worth far less than, say, a 1972 dollar.

The limitations of using per capita income figures to measure
progress in overcoming the worst *consequences* of absolute poverty
can be illustrated by noting that in the early 1970s Sri Lanka,
with a per capita income of $ 130, had a life expectancy roughly
comparable to that of Washington D.C., which had a per capita
income well over $ 5,000. Hong Kong (per capita income $ 1,610)
and Taiwan ($ 810) - which have pursued policies that combine
rapid economic growth with cost effective address of basic needs
- both have longer life expectancies (71 and 69 years, respectively) and lower infant mortality rates (18 and 26 per 1000 births
respectively) than Washington, D.C., with its life expectancy of
66 years and infant mortality of 29.

It is because of results such as these that there has been an
increasing tendency to look beyond income statistics, useful as
they may be, and beyond composite indicators that incorporate
both performance data and income figures. (6) The Director
General's Report to the World Employment Conference defined basic
needs in terms of adequate food, shelter, clothing, certain
household effects, safe drinking water, sanitation, public transport, and health and education facilities. Yet these, too, can
vary greatly from country to country and from region to region.
The shelter and clothing required in a tropical country such as
Sri Lanka is very different from that required in much of Nepal or
Afghanistan, with their rugged winters. This explains in part the
increasing tendency to speak of development progress in terms of
certain end results that are universally sought - for example,
life expectancy, infant mortality, and literacy - rather than in
terms of such inputs as calories, health services, or shelter.
Thus the Tinbergen group in the RIO Report called for the "attainment of the following national objectives for all countries by
the end of this century": a life expectancy of 65 years or more
(compared to the low-income countries' present average of 48
years); a literacy rate of at least 75 per cent (compared to 33
per cent for the low-income countries today); an infant mortality
rate of 50 or less per 1000 births (compared to 125 today); and a
birth rate of 25 or less per 1000 population (compared with 40
today).

The first three of these targets were achieved by Sri Lanka, Taiwan, and South Korea while their incomes were very low. The fourth
target - a birth rate of 25 or less per 1000 - is better than
these countries achieved while their incomes were still below the
$ 300 per capita level, although each of them did reduce the birth
rate at least to 30 per 1000.

The Overseas Development Council's rough but useful new measure of
progress toward meeting basic human needs - the PQLI - closely
parallels the social indicators used in the RIO Report for stating
the minimum targets for the year 2000 and provides a composite
indicator for measuring progress toward these goals. After examining a large array of social indicators, the ODC selected three
- infant mortality, life expectancy at age 1, and literacy - that
appeared to adequately represent the wider range of conditions that
a "minimum human needs" program seeks to improve and consolidated
them into a simple, composite index on the arbitrary basis of
equal weights. Because these variables are indexed on a scale of
1 to 100, keeping both upper and lower limits stable, progress is
assessed against a fixed target. (7) And because these indicators
measure different aspects of world development, and yet together
provide information about how the benefits of development are
distributed, combining them into one index provides much more
information on success in reducing the worst aspects of poverty
than does GNP alone or than would any of the social indicators
alone. Sweden, with a PQLI of 98, has the highest rating; Guinea-
Bissau, with 11, has the lowest.

The data for the three indicators, while still uneven in quality,
are widely available and express relatively unethnocentric
objectives. Improvements in the social conditions they describe
are fairly universally sought. In addition, the indicators have
the advantages that they do not make any assumptions about the
special patterns of development and that they measure results
rather than inputs. Because the results they measure reflect more
or less universal objectives, they are appropriate standards for
performance comparison among countries. Life expectancy and infant
mortality seem to be very good indicators of important aspects of
social progress. In essence, they represent the sum of the effects
of nutrition, public health, income, and the general environment.
At the same time, they reflect quite different aspects of social
interaction. Preliminary work suggests that infant mortality
rather sensitively characterizes the position of women within the
society; life expectancy is a reflection of general environmental
characteristics. Literacy is both a measure of well-being and a
skill that is important in the development process; the extent to
which poor groups are literate helps determine the extent to which
they do share or will be able to share the benefits of economic
growth. And literacy does not become widespread without sufficient
advancement in a society to make it a widely desired skill.

Table 1 shows that when the development progress of countries is viewed in terms of life expectancy, infant mortality, and literacy, rather than in terms of income, the picture that emerges is different from the usual. While levels of per capita GNP and physical well-being ususally show a close correlation, a number of striking exceptions indicate that low income and the worst consequences of absolute poverty need not go hand-in-hand. The life expectancy, infant mortality, and literacy rates of Sri Lanka are those of the United States in the late 1930s, but they were achieved at a per capita income level of $ 130 - in other words, while a substantial proportion of the population had incomes below that normally defined as "absolute poverty". These exceptions also show that relatively high per capita income does not necessarily reflect widespread well-being - as in the case of Gabon and Iran.

Table 1: *The development progress of selected countries.*

	Average per capita GNP ($, 1974)	PQLI Achieve- ment	Life expectancy at birth (years)	Infant mortality (per 1,000)	Literacy (%)
Low-Income Countries	152	39	48	134	33
- India	140	52	50	139	34
- Kerala, India	110	72	61	58	60
- Sri Lanka	130	83	68	45	81
- Afghanistan	110	18	43	182	8
Lower Middle-Income Countries	338	58	61	70	34
- Malaysia	680	59	59	75	41
- Korea, Rep. of	480	79	61	47	88
- Cuba	640	85	70	29	78
Upper Middle-Income Countries	1,091	68	61	82	65
- Gabon	1,960	21	41	178	12
- Iran	1,250	39	51	139	23
- Algeria	710	43	53	126	26
- Taiwan (ROC)	810	87	69	26	85
High-Income Countries	4,361	93	71	21	97
- Kuwait	11,770	65	69	44	55
- United States	6,670	94	71	17	99
- Netherlands	5,250	97	74	11	98

Looking at indicators of social conditions as well as at per capita income - and using the PQLI as a surrogate for life expectancy, infant mortality, and literacy - suggest that there is a dual challenge: (i) that of ensuring that progress in meeting basic needs at least parallels progress in improving per capita GNP; and (ii) that of accelerating progress in meeting basic needs to the point that by the year 2000 all countries will have met the "minimum floor" proposed by the Tinbergen study of a life expectancy of 65 years, an infant mortality rate of 50 per 1000 births, and a literacy rate of 75 per cent. Achieving these levels of progress would result in a PQLI rating of 78.

Improving Physical Well-Being is Complex

Targeting change toward attaining improvement in social indicators

raises the broad issue of what inputs are required to achieve
desired results. The complexity of advancing physical well-being
- particularly of extending life expectancy and reducing infant
mortality - is evidenced in the chart below, which suggests that
the two principal requirements are improvement in nutritional
status and reduced illness and infection. This, of course, raises
the further question of what variables affect these two requirements and what the relative weights of the variables are under a
variety of circumstances.

Figure 1: *Inputs for advancing physical well-being*

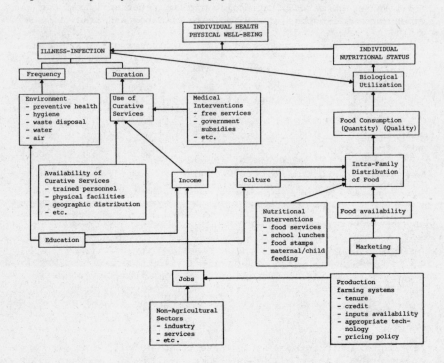

A determining factor in the amount of nutrition any individual
gets is whether he or she has sufficient resources to obtain what
food may be available. For even if there is plenty of food, as in
India in the mid 1970s, those in the poorest third of the
population may not be able to get it. The availability of medical
services is similarly restricted. Thus, in most countries, the
need for jobs assumes great importance. In Taiwan, which has
70-80 workers per 100 acres of cultivated land, agriculture
obviously is supporting more people than in northern Mexico, which
employs 3-4 workers per 100 acres. Taiwan - like China and South
Korea - undertook land reform and other programs to create the

the jobs that provide the incomes with which families can buy nutrition and health services.

In Sri Lanka, the villagers did not initially have the kind of power needed to bring about land reform. But they were able to tax the rich and then to make widely available for twenty-five years medical interventions and such nutritional interventions as two pounds of free grain per week. After several decades of emphasis on primary education and more than a decade of widespread health services and food subsidies, a vigorous citizenry was able to force land reform and other measures. This is a perfect example of a "virtuous circle". A somewhat similar process has been going on in Kerala, which is one of the lowest income states in India. Kerala now has a 61-year life expectancy - in contrast to India's overall life expectancy of 50.

More social science research is required before there will be even a basic consensus about the principal variables, and about their relative weights, that have made possible rapid progress in improving social conditions in such countries and regions as China, Sri Lanka, Taiwan, and Kerala. The need for this understanding is urgent. If all developing countries had the death rates of 10 per 1000 and birth rates of 30 per 1000 that these countries attained while their per capita incomes were under $ 300, about 11 million fewer people would be dying - and there would be about 20 million fewer births - each year.

Rates of Change

Is it appropriate to talk about an annual reduction in percentage terms in the disparity that exists between some countries today in terms of PQLI and its components and the levels attained by the most advanced countries? If so, what might be appropriate targets that are comparable to the 3 to 4 per cent annual improvements now sought internationally in food production and in per capita income? How feasible is it to attain the RIO targets - equivalent to a PQLI of approximately 78 - for all countries by the year 2000, when achieving these targets would require a better than 4 per cent improvement for some countries?

As noted, analyses of the inputs (and their relative weights) needed to achieve specified levels of well-being are still at a very rudimentary stage. The historical record, however, as evidenced by the examples below, offers encouraging evidence that sustained improvement in life expectancy, infant mortality and literacy has been achieved under a variety of circumstances.

An analysis of *infant mortality* trends since 1920 brings to light over fifty countries that have managed to reduce their infant mortality rates by more than 50 deaths per 1000 births in a period of some twenty years. More than twenty of these countries had reductions of over 80 deaths per 1000 births. Moreover, it appears that once an attack on high infant mortality rates is launched, success can be seen quite quickly.

A goal of 3.5 per cent reduction annually in infant mortality
disparities seems appropriate and would appear to be sustainable.
Large long term reductions generally consist of a large initial
decrease, with the pace of reduction slowing gradually. In Sri
Lanka, for example, rates fell from 132 per 1000 in 1943 to 92 in
1948, a period of just five years; they then continued their downward trend more slowly, to reach 56 in 1963 and 45 in the early
1970s; in the first five years, they fell by 25 deaths per
1000 births, and in the second five years by another 22 per
1000. There are many more such examples, and they are not
confined solely to the Asian continent; Romania, for example,
exhibited reductions of 54, 27, 15, and 13 deaths per 1000 births,
respectively, in each of the five-year periods between the late
1940s and the late 1960s, for a total reduction of 109. It is
worth pointing out that Romania accomplished this with a per
capita GNP estimated by the World Bank to be only $ 440 in 1965.

Examples of dramatic reductions are available on every continent
- in countries that are heavily urbanized and densely populated
and in those that are rural and more sparsely populated.

Furthermore, large reductions among certain ethnic groups and in
particular geographic regions *within* countries reinforce the
suggestion advanced here that it is the degree of commitment, and
not income or cultural factors, that is most important to success
in this effort. For example, in the United States, reductions in
infant mortality of 70 per cent have been documented among
American Indians in the last twenty years, largely as the result
of sustained attention to the problem. Targeted programs have
reduced infant mortality from 63 per 1000 in 1955 to about 18 per
1000 today. And, the city of Newark, New Jersey (with a population
of 382,000), managed through strong local efforts to reduce its
infant mortality from 42 to 22 per 1000 between 1965 and 1975 - a
reduction of almost half in just ten years.

A 3.5 per cent annual reduction in *life expectancy* disparities
also appears attainable in terms of the historical record. Since
the disparities are largest in the initial years, the largest increases in life expectancy would be required in the beginning
stages of the effort, with progressively smaller absolute
increases required in later years.

An analysis of selected experiences suggests that with sufficient
effort, a 3 to 4 per cent annual reduction in life expectancy
disparities can be attained even for the poorer countries. Sri
Lanka, a country which has shown dramatic improvements in all the
social indicators, recorded a life expectancy of 46 in the
1945-47 period. Twenty years later, life expectancy had risen by
18 years to 64. And Sri Lanka's increase occurred despite its low
per capita GNP of approximately $ 100 in the mid 1960s. Other

countries with higher per capita GNPs have recorded similarly dramatic increases: Japan rose from 48 years to 66 years in the twenty year period preceding 1955; Puerto Rico rose from 46 years to 70 years between 1940 and 1960. Typically, large increases in life expectancy come while a country is experiencing economic growth and advances in the levels of income, as in the case of Japan. However, the experience of Sri Lanka, and of China, where life expectancy is estimated to have risen from 45 years to 62 years between 1950-55 and 1970-75, despite a per capita GNP of less than $ 300, demonstrates that this need not be the case. In Sri Lanka, these results seem due in considerable part to a wide-spread availability of low cost health and malaria prevention services and the provision of a subsidized weekly grain ration.

For countries such as Angola with very low life expectancy (41 years), a halving of the disparity would raise life expectancy to only 58. Major efforts would be required for such countries to reach the RIO year 2000 target of 65 years.

Documented trends in *literacy* are difficult to find. UNESCO publications provide statistics for only a few years; where data are complete, it is typically for the more developed countries whose populations have been almost totally literate for many decades. However, Sri Lanka does have reliable statistics dating back to the beginning of the century and covering years in which real efforts were being made to increase the educational level of the population. In 1946, 57 per cent of the population was literate; in the next twenty-five years, literacy rose to 78 per cent, with an increase of 14 per cent in the first seven years and smaller increases thereafter. Improvements in women's literacy rates are even more impressive than the overall record.

This brief survey of the historical experience of selected countries that have been notably successful in making specific improvements in the physical well-being of large segments of their populations - as well as the evidence summarized in the table below - suggests that annual reductions of 3.5 per cent in the PQLI disparities, with a view toward halving disparities by the year 2000, between individual developing countries and the most advanced countries are difficult but not impossible to obtain. However, increased international cooperation will almost certainly be essential if the low-income countries are to attain these targets. For those countries that presently have the lowest PQLI ratings, attainment of the RIO minimum targets will be more difficult but again not impossible.

Table 2: *PQLI of Selected Countries*

		1950s	1960s	1970s
Algeria		32	37	43
India		26	36	42
Egypt		30	39	45
Brazil		54	63	68
Sri Lanka	45 (1946)	62	77	83
Taiwan	55 (1948)	69	81	87
Poland	54 (1935)	75	87	92
United States	84 (1940)	91	92	94
France	83 (1945)	87	93	96
Norway		95	96	97

Conclusion

Recent years have witnessed greatly increased national and international acceptance of the idea that advancing equity is as
important as increasing output and that these should be twin goals
of development. There also has been growing acceptance of Jan
Tinbergen's emphasis on justice - of the notion that priority
should be given to meeting the minimum needs of the poor.
Achieving equity and justice has suffered, however, as a result
of being measured primarily in terms of income rather than in
terms of human goals. The lack of adequate capacity for measuring
the social condition has contributed both to continuing confusion
in the discussion of how to combine equity and growth and to
continued deemphasis of equity and justice goals in both developed
and developing countries. The RIO Report's year 2000 targets for
life expectancy, literacy, and infant mortality; the PQLI; and
now this essay's proposal for percentage targets for the annual
reduction in disparities in basic social indicators are all
attempts to facilitate discussion of equity and justice issues by
policy-makers, planners, and the general public.

A second point warranting emphasis in this conclusion is that the
objective to be sought is that of combining equity and growth in
a symbolic relationship without improving one at the expense of
the other. It would have been useful if the goals of Development
Decade II had encompassed the target of, say, a 3.5 per cent
annual reduction in the disparities that exist between poor countries and rich countries in life expectancy, infant mortality,
and literacy in addition to the target of a 3.5 per cent annual
increase in per capita GNP for the developing countries. The
international goal for the balance of this century should be to
achieve both these targets and the RIO targets, thereby doubling
per capita income in the developing countries and at least halving
PQLI disparities between the poorest and the richest countries by
the year 2000.

Far more knowledge is required if the worst aspects of poverty are
to be overcome by the year 2000 - more knowledge not only of the

variables that affect progress in meeting basic needs, but also
of the types of technology that have relevance for the poor. For
example, vast amounts are spent for research on cancer, which has
little relevance for poor countries and poor people; almost
nothing, however, is spent on schistosomiasis, a disease that
affects 400-500 million of the poorest people in the world.

Research priorities and results, in short, should be analyzed in
terms of the potential contribution any given research project
can make toward improving a nation's PQLI rating as well as its
income. Those engaged in national and international research in
the physical and social sciences should keep in mind the following
question: Who is really going to benefit from this - those who are
already comparatively well off or those who are most in need?
This essay seeks - in the spirit of Jan Tinbergen - to advance
our capability to help those most in need while advancing the
well-being of all.

Notes and References
(1) Jan Tinbergen (Coordinator): *Reshaping the International
Order*, E.P. Dutton and Co., New York, 1976.
(2) For a fuller description of the index and PQLI ratings for all
countries, see Martin M. McLaughlin and the staff of the Overseas
Development Council: *The United States and World Development:
Agenda 1978*, published for the Overseas Development Council by
Praeger Publishers, Inc., 1978.
(3) For an earlier presentation, see *The Changing World Order and
the World's Poorest Billion: A Fresh Approach*, by James P. Grant;
paper presented to the 25th Pugwash Conference, Madras, India,
January 1976.
(4) Report of the Director General of the International Labour
Office: *Employment, Growth and Basic Needs: A One-World Problem*,
International Labour Organization, Geneva, 1976.
(5) *Employment, Growth and Basic Needs*, op.cit., gives a good summary of different income approaches to measuring basic needs, see
pp. 16-20.
(6) See *Contents and Measurement of Socioeconomic Development*, A
Staff Study of the United Nations Research Institute of Social
Development, Praeger Publishers, New York, 1972.
(7) For example, for the life expectancy at age 1 index, 77 years
was assigned the upper limit of 100 (Sweden achieved the most
favourable national figure of 76 years) and the most unfavourable
performance in 1950 (38 years in Guinea-Bissau) was assigned the
lower limit of one. Use of the worst performance in 1950 as the
lower limit of the index rather than the current worst performance
(41 years for life expectancy at age 1) allows for comparisons
across time without resulting in negative ratings.

Decision-Making for the New International Economic Order

Johan Kaufmann

Introduction

Optimalized decision-making, which implies an optimalized negotiating framework, has long been a concern of Jan Tinbergen. He
has distinguished four levels of decision-making in relation to
the New International Economic Order: (1)

- the local level;
- the popular level (e.g. civil rights movements, women's liberation);
- the intermediate level (e.g. the non-aligned countries);
- the international level.

This writer believes that at the present time the various levels
operate with less than optimal efficiency, are not sufficiently
interlinked, and offer no systematic contribution to the realization of the New International Economic Order which itself is
as yet loosely defined.

The RIO Report (Reshaping the International Order) has proposed
"packages of proposals for comprehensive negotiation", covering:
i) proposals aimed at removing gross inequities in the distribution of world income and economic opportunities;
ii) proposals to ensure more harmonious growth of the global
economic system; and
iii) proposals to provide the beginnings of a global planning
system.

Participation of people at the local level is convincingly
stressed by Alger: "World order proposals tend to build either
from the top down (i.e. with global institutions) or from existing "nation-states" up. Neither of these modes is concerned with
how sub-national communities would link to proposed global structures. This may be because these future world orders have been
primarily the creations of cosmopolitans - scholars and other
elites - who do not relate to the world from local communities
but as part of a national governmental and non-governmental elite
and perhaps also as part of a cosmopolitan transnational or
international elite that is selected from various national elites.
We have uncovered very suggestive evidence that participatory
linkages of people in local communities, rather than more traditional educational experiences, may be the key. The root of
the problem is that the public is not consciously linked to present global systems though they live in a sea of transnational
linkages in the form of food, clothing, medicine, information,
music, films and a host of manufactured goods." (2)

What is the New International Economic Order?

Superficially, the answer is easy: the NIEO is the Declaration and Plan of Action adopted at the Sixth Special Session (res. 3202-S-VI of 1 May 1974), supplemented by the Charter of Economic Rights and Duties of States (res. 3281-XXIX of December 12, 1974) and followed by resolution 3362 (S-VII) on "Development and International Economic Co-operation" adopted at the Seventh Special Session of the General Assembly (September 16, 1975). This, however, is a non-answer, both because of the vagueness of many of the precepts in these texts, and because a number of important governments do not accept, or only in part, the policy recommendations in these texts. In the case of the Sixth Special Session this non-acceptance took the form of a series of formal reservations.

To illustrate this, let us take as a random though important example the following provision on raw materials, taken from resolution 3202-S-VI:

"iii) Expeditious formulation of commodity agreements where appropriate, in order to regulate as necessary and to stabilize the world markets for raw materials and primary commodities;

iv) Preparation of an over-all integrated programme, setting out guidelines and taking into account the current work in this field, for a comprehensive range of commodities of export interest to developing countries".

The Seventh Special Session (in par. 3 of res. 3362-S-VII), and the 4th. UNCTAD Conference (in res. 93(IV)), provided elaboration.

General Assembly resolutions by their nature (with a few exceptions) do not constitute binding legal commitments. Frequent use of the words "where possible", "where appropriate" and "adequate", which enable each government to follow its favourite interpretation, render agreed specific international action more difficult. Not much has therefore actually happened.Few new commodity agreements have been negotiated; as of February 1978 no agreement on an integrated commodity programme, especially not on the "Common Fund", had been reached. Does this confirm that specific economic agreements do not find sufficient economic impulse from general precepts? My answer to this question is a qualified yes: general precepts help to "conceptualize", and they provide material for those who wish to make propaganda for "the good cause", but they are not sufficient to achieve internationally negotiated and agreed action.

The result of the Seventh Special Session, i.e. resolution 3362 (S-VII), has been described by the Netherlands Minister for Development Cooperation, J. Pronk as "a commitment to commit". (3)

This is semantically, perhaps morally, but not legally, true. Without a timeframe, and without real agreement on fundamental objectives and principal means to achieve these objectives, the significance of the commitment is limited, and potentially negative, if frustration and anger over non-results lead to negative action making subsequent agreement even more difficult.

If there is no agreed definition of the New International Economic Order, the negotiating process is obviously rendered more difficult. Every sub-goal has to be negotiated in cumbersome talks; simultaneously or subsequently instruments are tackled; often (sub-) goals and instruments get mixed up. On top of this, semantic and conceptual difficulties negatively affect the process of decision-making which more often than not becomes non-decision-making.

Institutional Format

There is no agreement on the institutional format for dealing with inter-linked issues. In the old (and still existing) system of sectorally divided specialized agencies, there was little disagreement on which international institution was "competent" to deal with a particular negotiable problem: FAO for agriculture, WHO for health, GATT for trade, IMF for monetary problems, etc. Three developments have shattered this tranquil picture:

i) Developing countries have successfully pushed for institutions which they could consider more responsive to their stated needs: UNCTAD is the typical example.

ii) A number of problems, recognized as being of worldwide importance, are being dealt with at worldwide conferences, some of which created new institutional machinery, including new sectoral financing funds. The World Food Conference created a World Food Council and the International Fund for Agricultural Development; the Environment Conference created the U.N. Environment Programme (UNEP), and the U.N. Environment Fund; the HABITAT Conference (Vancouver) resulted in Habitat (Centre for Human Settlements), including a Housing and Human Settlements Foundation.

iii) Problems are being recognized as interlinked, and many feel that they should be dealt with as a whole (as is implied in the "package" approach of the resolution of the Sixth and Seventh Special Sessions), but generally acceptable machinery for dealing with the package approach has only recently been adopted, in the form of a new Committee of the Whole which is supposed to assist the General Assembly by acting as the focal point in:

"(a) Overseeing and monitoring the implementation of decisions and agreements reached in the negotiations on the establishment of the New International Economic Order in the appropriate bodies of the United Nations system;

(b) Providing impetus for resolving difficulties in negotiations and for encouraging the ongoing work in these bodies;

(c) Serving, where appropriate, as a forum for facilitating and
expediting agreement on the resolution of outstanding issues;
and

(d) Exploring and exchanging views on global economic problems
and priorities;"(4)

The net result is still one of decision-making confusion, because
there are no clear responsibilities as to who deals with what,
and the more or less defined responsibilities of each organization overlap with those of others. This applies to UNCTAD and
ECOSOC, although in practice their work has been different. For
reasons perhaps more historic and psychological than factual,
UNCTAD remains the preferred organ of the developing countries,
ECOSOC that of the developed countries, although the former
have a large majority in ECOSOC also.

Confusion and overlap exist both on the level of the intergovernmental bodies and on that of the Secretariats which operate
without anybody providing for real direction and coordination.
The resolution on restructuring the economic and social sectors
of the U.N. system, adopted at the 32nd session of the General
Assembly (resl 32/197) intends to initiate a process designed to
remedy this situation.

Additional Implementation Constraints
A number of additional constraints hamper the implementation of
a New International Economic Order.

i) Semantic confusion often prevails and hampers conceptualization: because there was no agreed definition of the NIEO, several
countries objected vigorously every time the term NIEO, especially if preceded by "the" rather than by "a", and if written with
capital letters, was used in some draft resolution. These objections, as a minimum, meant loss of time in reaching agreement
and, as a maximum, blocked or rendered ineffective any decision-
making. As this is written, this problem has largely disappeared,
mostly after the United States accepted the term, although interpreted in a special way: "The international economic order is a
system of relationships among all nations. The process of change,
therefore, must be through an evolving consensus that takes into
account the economic systems, the interests and the ideas of
all countries. Thus we are talking about a process, or a broad
framework for dialogue and progress, as much as an "order". (5)

Suggested remedy: The U.N. might look at the pros and contras
of establishing an Ad Hoc Committee on Concepts and Definitions,
composed of scholars and practitioners, and enlarged for particu-

lar purposes with sector-oriented experts, to work towards agreed
definitions. U.N. draft resolutions providing definitions might
be referred to this Committee taking care that this would not
become an excuse for delaying action. Although definition-making
would not overcome fundamental problems, it could prevent some
difficulties and much timeconsuming sterile discussion.

ii) There is a lack of confidence in worldwide bodies, such as
the U.N. General Assembly, or the UNCTAD Conference or Board, on
the side of large developed countries without whose cooperation
there can be no NIEO. This lack of confidence has encouraged experimentation with new mechanisms, such as the Conference on
International Economic Cooperation (CIEC). The CIEC, composed of
27 countries (19 developing and 8 developed), held out promise
for concrete results. It has led to considerable clarification
and to a special aid action for the poorest countries, but it did
not solve basic problems. (6) After the "failure" of CIEC, attention was focused again on the U.N. as an overall mechanism for
negotiating interlinked problems.

Suggested remedy: there is probably no general cure against lack
of confidence. Greater attention will have to be focused on
psychological factors which are often at the roots of lack of confidence.

iii) Nations hate to be left out of the negotiating process, yet
efficient negotiations require a small number of participants.
The CIEC experience was criticized by countries which felt left
out while those who were in may have overestimated their bargaining power. (7) In the U.N. everybody is "in", but at the U.N.
effective negotiations are exceedingly difficult (although not
impossible, as the negotiating results of the Seventh Special
Session and a number of other examples show).

Suggested remedy: Review by a larger body, in which all participate, can be combined with negotiation in smaller bodies. This
time-proven technique should be systematically applied in the
U.N. and outside it. Just as the results of the (non-U.N.) 30-
nation Committee of the Conference on Disarmament (CCD) are
reviewed by the First Committtee of the General Assembly (i.e.
by all member states of the U.N.), so economic issues negotiated
in smaller bodies can be reviewed by a committee of the whole.

iv) Nations do not like abrupt change and will proclaim that
their parliaments and/or their business or other sectors and/or
their public opinion will not accept it, especially if this
change seems to be sudden and rapid, and in particular in times
of unemployment or recession. This constraint involves the question of timing. The decisions of the Sixth and Seventh Special
Sessions are without a time framework; developing nations desire
the fastest possible change, the developed countries seem to play

for more time. Elections and changes of government contribute towards absorbing more time.

Suggested remedy: There should be agreed timeframes, intermediate between slowness and abrupt change, perhaps conforming to the old concept "with all deliberate speed". Governments and private organizations should endeavour to prepare public opinion for change, and of course take effective domestic measures to restructure their economies, including financial support for companies and the retraining of workers which must reorient towards a different activity.

v) Governments are disinclined to accept specific quantitative or policy commitments without escape clauses. The General Agreement on Tariffs and Trade, still in its way one of the more successful examples of international decision-making, continues to function, inter-alia, because of its escape clause machinery.

Suggested remedy: An effort could be made, perhaps in the framework of a new International Development Strategy, to create machinery to relate targets agreed in principle to "examination procedures" to which governments voluntarily subscribe. An effort should be made to define a fairly precisely defined "escape clause" in relation to each target, and to apply agreed "examination procedures" to the use of escape clause machinery. Care should be taken that the use of escape clause machinery is subjected to international scrutiny (as is done in GATT and in certain OECD agreements) so that a minimum of equitable burden-sharing is maintained.

vi) Governments have distinct short term views, often linked to parliamentary or presidential elections, and are therefore reluctant to accept long term policy changes, unless it is in their interest to do so, as was the case with the Treaty of Rome which created the EEC.

Suggested remedy: There should be an international effort where countries concert in convincing their parliaments to accept long term commitments. OECD countries might work out joint long term commitment procedures and then seek to convince Eastern European countries (perhaps through the Economic Commission for Europe) to join. A global long term "commitment" policy should be negotiated in a U.N. body and include OPEC and other nations.

vii) The negotiating methods of many U.N. bodies are distinctly anti-result biassed. There are several reasons for this, and the remedies are visible:

a) Speech-making and negotiation occur in one and the same meeting, thereby reducing the time available for the negotiation process:

Suggested remedy: there should be an effort to put speech-making in separate meetings not necessarily preceeding the negotiating meeting. Some of the more successful decisions of the U.N. Security Council were possible precisely because "explanations of vote" or statements took place *after* a consensus decision, which was negotiated in private sessions. In delicate negotiations on the NIEO, e.g. those on the Common Fund of the Integrated Commodities Programme, a similar practice might help.

b)The process of negotiating between groups, e.g. Group B (developed market economies) and the Group of 77 in UNCTAD, leads to automatic rigidities, in some cases to a confrontation between maximum demand and minimum offers. The position of each group, as experience shows, tends to cluster around the extremes, and not around the average, especially if important countries in each group take extreme positions.(8)

Suggested remedy: there should be an institutionalized practice that group positions are flexible, and small contact groups empowered to negotiate compromise resolutions should be created at the start of any negotiating meeting. This would avoid the dangerous technique of "five minutes before twelve"-decision-making, and may prevent frictions due to artificially arrived at group positions in situations where groups are in fact divided.

viii) Efforts to simplify U.N. structures, both intergovernmental and secretariat, should continue. The recent General Assembly resolution 32/197 is an important step in this direction. On the intergovernmental side, thought should be given to merging ECOSOC, the UNCTAD Board, and the new Committee of the Whole of the General Assembly into a single effective body. This could perhaps be done in 1980 when a new strategy may be promulgated at a new Special Session of the General Assembly. Each body could be permitted to continue to exist in legal terms, but with the provision of joint sessions.

On the financing side, governments should stop and think before creating another sectoral fund which happens to be attractive in terms of some specific objective or the likelihood of collecting money. Some of the existing funds might be merged, perhaps initially by bringing them under the umbrella of the UNDP Governing Council.

On the Secretariat side, a central unit, reinforced by the right people from the specialized agencies, should prepare "policy guidance material" useful to governments and to all parts of the U.N. system. This material could take the form of "options for policy action" each substantiated by cost/benefit analysis, statistical material, etc.

Towards a New Global Compact

Really successful negotiation of the NIEO must involve not only governments, but also the other actors. All should know what they are expected to do.

It is not easy to state how this should be done, without making the sort of errors critized in this essay. The work of the U.N. Commission on Transnational Corporations is an example of how private companies can constructively cooperate in and with a U.N. intergovernmental body. Non-governmental organizations of all kinds are supporting U.N. efforts in various directions. The U.N. global conferences have been accompanied by successful private fora.

Somehow, the new International Development Strategy should have a wider and stronger base than similar international efforts have had so far. With such a wider base a true New International Economic Order, instead of remaining a disputed ideal, can become an inspiring reality.

Notes and References

(1) See his summary of the work of the Study Group on Decision-Making at the 1975 Symposium on a New International Order, held at the Hague under the auspices of the Netherlands Minister for Development Cooperation, Report of the Symposium, p. 54. Cf. also Tinbergen's lecture *"Reshaping the International Order"*, International Institute of Labour Studies, Geneva, 1976, p. 11.
(2) Chadwick F. Alger: *People in the Future Global Order* (Trilateral Conference "Power and Responsibility of the Industrialized Countries in the Global Community", Tokyo, October 1977).
(3) See the Seventh Special Session of the General Assembly, Round-Up and Resolution, United Nations, New York, 1975, p.15.
(4) General Assembly resolution 32/174.
(5) Statement by Ambassador Andrew Young, United States Permanent Representative to the United Nations at the Sixty-third Session of the ECOSOC, general debate, 8 July, 1977, Geneva.
(6) See General Assembly document A/31/478 and add. 1, with the Report of CIEC.
(7) Cf. J. Amuzegar, *Requiem for the North-South Conference*, Foreign Affairs, October, 1977.
(8) For a more elaborate discussion of this phenomenon see Johan Kaufmann: *Conference Diplomacy*, Sijthoff/Oceana, Leiden/New York, 1968, chapter IX.

Use and Abuse of Science and Technology for Development

Alexander King

Introduction

Among the complex problems of reducing the disparities between
the rich and the poor countries of the world, one of the most
acute and most highly politicized issues today is that of the
transfer of technology. The highly industrialized and most
affluent nations have achieved their material levels on the basis
of an extremely efficient, sophisticated and all-pervasive
technology which is both capital and energy intensive and which
seeks an ever greater level of productivity in terms of output
per man hour or year. Indeed, from his first beginnings, technology has been man's chief agent in his struggle upwards from
subsistence. It has evolved gradually from the dawn of human
history when the first bone or flint tools were shaped, through
the discovery of the wheel, the lever, the plough, the use of
fire and the smelting of metal ores. It has always been encouraged for military ends and was given a formidable impulse
during the industrial revolution which coincided with the
beginnings of modern science. Indeed the fathers of the
industrial revolution saw in the marriage of the new science
with the industrial arts, the possibility of the universal
abolition of poverty. Unfortunately, the sciences were then too
primitive to contribute significantly and it was nearly a century
later that the marriage was consummated when the content of the
various sciences had built up sufficiently, with the discovery
of the laws of thermodynamics, the use of electricity and the
architecture of the chemist who was able to design molecules
with properties hitherto unknown in nature which provide the
dyestuffs, medicaments, synthetic textiles and construction
materials of today. This first, scientific revolution is now
giving rise to a second, based on electronics, with the promise
of still greater productivity and much less energy consumption,
but at an extremely high degree of sophistication.

When, in the decades which followed the Second World War, it
became obvious that the disparities between the rich and the poor
nations had become intolerable and deliberate attempts were made
to stimulate development in the countries of the Third World, it
was recognized that technology was a key factor, whether in the
production of food, industrial expansion, strengthened infrastructures, the conquest of tropical diseases or even in
education. It seemed obvious that the developing countries should
take advantage of the vast accumulation of technology elsewhere
and not have to repeat the laborious and costly process which had
been achieved elsewhere, while at the same time avoiding many of
the ills of hasty and undirected technology which had appeared
in the industrialized countries in the form of environmental
deterioration, loss of work satisfaction and all the social

difficulties of a hasty and thoughtless urbanism. Transfer of technology, defined as "a process through which the productive system of a country (public or private enterprize) acquires a technology produced in another country, for incorporation in these enterprizes" was therefore seen as an obvious and major tool of development.

Today, only some two percent of research and development for new technology takes place in the developing countries themselves and this suggests that they must rely on their imports from abroad. Why then has technology transfer not been achieved to a much more significant extent? The answer seems to me to lie not so much in the inadaquacies of the transfer system as such, the machinations of transnational enterprises or inequities in the terms of transfer, but in a failure on the part of both donors and receivers to appreciate that successful transfer is a somewhat complicated socio-economic process with many variables and social conditions beyond the mere introduction of packets of knowledge and technical know-how. This is equally true for the process of technological innovation in general, although the detailed conditions are necessarily somewhat different in the already industrialized societies, where the complex nature of innovation has only recently been appreciated. It may be useful, therefore, in relation to the development imperative, to say something about the relationship between technology and the economy and about technological innovation in general.

Science, Technology and the Economy
Until recently, economists have paid rather little attention to technology, it being implicitely assumed that new processes and products arise spontaneously, as it were, in response to the interaction of economic forces and particularly those of the market. Until relatively recently this has been true to a large extent, although by no means exclusively. This was because through the centuries and until the scientific revolution, most innovation resulted from invention and inventions were exploited essentially if and when the market was ripe for them. Many ingenious inventions were premature and were either ignored or had to wait until the market forces were propitious for their use. Thus the fork-lift truck and other materials handling devices had been perfected many years before the cost of labour in the industrialized countries had risen to a point at which it was profitable to use mechanized methods. With the discovery of electricity and the offerings of organic chemistry great new possibilities were opened up for pratical application, but many of the exploitations were still essentially those of inventors rather than deliberate efforts of scientific research. However, as the sciences advanced, invention and innovation became increasingly sophisticated and great new industries arose which were essentially based on scientific research applied through technological development.

It was only in the early 1960s, however, that the role of research

and development in economic growth became the subject of serious
study by economists. It was shown, for example, that of the economic growth of the United States during the first half of this
century, only about 40 percent could be explained by increases
in the traditional productive factors of capital and labour. The
remaining 60 percent, designated at first as the residual factor,
was assumed to be due to improvements in technology, materials,
management skills and higher levels of education, i.e. in the
quality of labour and of capital utilization. This recognition
of the importance for economic growth of technological improvements and of the human factor coincided with the enormous
increases in research and development expenditures in all the
industrialized countries which followed the end of the Second
World War, a period when it was accepted that science was a good
thing in itself, with the assumption that the more science that
was done in a country, the greater would be the benefit to the
economy - and presumably to society.

This generalization proved to be false and many examples can be
cited of huge efforts of research and development which proved
to be technically successful, but economically disastrous.
Incidentally, this facile notion that scientific activity
automatically results eventually in economic growth has been
swallowed by the elites in some Third World countries; academic
snobbery has indeed been a significant export of the industrialized world.

Recognition of the complexity of the process of technological
innovation followed from studies done by the OECD in the late
1960s on the so-called technological gap between the European
countries and the United States and the work of many academic
research groups. It was shown that no direct correlation existed
between the proportion of the national expenditure of a country
and its economic growth; indeed the extent of the national
technological effort seemed to have little effect on either
economic or trade performance. It appeared that diffusion of
technology across frontiers was sufficiently rapid to compensate
for inadequacies in the domestic research and development effort.
This appears to be true, however, only with regard to countries
above a certain technological threshold, with a mature industrial
infrastructure and a sufficient spread of research and development activity to enable them to scan world scientific and
technological advances and to rapidly and accurately select what
is appropriate to their needs. It certainly does *not* apply to
diffusion and transfer of technology from advanced to Third World
countries where both the level of scientific awareness and the
strength of industrial underpinning are well below the necessary
threshold. Until a real scientific and technological capacity can
be built up in the less developed countries, it is improbable
that the "normal" processes of diffusion can operate effectively.

The case of the Japanese industrial miracle, based on imported

technology, is extremely relevant here and shows how difficult
it will be for Third World countries to follow the same pattern.
Before the war even, this country had achieved a certain amount
of industrialization and a well disciplined population with high
manipulative skills, some excellent universities with research
facilities. During the occupation by the United States, far
reaching plans were made for the modernization and industrialization of the country. The first phase consisted of a thorough
build up of the educational system, the creation of many modern
universities and of a comprehensive network of research
institutions, which ensured that Japanese scientists were
thoroughly aware of all the main points of scientific advance
throughout the world, and of modern industrial development. The
Ministry of International Trade and Industry (MITI) was created
and elaborated a comprehensive national industrial policy in
close cooperation with industry which was encouraged to purchase
the most up to date processes and know-how wherever they could
be found in the world - in practice mainly in the United States
and Western Europe. At first, the world outside tended to
ascribe the success of the Japanese industrialization programme
to the well known capacity of this country for imitation, but in
reality it was due to much deeper causes; the seeds of advanced
industrialization had fallen on fertile ground and resulted from
deliberate, comprehensive and sustained policy based on a
thorough understanding of the inherent nature of the process of
industrial innovation and its articulation with the productive,
educational and social processes. The massive industrial and
research system was thus able first to assimilate foreign
technology of the most advanced type, manage it well and is thus
capable now of moving to the next generation of technological
development in which Japanese science and industry will itself
originate new products and processes.

There are many lessons here for other countries on the threshold
of industrialization. Successful industrialization cannot be
achieved by mere importation of foreign knowledge and know-how.
It requires a soil, propitious and fertile, for the imported
technology to take root and the preparation of this soil is a
long and laborious process.

Technological innovation is thus an extremely complex process
and it is of primary importance that its complexities be understood thoroughly by political leaders, managers and scientists
in the countries of the Third World. Successful innovation must,
of course, have the vital technological input, created domestically or purchased from abroad. But this is only the first step.
Success depends on many other factors including the availability
of capital, a suitable fiscal system, careful selection from
among the immense number of alternatives of those processes and
products which will be most useful to the society, entrepreneurship and management skills, marketing ability, the general level
of education and the national psychology and cultural traditions.

Thus, the availability of technology is the beginning, but is far from being the totality of industrial innovation in countries of all types, already industrialized or at the beginning of their development.

The Present Situation

The conditions for successful innovation in industry are by no means fully appreciated in the industrialized countries. In the Third World, a few countries such as Mexico and India are fully aware of the need for relating industrialization in an organic sense to the needs of society and of developing science and technology in intimate articulation with the productive process and with education, but generally the complexities of the innovation process are not understood, or are ignored. As a consequence the main preoccupation at present is with the availability of technology as such rather than with conditions favourable to its assimilation. This is not to say that much remains to be done to ensure that the developing countries obtain the technology they require on equitable terms and without political or economic strings attached. But this alone is far from sufficient and both the industrialized nations and their enterprises as well as the countries wishing to industrialize are to blame for the present superficiality of the arguments.

Both agree that just conditions of transfer should be established, but while the advanced countries of the market economy world insist that technology in the form of patent rights and know-how, being normal commodities, are commercial - as indeed they are within the free economy zone - many of the developing countries insist that they should have the right of access to technology of the most advanced types. Interpretation of the meaning of "right of access" varies greatly from country to country and, at the extreme, there are those who feel that the governments of the industrialized countries should be able to force their industrial firms to yield their technological secrets, which is impossible without breaking the capitalist and democratic system to which they adhere. There is little evidence indeed that industrial enterprises in the countries of state capitalism are any more willing to pass on their technology without payment or on less onerous terms. Furthermore, in many of the presently industrialized countries there is a real fear that in aiding in any substantial way the industrialization of the Third World, they are creating severe competition for themselves at a later date, an argument which is particularly difficult in times of economic difficulty such as the present, which influences trade unions even more than governments.

Be that as it may, there is a strong case for improving the terms under which the developing countries secure the technology they require and many possibilities exist whereby preferential terms might be achieved and many of the restrictions which often

accompany technological transfer be removed. In addition, there
is a case for agreement on a code of good practice for firms
operating in Third World countries and, indeed, also within the
other two worlds. Whether this will be a code dictated to the
firms through one of the United Nations Agencies, such as
UNCTAD, or evolved voluntarily by the firms themselves, still
remains to be seen. This is certainly a period of transition in
the capitalist system as a whole and industry is well aware of
the need to improve its public image within the industrialized
world as well as in the developing countries. The basic problem
is how industry, as one of the great social institutions, can
reconcile its need for annual profits with its responsibilities
to society. Many important enterprises well realize that it is
in their long term interest to do so and to be seen to do so.

While, as we have seen, the complex nature of the innovation
process is not generally understood, there is a growing recognition that imported technology can take root in a country at the
beginning of its industrialization only if the country possesses
an indigenous scientific and technological system. In the absence
of such capacity, foreign technology must remain isolated from
the fabric of national economic and social activity and will
depend for its evolution and renewal on further reliance on
foreign imports and thus constitute a type of technolgical
colonialism, with continuing backwardness.

How then can such an indigenous capacity be built up? The
simplest approach is the creation of more universities or of
some sort of industrial research institute, both excellent
measures if the new institutions are well conceived within the
cultural and economic framework of the country. Too often, however, Third World universities can be too isolated from the local
community, outposts of learning remote from local problems and,
particularly where their academic quality is high, preparing
candidates for the brain drain. Many people in these universities
have deep concern for the social and economic problems of their
country, but somehow find it difficult to get to grips with them
or to come to terms with the political and economic hierarchy.

As to the industrial research institute, this can be a mere
alibi, a prestige body standing somehow outside the realities of
national economic existence. Experience has shown that there is
a tendency for such institutes, especially when set up and
initially directed by foreigners, to wither away after a
promising start. Yet research institutes are badly needed in such
countries; the problem is how to relate them to ongoing indigenous
technological activity and to ensure that the knowledge they
generate or acquire by scanning the advancement of research
elsewhere is incorporated into the stock of *available* knowledge
of the country and put to use as it is required.

As in so many aspects of development, the countries of the Third

World differ enormously within themselves with regard to
existing capacity for science and technology to the extent of
making generalizations meaningless. Some, such as India, have an
extensive and sophisticated scientific manpower and institutes
of research of high quality. For such countries, the problem is
how to articulate the national scientific effort into the
totality of social and economic policy and, it must be admitted,
many industrialized countries have yet to find an effective
solution to this problem. Most countries possessing valuable
natural resources - oil or minerals for example - have an obvious
need, and frequently also the economic strength, to build up a
formidable technological capacity, but often lack the educational
infrastructure to do so quickly. In many instances it is of
primordial importance for the resource rich countries, especially
where their income comes from a single commodity such as oil, to
build the technological capacity rapidly, so as to diversify
their industrial possibilities, ensure improved supplies of water
and energy and to intensify agriculture while their major assets
are plentiful. The less well endowed countries have a much more
difficult task, at times starting from almost no scientific
effort and inevitably requiring much more external aid and
advice. In general it may be said that of the small fraction of
the world's scientific research and technological development
which is undertaken in the countries of the Third World, a much
higher proportion is in the form of fundamental research and,
indeed, the poorer the country, the smaller the proportion of
its tiny scientific effort is in applied research. This is understandable since there is little industry or other organized
economic activity to demand much research.

There is thus no easy path to the creation of a vigourous
technological capacity. It must be approached in many directions
simultaneously - in universities and technical schools, in
agricultural institutes and extension services, in industry and
in the public services - and must be supported by information
services which scan world development in science and technology,
selecting what is intrinsically important for the society in
question.

Appropriate Technology

Firstly, it should be stressed that this term should be understood at its face value and not used as a euphemism for simple,
intermediate or village technologies. Indeed, the concept of
appropriateness is just as relevant to highly industrialized
societies as to those at the beginning of their development.
Some technologically advanced countries have declared that the
further development which they consider necessary for economic
growth purposes must be socially acceptable, because of widespread recognition of the unwanted side effects of technological
development in the past. This is related to the present preoccupation of such countries with the process of technology

assessment, i.e. the attempt to foresee as far as possible the social and cultural as well as the economic consequences of new developments. Furthermore, a technological process which seems appropriate to national economic and social needs at one time may become less so at a later date, for reasons of obsolescence, demand changes, altered attitudes to environmental impact, conservation pressures, etc.

All countries, in fact, require a mix of different types of technology and the blend will differ greatly form case to case, in accordance with raw material and energy endowment, level of skills available, size of the local market and export potential, its general environment and cultural conditions. Thus, it is not surprising that a country such as Norway has been greatly influenced in its industrial development by its geography. Fishing developed from a craft to an industrial activity with ancillary activities, such as canning and freeze-drying, also to shipbuilding and later to the manufacture of sophisticated navigation devices. Its possession of metal ores and hydro-electric potential also gave rise to metallurgical industries, including the manufacture of ferro-alloys of a specialist nature which represent a means of energy export. All this has necessitated the emergence of a range of firms, from large science-based enterprises to small craft companies which co-exist with traditional fishing and agriculture and which are supported by a small but effective research and development capacity. A similar evolution can be seen in most countries.

For the countries of the Third World a similar mix is required; a mix which will differ greatly from country to country. All of them require a proportion of advanced industrial facilities such as steel mills and oil refineries, or at least easy and secure access to them. Such processes are usually capital intensive and their effectiveness often involves the economy of scale. Here, the small size of many of the developing countries can be a grave difficulty and it would be wise in such cases to construct such facilities to serve a whole region rather than a single small country. That is why proposals for regional cooperation are so important, such as the envisaged West African Common Market.

Then come a whole series of industrial needs, again often costly, but which need not necessarily be on a large scale, to achieve import substitution by the local manufacture of building materials, consumer goods, etc., and also for the exploitation of local materials and agricultural produce. By far the largest proportion of the technology required for such manufacture is freely available and widely diffused, the patents having run out long ago. But for the effective construction of the necessary plants as well as for their operation and modification to make possible the use of local materials, much know-how is necessary and is seldom available at the level required and hence has to

be purchased. It is here that the utility of a local technological
and research capacity is most evident. Where such exists it is
possible to introduce a diversity of new process and products
quite inexpensively. The question also arises as to the extent to
which technology transferred abroad can have a generalized influence in building up the capacity. There is much evidence that
the spill-over of imported private know-how diffused within the
enterprise in a Third World country is quite limited because of
the owners interest to keep it to himself for reasons of
competitivity. A wide variety of mechanisms seems to be necessary
to nourish the extent and quality of scientific and technological
knowledge available to the society as a whole, including that
available to the government and, for future needs, to the
educational system.

In many Third World countries there is already a great deal of
unemployment and underemployment. Present high rates of population
growth and existing demographic structures will moreover mean
that in many countries a doubling of the total population over a
35 year period will bring a threefold increase in work force.
This suggests that a major effort is required to introduce
effective and *scientifically sophisticated manufacturing processes*.
Ever since the industrial revolution, a main drive in industrial
development has been for ever higher levels of productivity of
manpower, entailing high per capita use of energy and capital.
This is not inherently necessary and it is essential to begin a
serious and sustained effort to develop processes which are
advanced and effective but which rely more on a plentiful supply
of manpower. While this may be essentially the task of the
developing countries, preferably in concert, some of the transnational firms might well be persuaded that it is in their own
long term interest to start such a development which might also
fit the trends for employment in their home countries.

Finally, it should be noted that many of the technologies just
mentioned as well as their products have little meaning to the
great masses of the population in many developing countries who
are engaged in occupations - agricultural, fishing or craft -
which have remained virtually unchanged over the ages. There is
great scope for the improvement of local tools and methods by
the application of well known scientific principles. This could
be done at a modest cost by constituting scientific field
services similar to the extension services of agriculture with a
very great multiplier effect due to the large numbers of people
involved.

The Selection of Technologies
All of our discussion so far is, however, secondary to two basic
questions: firstly, what technology from the enormous world
repository should be selected by a particular country and,
secondly, for what purpose is the technology required and for

whose benefit will it be used? These are, in a sense, the forbidden questions.

The existing approaches to development were launched with great hopes that at least the grossest forms of poverty might be abolished. Yet, after thirty years of resource transfer and aid of many types, hunger, unemployment and hopelessness are still the lot of the great masses of the people of the world and even where "development" has apparently succeeded, many people feel that their lives have been, in fact, impoverished under the dictation of impersonal forces over which they have no control. Although the rich fraction of the world has not itself succeeded in abolishing poverty, the fact that their overall prosperity has been achieved by the systematic pursuit of industrial productivity and economic growth based on science and technology has led to the general acceptance of this process as a model for the poor societies also. Has this been justified by experience? A second assumption has been that economic benefits "trickle down" from the rich to the poor. The persistent disparities between nations throw great doubt on the verity of this, while within a single country, the diffusion of wealth is extremely slow. Certainly the gross GNP and per capita income levels indicate that many of the countries of the Third World have achieved considerable development success, but, in general, development has not responded to the needs of the masses of the people, inarticulate, hungry and passive.

Indeed, much of the transfer of technology hitherto has responded to the appetites of the existing small elites, which are the same as those of the rich countries. History may well show that the greatest disbenefits of the transnationals to the developing countries did not reside in harsh terms and conditions or in interference in their internal affairs, but in introducing processes and products developed for quite other kinds of societies in the industrialized world. Yet the transnationals can hardly be blamed for this. The international trade system operates on the basis that sellers offer goods which they can provide (including industrial property) and it is up to the buyers to select what they want. Thus, much of the fault lies with those who wish to import and produce the products of the Northern affluent.

What is necessary then is a reappraisal by the leaders of Third World countries of the kind of society that they wish to see in the future and a recognition that the knowledge and techniques required to achieve this must be carefully selected and assimilated over the years within the national cultural framework. Within the desiderata, the need to alleviate poverty remains an essential objective, but this does not necessarily mean development on the pattern of the existing industrial nations. Cultural integrity and diversity demand a range of alternative paths to a series of different cultural evolutions.

Within this concept the aid of technology is unquestionably
essential. But it must be appropriate in the larger sense we
have indicated and be seen as part of the socio-economic cultural
process. The industrialized countries could certainly be induced
to subscribe to and aid such a process, but whether it could
succeed in the present social structures of many of the developing countries is the subject of another essay.

The Age of Aquarius

Elisabeth Mann Borgese

The New Order for the Oceans

We are both commentators and actors in the drama of Reshaping the
International Order. When we are commentators, we sit back and
watch a scene or an act of the play of our own life: a strange
experience, with an eery feeling of the flow of time, the meaning
of history, and the purpose of life.

Rereading today our own contribution to the RIO Report, on Ocean
Management, gives us at once a sense of inadequacy: the problems
before us are so new and so complex, and our approach seems somewhat too structural, too legal, in its attempt to cope with them.
But, on the other hand, yes, we were right. The oceans *are* our
great laboratory in which a breakthrough *can* be made towards the
new international order we are all seeking, which should govern
a world that is made by the labor of all its inhabitants, not
just a few in a few countries, and in which

● war has become as obsolete as slavery and witchcraft have become in the recent past;

● peace is not just the absence of war but is based on equity;

● the spectre of world hunger is exorcised;

● science and technology have become the servants, not the demons,
of mankind;

● people produce in order to consume, rather than consume in order to produce;

● people stop sawing the branch on which they are sitting by
wrecking the environment which is theirs and their descendants;

● all, rather than a few people benefit; which implies a rethinking of the concept of ownership;

● people can manage their own lives and fortunes by participating
in the making of decisions that affect them; and

● decisions are made at the level where they comprise all people
affected by them, neither higher nor lower; which implies a rethinking of the concept of sovereignty.

Since the writing of the RIO Report, the Third United Nations
Conference on the Law of the Sea has moved through two more
sessions: laborious, quarrelsome, frustrating sessions. Sessions

burdened with all the political problems besetting the world today, in addition to those arising from its own concerns. Sessions
heated by personality conflicts and shaken by internal changes
within distant countries. But in spite of itself, the Conference
has been moving and, by untried and unprecedented methods, it
has now produced a text, the *Informal Composite Negotiating Text*,
the like of which the international community has never before
had to consider. Although still full of incongruences, holes,
technical weaknesses, the Composite Text is in fact a Draft Ocean
Space Convention. It will be "formalized" in due time, i.e.,
become *the* official Conference document whereas, at the present,
informal stage, it represents the work merely of the Conference
President, the Committee Chairmen, and the Bureau. When it has
been "formalized", it will be amended in detail, but the broad
outlines of the new order for the oceans are already clearly discernible.

Unresolved Issues

Among the still unresolved issues, the most important ones are
those concerning the regime of the deep seabed and the system
of production in the international area - the potential nucleus
of a New International Economic Order - and, on the other hand,
the question of access of States with little or no littoral (the
so-called landlocked and geographically disadvantaged States) to
the waters under coastal States' jurisdiction, called "Exclusive
Economic Zones".

Seabed mining. The provisions for the system of mineral production
in the international area contained in the Composite Text are
conceptually defective and practically inapplicable. As they
are, they are neither acceptable to the industrialized States, who
alone possess the technology and the capital required for deep
seabed mining, nor to the developing countries, who seek their
fair share of the Common Heritage of Mankind and to participate
in the management of these resources. The Text is based on a
curious sort of compromise between the positions of these two
major groups of States: not by reconciling or synthesizing them,
but merely by adding them up. Thus the industrialized States
wanted a licensing system under which their companies would essentially have a free hand after payment of certain fees to the
International Authority and obeying certain general guidelines
with regard to the Authority's resource policy. This position
was unacceptable to the developing States and was considered
contrary to the principle of the Common Heritage which assumes
common management of the resource.

To embody this principle, the developing countries proposed a
public international Enterprise as the operational arm of the
International Seabed Authority: an Enterprise modelled essentially after the nationalized mining enterprises in Latin America.
But the Authority is no State; it was to have neither technology

194

nor capital, and if the industrialized States and their private
consortia refused to cooperate, the system simply was unworkable.

The "compromise" added these two alternatives: there was to be
an "Enterprise" as the operational arm of the Seabed Authority,
and there was to be free access for States and consortia under a
licensing or "contract" system. The addition of an unacceptable
and an unworkable system was to result in a workable and acceptable one!

The difficulties that arose in fact turned out to be unsur-
mountable. How was the Authority's Enterprise going to be financ-
ed? How was it going to obtain its technology? If the industrialized States and their companies were free to mine what they
needed, who needed the Enterprise? Rather than an embodiment of
the principle of the Common Heritage of Mankind, was it not to
become a status symbol of poor nations? Like a restless sleeper,
the huge Conference tossed from one side to the other: on the one
side, imposing financial burdens and obligations of technology
transfer on the industrialized States which should have enabled
the Authority's Enterprise to get off the ground but which were
unbearable to the industrialized States; on the other side, trying to make their demands bearable to the industrialized States,
but then the Enterprise could not get off the ground. There was
no way out of the dilemma, as the compromise text grew longer,
more complicated, more involved, more contradictory, more
abstruse. Disillusioned, frustrated, the Conference was dragging
itself towards the end of a dead-end road.

But there are other roads. The Conference now has an Austrian
working paper before it which proposes an alternative system
aimed at meeting the objectives and objections of all major
groups of States. What it proposes is a unitary joint-venture
system based on the principle, not of an unsustainable competition between the Authority and established industry, but of
cooperation: established industry is structured into the system
by solid and well tried, familiar rules of the game.

States and their companies, whether public or private, have
guaranteed access to the international seabed area, but *only* in
joint venture with the Authority. In other words: each one of
the four or five international consortia, duly authorized by
their States of origin, must *form an Enterprise* with the Authority whereby the Authority must furnish *at least* one half of the
capital investment (including the value of the mineral nodules in
situ, which are the Common Heritage of Mankind), appoint *at least*
one half of the Board of Directors and obtain *at least* one half
of all profits. Companies are obviously quite used to working
under such a system which offers them the advantage of reducing
their capital investment and sharing their risks. On the other
hand, this system offers to developing countries the possibility

of *broad participation in all Enterprises*, through appointment, by the Authority, to the Governing Boards; and it offers the Authority the possibility of *control* and of *broad financial participation*, besides, of course, the general control it can exercise through its political organs (the Council and the Assembly).

The system vastly facilitates the problem of "financing" the Enterprises (reducing the required Authority investment by a factor of at least four) and of technology transfer (which follows standard form under a joint-venture arrangement and raises no particular problems). What is more, the system would be applicable not only to the international area but even to areas under national jurisdiction which, due to the peculiar boundary provisions proposed in other parts of the Convention, will contain at least 20-30 percent of the exploitable mineral nodules. In such areas, especially where they are under the jurisdiction of developing States (for example Mexico), the coastal State would not have to depend on private consortia for the exploitation of its resources but could enter into joint venture with one of the Authority's "Enterprises" which would plow back its share of profits into international development.

The proposal has a number of other technical and political advantages over the "parallel system" belabored by the Composite Text. Among other things, the new proposal would greatly shorten and simplify the present text, freeing it of involved sub-paragraphs and lengthy annexes.

The Exclusive Economic Zone. Although the Composite Text made some major breakthroughs with regard to the legal status of the Exclusive Economic Zone, a number of basic issues remain unresolved. The rumblings of dissatisfaction are becoming more audible as the facts unravel. It is clear that by far the greatest advantage from the "grab" of the 200-mile Exclusive Economic Zone accrues to a few, already rich, coastal States, while the majority of poor developing States, including the poorest among them, get nothing. Apart from Micronesia, whose huge area can be calculated in different ways, the U.S.A., acquiring an economic zone of 2,222,000 square nautical miles, is the principal beneficiary, the next three being Australia (2,043,300 square nautical miles), New Zealand (1,409,500 square nautical miles), and Canada (1,370,000 square nautical miles). Some 25 States will acquire 76 percent of the total area of all economic zones. Of these 13 are developed States and together they will gain 48 percent of the total area of all economic zones; the 12 developing countries will together gain 28 percent of the total area. About 80 countries will gain nothing.

The question, however, is what do we really mean by "gain"? The rich and powerful coastal States "gain" what they already have: for the former freedom of the high sea bestowed on their might

the right to exploit marine areas as far as their technologies,
and their national interests, would reach: 200 miles out or further. Developing coastal States, on the other hand, formerly at
the mercy of the fishing fleets and factory ships of wealthy
distant-water fishing States free to deplete and pollute their
coastal waters, are now, at least theoretically, protected
against these inroads. But the big question is: what next? For
the problems of surveillance, enforcement, and management of vast
maritime zones are rather staggering. In many respects they are
bound to lead to periods of convulsion and transition.

When the dust - or the whirled up drops of water - will have
settled, however, the scene will look old rather than new. Continuity will have triumphed over change, the economic reality
(the balance of business) over political illusion (territorial
expansion).

The rich countries will continue to rule the waves and to exploit
the resources of the sea: within their own economic zones, the
no-man's land of the High Seas and in the economic zones of poorer coastal States. In these zones the rich States and their companies, whether national or multinational, will have made suitable bilateral arrangements, paying rent or royalties. This,
however, will not be substantial enough to make any dent in the
economic and social status quo. Production, as heretofore, will
be geared to the needs and interests of the industrialized countries, not to the needs of the poor, not toward a redistribution
of resources, technologies and skills. If the economic zones of
poor coastal States are not exploited by the companies of the
rich, they will be underexploited: for it will take a considerable time for poor coastal States to develop the technologies and
social infrastructures needed to manage large expansions of
ocean space. Who, under these circumstances, will be able to
resist the pressures and blandishments of the rich? Nature abhors
a vacuum.

The economic zone, however, is here to stay. If, with regard to
seabed mining, there still is so little agreement that it is
possible to turn around, leave the dead-end road, and try a
different approach, there has been, on the contrary, such wide
agreement on the Exclusive Economic Zone that it would be quite
impossible to turn back. Many States have indeed already unilaterally declared their economic zone, and, in the opinion of some
international lawyers, it has already become customary international law. To try to undo it would be futile - or wreck the
Conference.

But there are at least five sets of measures that can be taken,
at the Conference, around the Conference, beyond the Conference,
to make of the Exclusive Economic Zone a viable part of a New
International Economic Order. The first is a tidying up of the

boundaries of the economic zone. The second is the establishment of strong public international institutions to cooperate with developing coastal States in the management of their economic zone. The third is regional integration. The fourth is international taxation. The fifth is a pooling of surveillance and enforcement mechanisms.

The Limits of Exclusive Economic Zone. Three provisions still could be adopted by the Law of the Sea Conference to tidy up the boundaries of the Exclusive Economic Zone and to forestall further extensions of national claims. One would be a more precise definition of the baselines from which the economic zone is measured. These are presently very loosely defined, making it possible to enclose large marine spaces as "internal waters" and pushing the boundary of the Exclusive Economic Zone out much farther than 200 miles from shore.

Secondly, something ought to be done about the definition of islands. According to the present proposals, tiny islands or rocks have the same right to an Exclusive Economic Zone and a continental shelf as big, populous islands or continents. Tiny islands thus acquire sovereign rights over enormous areas of ocean space: certainly an anomaly, and not part of a rational economic order. Such tiny islands or islets should be treated differently from islands who depend on their marine resources for their livelihood. This, too, could still be achieved.

Thirdly, the limits of the legal continental shelf should be clearly defined. For reasons of clarity, simplicity, and equity, the limit of the legal continental shelf should coincide with that of the Exclusive Economic Zone, that is, 200 miles from clearly defined baselines. It should *not* extend beyond 200 miles. This, however, cannot be obtained today. National claims have been staked way beyond 200 miles and they will not be given up. The number of States, however, who would profit from an extension of the continental shelf beyond 200 miles is rather small: twenty States, at most.

If a vote were to be taken today at the Law of the Sea Conference on the question of the outer limits of the continental shelf, it is very likely that a majority of States would be in favor of legal continental shelf boundaries coinciding with those of the Exclusive Economic Zone. Such action by the majority, however, could be blocked by a third of the members of the Conference who could be mobilized in favor of a legal continental shelf extending to an open-ended continental margin, even though a majority within this blocking third would, themselves, gain little or nothing from their position. Thus there would be no solution and the present article of the Composite Text (Article 76), with its highly unsatisfactory definition of the continental shelf, would not be adopted. But no solution to this problem may be better than a bad, inequitable, irrational and impractical one. After all, we have lived with the Geneva Conventions for twenty years without an agreement on the limits of the territorial sea. And today, agreement on this issue has been reached relatively easily. Perhaps we may have to live for some time without agreement on the outer limit of the legal continental shelf. This would cause grave inconveniences, by rendering delimitation of the continental shelf between States lying adjacent or opposite each other more difficult; but it would not essentially change the situation with regard to the International Seabed Authority since, according to the present proposals, the boundaries between coastal States and the international seabed area are determined by unilateral declarations by the coastal States. A general agreement on the outer limit of the continental shelf might be reached ten, fifteen years from now, when the Seabed Authority will be an established fact. It might be easier at that time to find a rational and equitable solution than now while the international area is still a legal vacuum and national claims tend to expand to fill it.

International Institutions. If the Exclusive Economic Zone is to be of use to developing countries, there should be *public international institutions* to assist them in the exploration and exploitation of their resources - lest they were to fall back on multinationals and consortia. Existing international institutions must be restructured, on a global and regional basis, and new ones must be established wherever necessary.

This applies, in the first place, to the international institutions dealing with fisheries. The body established within the United Nations to deal with fisheries on a global scale is the Committee on Fisheries (COFI) of the Food and Agriculture Organization (FAO). This institution should be upgraded, restructured and strengthened so that it can operate at the same level of, and in cooperation with, the future International Seabed Authority. This process of restructuring is already in course. To be complete and effective it should cover at least (a) universalization of membership (which presently is limited to members of FAO and thus excludes the Soviet Union); (b) establishment of a system of licensing for fishing in the international area (regulation of catches in the Exclusive Economic Zone is impossible unless catches are equally regulated in the international zone); (c) establishment of an independent Secretariat, separate from that of FAO; (d) establishment of an operational arm or "Enterprise system", somewhat analogous to that of the International Seabed Authority, to manage living resources in the international area and assist developing coastal States in the exploration and exploitation of the resources of their Exclusive Economic Zone; (e) establishment of an independent international fisheries research capacity; (f) establishment of a dispute settlement machinery as required by the Composite Text; and (g) independent financing, preferably through international taxes.

Besides the restructuring and strengthening of COFI, it is
essential that the regional fisheries commissions be reorganized
and adapted to the requirements of the new Law of the Sea and
that the system of regional commissions be properly coordinated
with COFI.

Developing coastal States will need increasing assistance from
the Inter-Governmental Maritime Consultative Organization (IMCO)
for the regulation of navigational traffic and the provision of
navigational aids in the waters under their jurisdiction where
they now bear the responsibility for the safety of ships in
transit. This means that IMCO must be strengthened and the participation of developing countries in all its organs must be increased: this process is already in course and will continue.
Furthermore the problems of the economics of shipping and of a
more equitable participation of developing countries in freight
carriage can only be solved by structural changes in the international machinery.

Similar considerations apply to scientific research and to the
protection of the environment. Most coastal States do not have
the marine scientific capacity for the research needed as a
basis for rational ocean management. Either they have to rely on
the great powers to carry out such research in their waters and
on their shelves, which often may be politically undesirable, or
there will be no research. The only way out of this dilemma is
to internationalize scientific research as far as possible, that
is, to give to international scientific institutions an independent research capacity.

An interesting beginning in this direction has been made with
Aricle 248 of the Composite Text. This provides, in effect, for
two different regimes for scientific research in areas under
national jurisdiction. Research carried out by States or private
institutions is to be subject to a *consensus* regime, that is, the
coastal State must explicitly authorize, and, under certain conditions, has the right to refuse to authorize, scientific
research in its Exclusive Economic Zone and on its continental
shelf. Research carried out by an international institution is
subject to a regime of *notification* only: that is, the coastal
State must be notified in due time when the expedition is to
arrive. It has no right to refuse authorization provided the
coastal State has approved the project when it was adopted by
the international institution of which the coastal State is a
part. Here sovereignty is exercised through participation in the
making of decisions affecting a country, in an international
forum. In this sense Article 248 is a breakthrough. It will
impose structural changes on the Inter-governmental Oceanographic
Commission (IOC) of UNESCO which is the body, within the U.N.

family, with the greatest responsibility for marine research. It will give a new impetus to the internationalization of research with benefits not only for science and development but also for peace.

While the Law of the Sea Conference can give, and is giving, an initial impulse to the process of restructuring and strengthening of the international institutions dealing with the major uses of ocean space and resources and to the creation of some integrative machinery for the harmonization and integration of their policies, this development, obviously, points beyond the scope of the Conference. It must be carried out by the institutions themselves.

Regional economic zones and "matrimonial seas". An additional measure for making the Exclusive Economic Zone a viable part of a new international order is to merge them, where appropriate, into *regional economic zones* or "matrimonial seas". This is the only solution for enclosed or semi-enclosed seas, like the Mediterranean or the Caribbean, where national economic zones would be exceedingly complicated to delineate and would make rational resource management totally impossible. Cooperation, through an appropriate regional institutional framework, should extend to all marine activities, from the management of living resources and the protection of the environment to scientific research, from navigation to the mining of minerals. The Composite Text provides for regional cooperation in enclosed and semi-enclosed seas but omits reference to oil drilling and seabed mining, taking account of the particular sensitivities of States with regard to their sovereignty over their continental shelves. Yet, the regionalization of the continental shelf would, in some cases, be the only hope for the maintenance of peace and the effective exploitation of the resources.

The establishment of regional regimes need not be limited to enclosed or semi-enclosed seas; they can be conceived as part of land-based regional economic development, such as the EEC or African or Latin American common markets. The extension of such common markets to "matrimonial seas" holds by far the greatest promise for the solution of the problems of landlocked and geographically disadvantaged States which would participate in the marine common markets on an equal footing. The development of regional regimes, likewise, transcends the scope of the Law of the Sea Conference. Such regimes must be established by the countries belonging to the region.

International taxation. In 1970 the International Ocean Institute published a plan for the establishment of an *Ocean Development Tax*: that is, a small levy - say one percent - *on all major uses* of the oceans, be it the production of offshore oil and gas, commercial fish production, navigation or the use of cables and pipelines. Such a tax should be collected by States and paid to the international ocean institutions, or, in other words, States' contributions to the international community would be assessed on the basis of their uses of the oceans. The tax would be based on a *functional* criterion, (the use of the oceans, anywhere), not on *territorial* criteria (there would be no distinction between areas under national jurisdiction and international areas).

During the last decade, the idea of an international tax of this sort has cropped up again and again. First, Canada espoused it in the Seabed Committee with regard to minerals only. While the Law of the Sea Conference, in the Composite Text, has given a territorial aspect to the proposal and restricted it to the continental margin beyond the 200 mile limit of the Exclusive Economic Zone (from which there will be no revenue for the foreseeable future), the U.N. Environment Programme (UNEP) has more recently embarked on a study of the modalities of collecting an international tax. On the non-governmental level, the RIO Report advocates international taxation as a means to achieve automaticity of transfers and redistribution of international income.

In some proposals, the tax is to be levied from the richer countries only and to be paid to the poorer. Such a distinction - institutionalizing the development gap - would tend to freeze the status quo. The law, however, must cover both rich and poor nations, this being the real essence of "sovereign equality". This, obviously, does not mean that poor nations will pay as much as rich. In the first place, the big users of ocean space and resources are the rich nations. Secondly, the tax rate can be modified by income-per-capita factors so that poor nations will in practice get much more than they pay. In a New International Economic Order the emphasis must be on sharing what is common; the idea of donors and recipients does not accord with the principle of self-reliance.

An ocean development tax of the kind referred to would put billions of dollars annually into the treasury of the international community to spend on international development and assistance to developing countries. It could be a tool of substantial importance in development strategy. It could also, to a large extent, *compensate* landlocked and geographically disadvantaged States for the vagaries of geography that have been invoked in fashioning the iniquities of the Exclusive Economic Zone. An ocean development tax may be an idea whose time has come.

Surveillance and enforcement. One of the problems developing countries have to face in planning for the management of their Exclusive Economic Zone is that of surveillance and enforcement: and the larger the zone, the worse the problem. Rich countries, like the U.S.A., are spending billions of dollars reinforcing their

coastguards, acquiring helicopters, linking up with satellite
surveillance, installing tracking devices. But what can a poor
country do? Expenditures on warships in Third World countries
are rising much steeper than in the rest of the world. During
the period 1970-1976 they have been growing trice as fast as
the world total. While this development is partially due to the
rise of tension in international affairs, it is, undoubtedly,
also related to the need to protect the resources in the newly
acquired economic zones. What is being spent on warships,
however, cannot be spent on fishing fleets, and the arms race
directly impinges on the development of the zone.

Developing countries thus would do themselves a great service
if they pressed for the *internationalization of surveillance and
enforcement instruments*. Regional surveillance by planes, helicopters and satellites would be cheaper and more effective than
national surveillance. Even coastguard contingents could be inter-
nationalized for regional enforcement purposes. This may be a
long-range development and cannot take place everywhere at once
but it would, again, contribute toward making of the Exclusive
Economic Zone a viable part of a New International Economic Order.
It would contribute both to development and disarmament.

The forum on which decisions leading to this kind of development
can be taken is not the Law of the Sea Conference. It must be
done on the regional level.

The Common Heritage of Mankind
The Law of the Sea is, thus, far more complex than the Law of the
Sea Conference. It is in fact far greater than the oceans. It is
world law, world order in the making. The Conference has a unique
opportunity: it may be the point of break-through. There is no
other place that brings together so many world issues, no other
instrument that can redirect and accelerate them as effectively.

The motor force that engendered the Law of the Sea Conference
and keeps it moving is the new and revolutionary concept of the
Common Heritage of Mankind, the concept, that is, of space and
resources which cannot be appropriated by any one; which must be
managed for the benefit of mankind as a whole with special consideration for the needs of developing people; which can be used
for peaceful purposes only, and which must be transmitted to
future generations. Applicable first to the international seabed
and its mineral resources, the concept must, perforce, be expanded to ocean space as a whole and to its living resources; for
ocean space is an indivisible system and it is impossible radically to transform one part of this system without affecting all
other parts. The concept of the Common Heritage of Mankind transcends the traditional principles of sovereignty over territorial
waters and freedom of the high sea. It transcends the concepts of
sovereignty and ownership. It transforms the structure of inter-

national relations: there will no longer be "owners" and "non-owners" among nations, nor "donors" or "recipient" States; but rather people who will share what is commonly owned or owned by none, such as resources in science and technology and in means of production. The concept of the Common Heritage of Mankind is already being extended from marine spaces and resources to outer space and celestial bodies, with consequences for international law and the structure of international relations which are only beginning to be explored. From ocean space and outer space it is being reflected on the ice of Antarctica, the minerals in its shelves, the abundant living resources of the Southern Ocean. Finally, it is inevitable that the concept of the Common Heritage of Mankind be extended to the resources of the earth, within States; for the structure of internal social relations and the structure of international relations are inseparately and intimately linked, and one cannot change one without changing the other. The concept of the Common Heritage of Mankind, or social ownership as it is called in some countries, thus will become the basis of the New International Economic Order, and there can be no New International Economic Order without this concept.

The replacement of the old regime based on ownership and sovereignty by the new one based on the principle of the Common Heritage of Mankind may be spasmodic at some times and places: but it is not violence that displaces the old concepts. It is science and technology, the growing impact of human activities on the natural environment, the shrinkage of spaces, that impose on our generation a new awareness of unity and solidarity, beyond the distinctions between what used to be seen as "internal" and "external", "ownership" and "non-ownership", "man" and "nature".

The New International Order, including the New International Economic Order, is the institutional or constitutional embodiment of this new awareness.

Most of us who were there when the call for the new Law of the Sea was first issued had only a dark inkling of what we started.

Dynamic Division of Labor and the International Order

Saburo Okita

Introduction

When thought is given to the future international order, the
relationships between rich and poor countries, the North and the
South, are of obvious importance; hardly less important, however,
is the order among the rich and among the poor countries. In
particular, the principle of free trade, which has been a regulating force in the market economy countries, has felt the brunt of
both prolonged stagnation of the world economy and high unemployment rates in the industrialized countries – pressure which seeks
to modify the working of the principle of free trade. Moreover,
when consideration is given to the diversity which is becoming
common among the developing countries, it becomes evident that
there should be different policies for different economic groups
of countries. Even though it is possible to think of the South as
a political monolith when discussing North-South issues, it would
be quite difficult to entertain similar thoughts in an economic
context.

The developing countries may be divided into four categories:
(i) the oil exporting countries; (ii) the rapidly industrializing
developing countries; (iii) the intermediate developing countries
which account for the largest part of the Third World and which
heavily rely on exports of primary commodities, and (iv) the low-
income developing countries.

The members of the oil exporters' category do not necessarily
have similar economic conditions. Indonesia and Nigeria, for
example, belong to OPEC but also have features of the fourth
category. Circumstances thus defy neat division into four categories. Many of the oil exporters are now important capital
exporters. Nevertheless, with regard to their domestic economic
development, they must, because they still display aspects of
underdevelopment, receive technology, know-how and other inputs
from the advanced industrial nations.

Typical examples of rapidly industrializing developing countries
exist in Asia and include South Korea, Hong Kong, Taiwan and
Singapore, as well as in Latin America: Mexico and Brazil, to cite
just two. These countries have succeeded in rapidly expanding industrial output and in attaining rapid growth of their GNP and
export trade. What is necessary for these countries is that the
industrially advanced nations open their domestic markets to
goods exported from this category of countries while also
providing capital which they require for development. This supply
of capital need not necessarily be on soft aid terms but may be
at commercial or near commercial terms, the important point being
the access to supplies of capital rather than the cost of that

205

capital. In the case of low income countries, what is necessary
is a transfer of resources from developed countries at very soft
terms or in the form of grants.

The basic approach to the provision of development aid should be,
according to the Pearson Report, to provide assistance to those
developing countries which can effectively use it: "Increases in
foreign aid should be clearly aimed at helping the developing
countries to reach a path of self-sustained growth at reasonable
levels ... Countries growing at a rate of 6 per cent per year
will be able gradually to raise their rate of capital formation.
If they give adequate attention to the fostering and promotion
of exports, they should, before the end of this century, be able
to participate in the international economy as self-reliant partners, and to finance the investments and imports they need for
continued rapid growth without foreign capital on concessional
terms ... This is why increases in development aid should in
the future be closely linked to the economic objectives and the
development performance of the aid-receivers". (1) The approach
suggested by the Pearson Report may thus be called the provision
of aid according to the "efficiency principle".

However, later criticism held that this efficiency principle was
of little use in dealing with the poorest countries. If performance in these countries is poor and they are assigned low
priority as aid recipients, then the gap separating those poor
countries from the others would be made wider.

Consequently, in the past few years, the argument that international aid should preferably contribute to the direct improvement of the living standards of the impoverished masses in the
poor countries has become stronger. The emphasis on the fulfillment of "basic human needs" is typical of this new argument. It
can be viewed as being based on the pursuit of income redistribution
on a global scale; as a "welfare principle" by which aid is to
be provided.

The Rapidly Industrializing Countries
Some of the developing countries, when domestic and external conditions are favourably combined, experience explosive economic
growth, as is shown in the case of the Japanese economy in recent
years as well as the experience of several other countries. About
ten years ago, I wrote: "Japan's economy, though highly developed
in many ways, still retains various elements of backwardness and
this semi-backward stage of development has occasioned conditions
conducive to rapid growth. In view of the recent experience in
Japan, some of the newly developing countries may also succeed in
the future in creating a favourable combination of factors for
economic growth. In the course of transition from an under-
developed to a more developed stage of the economy, there is a
possibility of realizing a process of "virtuous circle" accompanied with an explosive, rapid economic growth". (2) I advanced a

similar view in a collection of essays in honour of Thorkil
Kristensen, first Secretary-General of the OECD. (3)

Development has been particularly remarkable in East and Southeast Asia. Recapitulating the process whereby Japan caught up
with the Western nations by dint of her economic growth and
development, in recent years some of the East and Southeast Asian
countries have been rapidly catching up on Japan. In 1976, the
total exports to South Korea, Taiwan, Hong Kong and Singapore
amounted to 43 per cent of Japan's total export trade. Traditional
markets for Japan's textiles and other light industrial products,
such as the United States, are rapidly being captured by these
newly industrializing countries. Moreover, their exports to the
Japanese market have increased sharply, necessitating structural
adjustments in Japanese industry.

In the case of the countries of North America and Western Europe,
conditions requiring adjustments are present, due to both an
increase in the import of labour-intensive products from the rapidly industrializing countries as well as an increase in the import
of more advanced industrial goods from Japan. These conditions are
exerting forces which are shaking the very principle of free
trade, which the developed countries have been strong to advocate.

Further, an international order desirable for those developing
countries possessing the ability to produce high quality products
for export at low costs, necessitates that the importing countries
impose as few constraints as possible, in accordance with the
principle of free trade. Regarding this, the RIO (Reshaping the
International Order) Report observes: "The industrialized countries, on their part, will have to introduce *policies of adjustment*, develop specialization in knowledge-intensive products and
gradually introduce and enforce environmental protection standards.
This implies a further reduction or even abolition of the tariffs
imposed by the industrialized countries on the semi-manufactured
and manufactured products of the Third World, a trend that would
contribute towards combating inflation in the industrialized
countries. Likely to be of even greater importance is a *reduction
of non-tariff barriers* since these form a major hindrance to
intra-industry trade. If this is not possible without the
inclusion of some escape clauses, it should be ensured that temporary protection mechanisms are *degressive*, i.e. are in accordance with a specific time-table and strictly connected with adjustment measures". (original italics) (4) In this sense, these
developing countries may consider that the old economic order
offers advantageous conditions for future development.

The Lima Declaration of 1975 contains the objective of increasing
the Third World's share of world industrial output from the existing level of 7 per cent to 25 per cent by the year 2000. Generally
speaking, it may be possible that this objective be attained by
those developing countries which are attaining dynamic growth

through the international division of labour; countries which will further expand their exports to the advanced nations and, moreover, be joined by more countries which enter their group.

In the advanced industrial countries there is at present a gradual transition from demand for goods to demand for services. At the same time, as incomes are rising, society's industrial discipline is tending to become weaker. As an overall trend, while interest in the production of more goods is waning in the rich countries, in the developing countries increasingly wide segments of the population are receiving better education and acquiring new technical skills, and production efficiency is improving. At the same time in these countries, the demand for the fulfillment of material needs and desires, such as for food, textiles and fertilizer, is at a very high level. Moreover, in many of the developing countries there is a relative abundance of labour and in particular, as a recent result of demographic trends, the forthcoming increase in the youthful section of the workforce will constitute a favourable condition in regard to production.

However, if the Lima Declaration objective is to be attained, it is vital for the developing countries that the developed countries adhere to the principle of free trade. There is a strong tendency for old industrial countries to be reluctant to adapt to rapid change. In these countries, social structure is becoming rigid and political and social resistance to rapid change in the industrial structure is present: even though it may be objectively seen as desirable economically to move toward utilizing comparative advantages, political and social factors may prevent it. But if the advanced industrial countries move toward a hardened stand on protectionism, the result for world economic development or for the economic welfare of individual nations will be stagnation. As was experienced during the interwar period, the erection of trade barriers leads to a decline in world trade, stagnation in economic growth, an increase in unemployment and, in total, a brake on the economic activity of the entire world.

Therefore, it becomes necessary, when giving thought to a future international order, that we adopt the standpoint of seeking to facilitate the responses of the world's countries to a dynamic international division of labour. For the rapidly industrializing countries, while adherence to the principle of free trade is desirable in principle, as a matter of practical concern exporting countries may at times be obliged to accept voluntary export restraints and orderly marketing arrangements in order to make adjustment policies feasible for the advanced industrial countries. The importing countries on their part may resort to safeguard measures.

Moreover, the emergence of rapidly developing LDCs will also present a problem in terms of splitting the existing groups of countries - notably the Group of 77. Although this group shares a

common historical background, some of its members have attained
very high rates of economic growth. From the viewpoint of attaining a rational, new economic order, reclassification of developed
and developing countries will be required from time to time.

One way of approaching this would be to classify those developing
countries which have surpassed a certain level of per capita GNP,
say $ 1,000, as belonging to the "intermediate stage" of develop-
ment and those countries which have passed, say, the $ 2,000, as
"developed".   The intermediate countries would be exempt from
both the obligations imposed on developed countries and the
privileges given to the developing countries under UNCTAD
resolutions.

From the viewpoint of the developed industrial countries, a
boomerang effect may be anticipated for the rapidly industrializing countries. When these countries rapidly acquire technical
and managerial skills from the advanced industrial countries,
because they are well endowed with abundant and low-cost labour,
it becomes possible for them to rapidly improve the export
competitiveness of their industrial products. As these countries
are using capital and technology imported from developed
industrial countries and are becoming their competitors, at least
in the short run they may constitute a potential threat to the
industries and employment in the advanced countries. That is, the
boomerang thrown by the developed industrial countries may well
return to strike them. Of course, from the viewpoint of the world
economy, this effect is not undesirable: poor countries would
acquire capital and technology from the richer countries,
gradually develop and increase incomes and then increase their
imports of more sophisticated products from the industrialized
countries. For countries faced with this problem, the conditions
exist which could lead to the adoption of protectionist practices:
on the basis of the dynamic international division of labour, however, the developed industrial nations have, in the long run, no
choice but to strive to open up new frontiers.

Intermediate Developing Countries
The intermediate developing countries are, essentially, countries
with a high dependence on the export of primary commodities.
Among them, countries which are exporting primary commodities
under internationally advantageous conditions are attaining
relatively high economic growth rates and some of them have
gradually moved into the stage of industrial development. Examples
include Malaysia, the Philippines, Thailand and some countries in
Latin America. For these countries the subject receiving most
attention is the stabilization of revenues from the export of
primary commodities, especially through the vehicle of commodity
agreements. These agreements are beneficial to importer country
and exporter country alike since they smooth out market price
fluctuations, which otherwise could be volatile, and a number of
these agreements has already been signed. If the terms are

improved in favour of the exporting developing countries then trade in primary commodities will have the function of redistributing income, by transferring it from relatively wealthy countries to relatively poor countries. If this element is overemphasized, however, it will make it difficult for exporting and importing countries to reach necessary agreement.

Regarding issues related to trade in raw materials, there are resource-rich rich countries, resource-poor rich countries, resource-rich poor countries, and resource-poor poor countries. Given this, increases in the relative prices of primary commodities will not by themselves automatically resolve the North-South problem. Since such agreements could be beneficial to resource-rich rich countries but not to resource-poor poor countries, caution is required regarding the selection of the commodities to be the subject of agreements, and to the implementation of the agreements.

The promotion of efficient and equitable resource development would be beneficial to the entire world. It opens the way for international institutions, international taxation and the development of resources without excessive dependence on transnational corporations which have hitherto dominated many development efforts. When there is a transfer of resources through the vehicle of a commodity agreement, the incidence of such a transfer is sometimes arbitrary; it may favour a country possessing resources and not a country lacking resources. In other words, it need not necessarily be in the interest of all the poor developing countries. This makes it advisable to study the possibilities of a transfer mechanism which functions more equitably among countries. One such mechanism is compensatory finance for export earnings. A suitable step in this direction would be expansion to a global scale of STABEX (Stabilization of Export Earnings), created under the Lóme Convention.

Also important to the countries within this group is the promotion of the processing of primary commodities with a view to obtaining a larger share of the total value-added. On the part of importer countries, it is necessary to modify the existing tariff escalation structures by which taxes are levied on products in direct relationship to the extent of processing prior to importation. For the countries of this group, then, increased processing of export products must be promoted. Hereafter, we may expect that a number of the countries within this group will join the group of rapidly industrializing countries. Further, it is also necessary to give thought to the expansion of markets through regional cooperation, and by promotion of trade among developing countries to eliminate the problem of small domestic markets which is an impediment to effective import substitution policies.

Low Income Countries
The problems of low income countries are central to the entire North-South problematique, and the eradication of absolute poverty

210

is a joint responsibility of all nations, rich and poor alike. It is generally accepted that a nation should seek to eliminate poverty from within its own borders; the extension of this welfare state concept to the global level can also be considered perfectly logical as an objective of human society. Such a viewpoint is contained in the growing recognition of the necessity, as expressed in discussions on "Basic Human Needs", to aid the poor people of the poor countries so as to help them attain at least the minimum standards of living which each deserves as a fellow human. Included in basic human needs are adequate nutrition, medical care and basic education. Although it is difficult to adequately describe all basic human needs in specific, quantitative terms, I believe that the world has been entrusted with the task of fulfilling them on a global scale.

Aid for the fulfillment of basic human needs has sometimes been criticized as being cast into a bottomless hole. Certainly, if poor countries were to rely for a prolonged period of time on aid in order to maintain certain standards of living and to meet the basic human needs of their people, there would be a danger of becoming firmly locked into positions of dependency. Nevertheless, poverty and malnutrition, because they threaten human existence, are adverse elements of the highest order and it will not do for us to ignore the vicious circle of poverty, malnutrition and low productivity. On this, I made the following statement in delivering a McDougall Memorial Lecture at the FAO: "We find very often in developing countries a vicious circle of malnutrition and poverty. Food is like fuel for engines. Without a sufficient amount and adequate quality of fuel, engines will not work. Moreover, in the case of the human body there is a minimum requirement of calories just for keeping the body alive. Intake of calories over and above such a minimum can only be converted into work. If food is insufficient people cannot work efficiently. Moreover, insufficient food both in terms of quantity and quality during childhood affects the health conditions of the next generation. Malnutrition also makes the human body susceptible to many kinds of disease, thus reducing the efficiency of work by individuals and by their society". (5) It must be recognized, therefore, that satisfaction of basic human needs, such as through the improvement of nutrition, also has productive effects through an improvement in the quality of labour.

A more fundamental policy would be to provide aid for assisting local food production. From the viewpoint of relative production costs, it can be argued that production of rice in Australia or the United States under conditions of mechanized agriculture would be cheaper than production of rice in small scale units in South and Southeast Asia. But the production of rice in Asia also means the creation of more employment opportunities and more income. Given the rapid rate of increase of the labour force in the Asian region, it becomes evident that there must be more absorption of employment in the agricultural sector.

A survey by the World Food Council indicates that the shortfall in the food supplies of all developing countries will increase from 16 million tons in 1969-71 to 85 million tons in 1985. Of this, the shortage of rice will increase from 3 million tons to 39 million tons. This shortage will be concentrated in the Asian region. In this respect it should be noted that the per hectare yield in South and Southeast Asia is one-third that of Japan and half that of Korea and Taiwan. It would thus appear that there is ample possibility of increasing food production through the improvement of per unit area yields.

The Task Force Report, *Expanding Food Production in Developing Countries: Rice Production in South and Southeast Asia*, submitted at the Bonn session of the Trilateral Commission, recommends that a program be established for doubling rice production in South and Southeast Asia over a 15 year period by investing in water control - especially in irrigation - which would increase the effects of cultivation of high yielding varieties and in the use of fertilizers. The cost of this 15 year program would be $ 54,000 million. The annual cost - $ 3,600 million based on simple arithmetic - would be about double the current annual investment in irrigation in the region by national and international bodies. Of course, the supply of all the requisite inputs must be integrated and, in particular, the production of high yielding varieties of rice would require a high level of technology. A considerable expansion of agricultural research and extension activities would thus also be required.

This investment in Asia would contribute substantially to increasing both employment and incomes; it should also be evaluated for the effects it could have in fulfilling basic human needs through local increases in production.

The fulfillment of basic human needs is an important element in the North-South issue. It should not, however, be presented as a substitute concept for the efficiency principle described in the Pearson Report: both are vital in the total development aid effort.

Conclusion
In today's world we have economic stagnation, idle production facilities and unemployed manpower in the developed industrial countries. At the same time we witness a great demand for investment - in food production, industrialization, infrastructure - in the poor countries. In a paper prepared for the United Nations I observed the following: "The developed industrial countries are increasing their investment in domestic road and housing construction, and seeking to stimulate personal consumption, but if a part of that were directed, for example, to construction of irrigation projects or buildings of the fertilizer industry in developing countries, the purchasing power of those countries would be augmented, the exports of developed countries would be

increased, and imports by developed countries of primary products from developing countries would also be expanded thereby contributing to improvement of world economic conditions ... Just as the New Deal policy adopted by the United States of America during the 1930s increased public investment and contributed to the recovery of the economy, what is needed at the present time is the implementation of a Global New Deal by which means policies could be adopted for investing in increasing production - especially of foodstuffs - in developing countries and, also, for preventing facilities and labour in developed countries from being made idle". (6)

In the global investment policy which would be needed for this task, the constraints imposed by available resources would need to be fully considered. For example, as part of the Global New Deal, investment policies should be directed at raising production ceilings for renewable resources, such as foodstuffs, at the development of the related infrastructure, as well as at the development of non-exhaustible sources of energy. At the same time, at least in the medium term, we should shift our emphasis away from the use of petroleum for fuel to other sources of energy, such as natural gas, coal and nuclear power.

Today we must deal with the problem of linking the surpluses in savings accumulated in the industrialized countries and OPEC members to the investment needs of the developing countries. Consequently, we must think in institutional terms of combining measures to combat the recession in the advanced countries, to utilize the capital accumulated in oil producing countries, and to meet the investment needs of the developing countries. While it is desirable that the growing surpluses in the oil producing nations are effectively mobilized for productive uses on behalf of the development of the world economy, since those surpluses only represent a conversion of the non-renewable resources possessed by those countries into currency, it is understandable that those countries would want to have hedges against the depreciation of currency value and would want to use the currency as profitably as possible. As one desirable direction, oil capital may be provided to a greater extent than at present to the rapidly industrializing developing countries as development funds, at commercial or near-commercial rates.

With regard to the intermediate income countries, the capital surpluses of the oil producing countries should be used together with the private capital of the advanced industrial countries and their concessional government-based aid. In addition to this, a semi-soft capital supply, such as through the Third Window of the World Bank, may be encouraged.

Regarding the low income countries, it is necessary to work toward the satisfaction of basic human needs through the provision of aid funds on very soft terms or as grants. Perhaps the creation of a "World Welfare Fund", which would pool the resources and distribute them according to needs, would eventually become necessary in order to avoid direct bilateral dependency in the supply of basic requirements.

The slowdown in the economic growth of the developed countries is projected for the future of the world economy. According to conventional thinking, economic recession in the advanced industrial countries causes stagnation in world trade and a slowing down of both the exports from and the economic growth of the developing countries. If the gap between the advanced countries and developing countries is to be narrowed, or if international targets, such as that adopted by UNIDO, are to be achieved, a means must be found for enabling the economies of the developing countries to grow quickly, even if economic growth in the developed countries slows. That is, the economic growth of the developing countries should not be directly governed by economic growth in the developed countries. Ways to achieve this include the expansion of production and consumption in domestic markets and the promotion of regional cooperation among developing countries. On the part of the developed industrial countries, it is necessary to embark on institutional reforms in order that acceptable employment conditions may be attained in a low-growth environment. These are the basic long range policy issues which both the developing and the developed countries will have to face in the course of coming decades.

Notes and References
(1) Lester B. Pearson: Report of the Commission on International Development: *Partners in Development*, 1969.
(2) Saburo Okita: *Causes and Problems of Rapid Growth in Postwar Japan and Their Implications for Newly Developing Economies*, Japan Economic Research Center Paper, No. 6, 1967.
(3) Saburo Okita: *Virtuous Circle of Accelerated Growth, The Case of Japan and Possibilities in Some Developing Countries*, in: "Essays in Honour of Thorkil Kristensen", OECD, 1970.
(4) Jan Tinbergen: *Reshaping the International Order*, Report to the Club of Rome, E.P. Dutton, New York, 1976.
(5) Saburo Okita: "Integrated Approach for Food, Nutrition, Population and Economic Growth", *Food and Production*, FAO, 1976.
(6) Saburo Okita: *Transfer of Resources from Developed to Developing Countries*, U.N., ECOSOC, E/AC 54/L.84, November, 1975.

Some Consequences for Industrialized Countries

Jan Pronk*

Introduction

Although the aim of building a New International Economic Order
(NIEO) was generally accepted at the 7th Special Session of the
United Nations General Assembly (September 1975) not much progress has been made in its implementation. The Conference on
International Economic Cooperation, held in 1976 and 1977 to
negotiate main elements of the NIEO, was a failure; nor did
UNCTAD IV produce concrete results. Moreover, in some specific
fields, for which perspectives were created by a chain of international conferences between the 6th and 7th Special Sessions,
a standstill seem to have been reached or even steps taken back-
wards.

This is due to a variety of reasons. The negotiation position of
the South, for instance, turned out to be weaker than was envisaged in the two years following the oil crisis. The negotiation
behaviour of these countries was also softer and more incidental
than might have been expected. Another reason was that it was
not clear how these countries would translate the economic benefits of a NIEO into real improvement in the standard of living
of the poorest strata of their populations.

However, the main reason why the efforts made to build a NIEO
have so far met with little success is the lack of political will
on the side of the industrialized countries. Most of them still
do not want to change the present system.

Elsewhere I have described why, in my view, a NIEO is necessary,
what its main elements should be, how it could be brought nearer
towards realization, and what the relation is between the NIEO
and a strategy to fulfill basic human needs in developing countries. I will not repeat those remarks here. In this essay I will
confine myself to some thoughts on the significance of a new
world economic system for the industrialized countries. In so
doing, I will give special attention to two aspects:
● the fact that a new international order is in the interest, not
only of the developing countries, but also of the industrialized
countries; and
● the conditions and consequences of a New International Economic
Order for the domestic policies of the industrialized countries.

The Interests

Given the fact that it was the developing countries that urged
the creation of a new international order it has, too easily,

---

* In close cooperation with Leo van Maare

been concluded that this new order is contrary to the legitimate interests of the industrialized countries. The demands for a new order have been too hastily viewed in terms of "they win, we lose". This zero-sum game approach only holds true for short term economic considerations. Any deviation from what the free market decides is, after all, detrimental to the most powerful actors in the market, that is the developed countries.

But there is more than simple short term economics. Although the market-system as such cannot cope with them, long term economic and political considerations are as valid and necessary for analysing whether a new international order is in the interests of industrialized countries or not.

In the short term, and economically speaking, a NIEO could very well be disadvantageous to the developed countries. Higher prices for raw materials and industrial redeployment will not be applauded by the public in the rich countries. However, an important lesson of the recession of the last few years is the increased degree of interdependence in the world. It is not only the developing countries that need crucial imports from industrialized countries, but increasingly the industrialized countries need the developing countries as sources of raw materials, energy and manufactures and also, in view of distinct signs of saturation and diminished growth possibilities in the industrialized world, progressively as export markets.

There are also political considerations. The proliferation of nuclear knowledge to developing countries and the power of OPEC countries to control, to a certain degree, the availability of crucial energy supplies have given new dimensions to the question of whether a NIEO is desirable from a peace and security viewpoint. I am convinced that it is. There is nothing more likely to provoke violence than a lack of perspectives for a better future. Poverty and unemployment are only bearable when there is hope for improvement in the not too distant future. If this hope is lacking, then violence enters the picture. Creating opportunities for the poverty stricken masses in the Third World by changing the existing order is, therefore, in the interest of all mankind, including its rich minorities.

If left to the charity and goodwill of the traditionally powerful industrialized countries a NIEO will not be brought about. Requests on this basis have traditionally received a negative answer. One may deplore it, but powerful nations will only cooperate in the building of a new order if they view it as being in their interest to do so. To a certain extent, this now seems to be the case. The oil crisis, the growing awareness of overall scarcities, the international recession, characterized by inflation, unemployment and monetary instability, the growing unity of the Third World, the unstable political and military situation in various parts of the world (e.g. the Middle East and Southern Africa) and the proliferation of nuclear knowledge together have shifted some of the power of the traditionally rich countries to the Third World. It is therefore in the interest of the traditionally rich countries to solve world problems in close harmony with the Third World.

Industrialized countries, having defined their own interests in the implementation of the NIEO, should accept its consequences for their own domestic economic policies. If they are not willing to do so, new instabilities in international economic relations will arise, especially in the fields of investment, production and employment.

The Structure of Production

It is desirable that every country specializes more than at present in the production of the goods in which it is most competitive. A rational distribution of production of this kind should take account not only of differences in location, natural resources, climate, etc., but also of the level of development that a particularly country has attained and the related availability or non-availability of production factors as manifested, for instance, in differences - sometimes considerable - in capital wealth and in wage levels.

Therefore, industrialized countries, with their relatively large reserves of technological know-how, highly skilled labour and capital, should concentrate on producing the goods dependent upon these factors. The production of goods by simpler and highly labour-intensive processes should, as far as possible, be entrusted to the economically less developed countries.

This is, of course, only an approximate picture. It applies only to the production of goods and services that are mobile (the so-called "international products"). Moreover, there are cost factors other than labour and capital: the availability of natural resources, transport costs, etc. An optimum division of labour should, therefore, be pursued, based on an optimalization of the various cost factors, and also taking account of some specific demand conditions.

Readjustments in the production structure of the industrialized countries are not a new phenomenon. Exports of manufactured products from developing to industrialized countries have increased considerably. However, this autonomous process leads to instability due to the stop and go manner in which the private investment decisions concerned are taken. And this instability leads to protective measures which impede improvements in the international division of labour.

Therefore, a restructuring policy is called for consisting of the following measures. Firstly, sector structure studies should be undertaken particularly of these industries confronted with serious difficulties or threatened by such difficulties.

Secondly, a system of indicative planning should be initiated to
guide investment and production decisions in these sectors in
order to implement restructuring of the sectors concerned within
a specific time period, which should be neither too long nor too
short (e.g. 10 years). Such a sector restructuring policy should
be concerned both with bolstering existing restructuring processes and with preparing for the future. Adverse effects of the
autonomous process on employment should be countered, compensated
for or eliminated by means of alternative investments.

As far as a forward looking policy is concerned, the course that
the restructuring process is to take should be recognized in good
time; it should be taken to anticipate the course of events so
that restructuring can take place with a minimum of negative
effects. At the same time, trade and other barriers erected
against the competing imports from the developing countries should
be removed in order to enable these countries to gradually take
over the production of those goods and services in which the
industrialized countries are not competitive and which are to be
cut back. This should also be done by means of planning and international consultation so as to avoid destroying the sections of
the production structure in the industrialized countries which
should be preserved but which are technically, economically or
institutionally linked to the marginal sections.

Employment

Even if planned properly, the readjustment of productive activities in the framework of a changing international division of
labour will, at least in the short term, add to the unemployment
in the industrialized countries. I say "add" because increasing
imports from so-called "low-wage countries" is by no means the
only or even the most important cause of unemployment. Increasing
scarcity and therefore higher prices for basic commodities,
including energy, saturation of demand for certain goods and services (in particular consumer durables), inflation, labour saving
investments and structural shifts towards the tertiary or commercial services sector where productivity increases are also
limited contribute to structurally lower growth rates and thus to
a worsening of the employment situation.

Given this multiplicity of unemployment causes in the industrialized countries, the way in which unemployment is tackled is clearly of crucial importance. After all, a rational and more equitable
international division of labour can only in the long run contribute substantially to employment creation in the industrialized
countries, whereas the adjustments needed in the short run will
lead to a deterioration in the situation. In this sense, the
address of present employment problems is a condition for the
establishment of the NIEO.

Two main employment policies have so far been implemented in the

industrialized countries. First, there is the old Keynesian policy of stimulating effective demand. In so far as this policy has
been aimed at stimulating private demand, its effects have been
insufficient. Part of the increased purchasing power is used for
imports or for the production of "nonsense goods" which does not
contribute to a structural and long term increase in employment.
Moreover, there seems to be a structural decline in both the
growth rate of private consumption and in the propensity to invest, which seemingly cannot be influenced by a policy of stimulating private demand.

Secondly, there is the neo-classical approach of the relative
decrease in production costs, in particular labour costs. In as
far as this approach leads to higher business profits, it is
becoming increasingly clear that there is no such thing as an
automatic link between higher profits and increased employment.
In a number of cases, higher profits are not reinvested (but consumed or transferred abroad) or are only invested in labour-
saving processes. Unless there are provisions for social assessment of the allocation of business profits, the neo-classical
approach is also bound to fail.

Conventional approaches seem thus to have either no effect or to
have effects which run counter to the interests of the weaker
sections of the population. New ways of dealing with unemployment
should be added to a more socialized application of the conventional approaches. I see two of them.

Firstly, a selective growth policy should be pursued with respect to production. Such a policy implies the provision of
government support to specific investments on the basis of certain criteria designed to reconcile the objective of growth and
employment with the need to be selective on the grounds of considerations with regard to the environment, the use of energy and
other scarce commodities, the spatial distribution of activities
and the international division of labour. Special instruments,
such as investment subsidies and investment controls, the promotion of technological innovation in some and of smaller scale
production in other sectors, are in this case necessary.

In the second place, new ways of dealing with the employment
problem should be applied to the consumption side. We see at
present tendencies towards a saturation of demand for certain
consumer goods. However, there is at the same time an unfulfilled
demand in the so-called developed countries for certain non-
material goods which cannot be bought on the market. There are
many unfulfilled needs in the spheres of education, health, welfare,
culture, urban renewal to mention but a few. They are rapidly
increasing, due in part to certain over-development tendencies in
the rich countries, and they lead to social inequities and to a
growing gap between economic growth and technological innovation

on the one hand and individual psychic well-being and social
welfare on the other. These needs have as yet not been identified fully, and virtually no progress has been made in their
measurement. This, together with the fact that they have in
common a lack of endogenous individual demand, points to the
need for a socialization of demand, whereby society itself
creates a demand for the satisfaction of needs that cannot be
fulfilled via the market. Such a creation of demand would
require an expanded service sector, in particular the non-commercial or "quartenary" sector, which offers important employment
possibilites. Here, perhaps, also lies an answer to the burning
question of where to find alternative investment opportunities
in a restructuring policy leading to a reduction in investment
in marginal sectors. Such a lack of investment in new sectors,
substituting declining ones, during the recession prevailing
since 1972 has constituted a serious impediment to the implementation of a new international division of labour as an essential
element of a NIEO.

The more effective use of conventional employment policies combined with the non-conventional approaches described above will
not solve but only lessen the unemployment problem. The structurally lower growth prospect will not enable a return to full
employment, not even when an integrated employment policy is implemented. The problem thus calls for more than the adaption of
employment policies: it calls for modifications to the very concepts of labour, consumption and our way of life.

When unemployment becomes a long term and structural phenomenon,
a better distribution of existing employment will be necessary.
This should not in the first place be achieved by decreasing the
number of hours worked per day because of the productivity losses
this will mean. A better distribution will have to be achieved
primarily by decreasing the number of years a person is involved
in the labour process. Earlier retirement, longer schooling, sab-
batical periods and re-education are among the ways to achieve
this. It will in any event require that the population of the
industrialized countries be prepared to afford a less central
position to materially productive labour. These countries have,
after all, entered post-industrial stages in their economic
development, with an increasing part of the national income to be
spent on collective services. The production of these services
in the transitional period is being left to volunteers. Their
efforts should be professionalized and rewarded. All this will
affect our way of life: less material consumption in general and
of "nonsense goods" in particular, creative leisure and more
consumption of education, culture etc.

A New National Economic Order
The required changes in the industrialized countries go further
than the structure of production and employment. The population

of these countries, and especially their economically weaker
parts, will only accept, let alone support, a NIEO if they are
sure that they will not become weaker as a result of change in
international economic relations. For that reason it is important
that the employment and income effects of this change for the
industrialized countries, which in the short run may be negative
and will only become positive in the longer run, are spread
among their populations in an equitable way, whereby the heaviest
burden is carried by the strongest shoulders. A policy aimed at
increased income equality and social security within the richer
countries is,therefore,a condition sine qua non for the construction of a NIEO, in itself the basis for attaining more equality
and security in the world as a whole. And it goes without saying
that such a policy should go hand in hand with policies aimed at
the economic, social, cultural and political emancipation of
women, minority groups and foreign labourers(the latter category
providing an additional human link between the industrialized
and the developing countries).

From what has been said concerning the required changes in investment, production, employment and income policies, it will be
clear that these changes imply an expansion of government activities. This points to the necessity of a change in the national
economic order of industrialized countries to enable them to
implement the right domestic policies, complementary to changes
in the international economic order. An increasing part of what
used to be private decisions will henceforth have to be taken
by the government, whether it concerns decisions on major industrial investments, the conversion of profits into employment, the
kinds of demand which should be stimulated, what constitutes
fair personal income, and so on.

According to some critics in the industrialized countries, the
government sector has already reached a critical limit. In their
view, an expansion of this sector would be detrimental to the
economic potential of the private sector. This criticism, however,
neglects the fact that the government sector itself is part of
the economic potential of society. The government produces goods
and services that contribute to national income and wealth and
its consumption is consumption by private individuals, but not
on the basis of the primary income distribution.

The centralization of decisions at the governmental level, however, requires a democratization of the decision-making process.
Participation by those affected by the decisions is essential.
The ultimate aim: the greatest possible material and non-material
welfare for as many people as possible. This aim cannot be attained in a decision-making process dominated by a small group of
powerful individuals remote from the masses; nor can it be reached by a government which takes decisions on a level far above the
heads of its people.

Creative thinking about the possiblilities of obtaining a higher
degree of participation in political and economic decisions which
must be made at higher levels is a very important challenge. It
is obvious that the educational system is in this respect very
important (and also to enable society to implement the necessary
employment and income policies).

Conclusion

In recent years, the link between the NIEO and policies within
the developing countries aimed at the satisfaction of basic
human needs has been stressed. That link indeed exists. It is,
however, equally important to stress the link between a NIEO and
the required changes in the policies and structures of the
industrialized countries. Without these changes a NIEO simply
cannot be brought about; without them the powerful interest
groups and the weaker sections of the population in the richer
countries can be expected to resist efforts aimed at the establishment of a NIEO.

For some decades now, Jan Tinbergen, on the basis of careful
research, has made proposals for changes both in the international economic system and in the structural policies within the
industrialized countries. Not only his ideas on "shaping a
world economy" and on an optimum international division of labour,
but also his creative thinking on employment policies, on income
distribution, on education and on an optimum economic regime may
serve to guide us.

It is high time. The spirit of 1974/1975 appears to have faded.
The power of the developing countries to demand a new international economic and political system is diminishing. That power
was based on oil, solidarity and reason. It is being confronted
by the industrialized countries' nuclear energy, arms deliveries
and sham deafness. It is crucial, therefore, that within the
industrialized countries a new process of awareness building
starts to identify longer term interests and to understand what
justice really means, both between and within nations.

Some Economic Theoretic Aspects of a NIEO: Prolegomena to Further Debate

Justinian F. Rweyemamu

Introduction

The turbulence in the world economy since the early seventies
that has sharpened the demands of the Third World countries to
establish a New International Economic Order has been extensively
discussed in many international fora. This note is not intended
to review these fascinating developments. Rather, my concern
is in establishing the fact that the economic profession has
discussed these new issues in the context of received economic
doctrine which is ill-suited to the task. I want to suggest that
the developments in the seventies call for a new paradigm. I will
restrict myself to two broad areas: international monetary reform
and commodity problems.

International Monetary Reform

It will be recalled that when the 44 Allied Nations convened the
U.N. Monetary and Financial Conference at Bretton Woods, New
Hampshire in July, 1944 to draw up at the articles of agreement
to establish the IMF and IBRD, most Third World countries were
colonies of some of the allied powers. As such, the objectives
of the two key financial institutions were clearly geared to
enhancing the interests of the dominant powers. The IBRD was to
provide long term capital for the war devastated economies of
Europe and Japan and the IMF was to foster international monetary
cooperation through the promotion of exchange stability, the
elimination of exchange restrictions and the correction of balance of payments disequilibria.

Over time the IBRD has grudgingly taken into account the interests of the emerging nations. Thus, the IFC became a member of
the World Bank Group in 1956, a soft window (IDA) was created in
1960 as a compromise to the establishment of SUNFED (Special
United Nations Fund for Economic Development), and in 1975 the
Third Window was added to the World Bank Group. But in spite of
these modifications, the modus operandi of the Bank vividly sym-
bolizes the Bretton Woods order. For the Bank is dominated in
terms of voting and policy orientation by the major industrial
powers. At present these countries hold 42.5 per cent of the
voting power, other industrial countries have 19 per cent and the
Third World countries (including OPEC) have 38.5 per cent. Of
course, even within the industrialized countries the voting
pattern corresponds more to the aftermath of the last war than
present realities. Thus the United Kingdom continues to have
twice the voting power of the Federal Republic of Germany! The
significance of voting rights is that they determine the pattern
of world distribution of production, surplus and economic power.

It would be misleading, however, to overemphasize the drawbacks

of the World Bank Group as a promoter of economic development of
the Third World. For one thing, since its inception, the Bank
reports to have lent US $8,535 million to the Western hemisphere
compared to US $4,593 million to Africa and US $8,515 million to
Asia. Secondly, the Bank, under President McNamara, has been
moving towards an appreciation and understanding of, and support
for, national strategies of meeting basic needs and self reliance.
More fundamental, however,   is the fact that the Bank is *not*
a primum mobile of international finance. At best it can function
as a benign aid mobilizer. The linchpin of international monetary
relations rests squarely with the IMF.

Perhaps it is no exaggeration to claim that the prime mover of
the accelerated expansion of industrial capitalism in the post
war period has been the IMF. By agreeing to have the domestic
currencies of a few countries also serve as international currencies, the rest of the international community (and particularly
all of the Third World countries) effectively gave up their
financial sovereignty. And the rhetoric of conventional economic
wisdom notwithstanding, this loss has not been to their advantage! One consequence has been that the wealthier a state, the
more reserves it gets (or creates!) and the higher its currency
has stood in relation to others. Professor Triffin has estimated
that the Third World, with over 70 per cent of the world population, received less than 4% of the US $126 billion of interna-
tional liquidity created during the last two decades. In this
respect, the introduction of the SDR facility heralded as a
"major" breakthrough of the First Amendment to the Fund's Articles has not improved matters significantly. By the end of 1974,
for example, 74.7 per cent of the SDRs created was allocated to
the rich countries.

The second consequence has been that Third World countries
exchange real goods for dollar IOUs! In this context, no amount
of "assistance" can be sufficiently mobilized to bridge the gap
between the rich and the poor! And it is, of course, no surprise
that indexation is discouraged by theoreticians who defend the
status quo. Moreover, this is also why all "aid" is a poor pal-
liative (which should not be discussed as an instrument of the
new order but rather as tidying up of the old order) and we cannot meaningfully compare the eight billion dollars the World
Bank gave to the Western countries with the eight billion dollars
it gave to Asia.

The New International Economic Order is about the equitable distribution of resources and power and of equal sovereignty. In
the monetary field, the New International Economic Order must
imply a guaranteeing of financial sovereignty through the *dena-
tionalization* of international currency and the establishment
of equitable trade on the basis of exchange of real value for
real value. The SDR, as presently constituted, does not meet

these conditions. In theoretical parlance, and this is my first major submission, the economic profession must seek a new basis for international exchange which can take either the form of a *neutral* international reserve asset (and thereby remove the undue influence of currency speculators) *or* the creation of regional banks of international settlements or undertaking international trade on a barter basis, or even establishing an exchange regime that is fixed according to the cost of feeding an adult over an agreed period in each country.(1)

It is needless to mention that the establishment of such an equitable basis for exchange would remove the major problems of the present order, namely terms of trade, aid, indexation, etc.

Commodity Problems

Turning now to the commodity issues, I would like once again to begin by examining the institutional framework. First, it is pertinent to mention that the Keynes plan to have a set of "common controls" or commodity organizations, overseen by a "general council for Commodity Controls" and funded by the International Clearing Union was rejected. (2) Attempts to set up an International Trade Organization (ITO) were unsuccessful; they merely resulted in the establishment of GATT in 1948 and the unsigned Havana Charter. Secondly, commodity production in the Third World has historically been largely controlled by transnationals.

A modest estimate suggests that the transnationals presently control two-thirds of the value of exports from developing countries in food, beverages and metals. Furthermore, the trade infrastructure (transportation, storage, insurance, etc.) has had even more metropolitan dominance. Thus, the functions of distribution and the price determination institutions (future markets, speculators, etc.) have been centred in the developed countries, the Third World having no say in the design and implementation of the rules of the game. Under these conditions the functioning of the commodity market institutions have been exceedingly unfavourable to Third World countries, especially in the post war period. In the more recent past, however, these adverse effects have spilled over to the economies of the dominant countries contributing, as Professor Kalder correctly suggests, to "stagflation" since in the long run there is a unique relationship between the growth of commodity production and trade and the growth of industrial production and trade.(3)

The fact that the link between commodity issues, industrial activity and monetary reform has only recently been rediscovered by Professor Kaldor and Samir Amin merely points to the malaise of received economic doctrine and its inability to deal adequately with dynamic problems of the world economy. What is more surprising is the diagnosis which conventional economic wisdom has made of the commodity problem. It concludes that it is the *attributes* of Third World commodities, as reflected in the price and income

elasticities, which account for the wide fluctuations and deteriorating terms of trade. There is no questioning of what lies
behind these elasticities, namely the deformed production structures of Third World economies or the monetary conundrum we have
noted above. If one trading partner produces and trades in a
basic good in the Sraffa sense while the other partner is unable
to produce it, the former will obviously have the possibility of
turning the terms of trade in his favour as he wishes.(4) On the
other hand, as Kaldor points out, "it is yet to be demonstrated
that a monetary system consisting of paper currencies convertible only into each other can even succeed in keeping their value
stable in terms of commodities. Though the role of gold has been
purely ephemeral ever since the 1920s, the formal though distant
link embodied in the Bretton Woods system sufficed to maintain
the illusion that dollars were as good as gold, and that commodities have a (long run) normal dollar price, around which their
market prices fluctuates. The formal demonetisation of gold, as
subsequent events have shown, has greatly weakend this stabilis-
ing force in the markets, and I do not believe that the regulation of the money supply, when "money supply' means current
account deposits and other forms of liquid financial assets,
could ever be an adequate substitute for direct convertibility
of money into commodities or that *without such convertibility* we
could, in an unregulated market economy, create a monetary medium
that is adequate for maintaining stability whilst giving a free
rein to the forces of economic expansion."(5)

The analysis of commodity problems by economists from the dominant countries has been hindered by the unbridled faith in the
inviolability of the free market. Yet it is now generally accepted that the market for commodities is not a perfect one; it is
characterized by monopolies with strong linkages not only in
production, marketing and distribution but with one another as
well. Nor is the necessary precondition to reap equitable benefits from free trade present, namely, equal distribution of
control between countries over basic resources and freedom of
access by all countries to all markets.

In the context of a competitive production regime with little
staying power and of a financially strong oligopolistic buying
regime with possibilities of stock manipulation, the establishment of a price level that is "remunerative" to producers and
"equitable" to consumers under the conditions of a free market is
quite remote. It is also obvious that such an institutional
framework is *not* conducive to establishing an equitable international system of exchange.

I would like to suggest that the economic profession should
approach the Integrated Programme of Commodities, that attempts
to put price stabilization, marketing and processing together in
one package (glued by a Common Fund!) and covers a broad range
of commodities so that on balance the majority of the Third World

could benefit, with the objective of ascertaining whether the scheme provides an equitable and beneficial framework in international economic exchange. After all, it must be realized that commodities constitute the only major bargaining card for the Third World. But commodities can become an effective instrument for it *if* a mechanism for exploiting monopoly power latent in an appropriate combination of commodities that allows intervention in commodity markets is established. This is the significance of the Common Fund negotiations within the framework of the Integrated Programme of Commodities.

In sum, the New International Economic Order is about equitable distribution on a global scale: the distribution of economic power. In the short term it will appear as a zero - sum game. Received economic theory has been particularly weak in its treatment of distribution issues; its treatment of equity problems is not likely to be more enlightened. But if the economic profession intends to make a significant contribution to the debate on the New International Economic Order, it will have to focus its attention on equity and distribution in production, surplus generation and exchange.

Notes and References

(1) For an elaboration of these ideas see the useful contribution of Alex P. Egom: *Money is An International Framework: An Inquiry into the Poverty of Nations*, Adione Inc., Copenhagen, 1977.
(2) J.M. Keynes: *The International Control of Raw Materials*, a U.K. Treasury memorandum written in 1942 and published twenty-two years later in *Journal of International Economics*, vol. 4, 1974, pp. 299-315.
(3) N. Kaldor: *Inflation and Recession in the World Economy*. Presidential address to the Royal Economic Society, delivered on 22 July, 1976 and published in the *Economic Journal*, 86, December, 1976, pp. 703-714. He concludes that "any large change in commodity prices - irrespective of whether it is in favour or against the primary producers - tends to have a dampening effect on industrial activity, it retards industrial growth in both cases, instead of retarding it in the one case and stimulating it in the other" (p. 706). See also Samir Amin: *Accumulation on a World Scale*, Monthly Review Press, New York, 1974.
(4) Basic goods are defined by Sraffa as those which are used either directly or indirectly in the production of *all* other goods in the economic system. See esp. Pierro Sraffa: *Production of Commodities by Means of Commodities*, Cambridge University Press, London, 1960. For an elaboration of this point see Oscar Braun: *International Trade and Imperialism* (mimeo) and Samir Amin, op.cit.
(5) Kaldor, op.cit. p. 714.

Can We Understand Each Other? The Need for a New International Information Order

Juan Somavía

Introduction

"It must be recognized that international information dissemination has long formed the subject of discriminatory practices.
Flows of information from the Third World to the industrialized
countries are controlled by a handful of Western news agencies;
information is subject to manipulation and can be and is used
as a means of perpetuating preconceived ideas, ignorance and
apathy. It serves to maintain systems rather than to transform
them.

Public opinion in the industrialized countries will not have real
access to full information on the Third World, its demands, aspirations and needs, until such time as information and communication patterns are liberated from the market-oriented sensatio-
nalism and news presentation which characterize them at present
and until they are consciously stripped of ethnocentric prejudice.
The widening of the capacity to inform must be viewed as an
essential component of attempts to create a new international
order and, as such, the monopolistic and discriminatory practices
inherent in current international information dissemination must
be deemed as one of the worst, though subtle, characteristics of
the present system. That there is a need for reform is obvious."

(RIO Report 1976)

Nevertheless, that there is a need for reform is not yet obvious
in the minds of many people, both in the industrialized and Third
World countries. The debate around the establishment of a new
international information order continues to be acrimonious and
highly emotional. It is clear that the resistance to change in
this field of international relations is far greater than in
economic matters. The control and orientation of the means of
international communications is an important instrument in the
maintenance and consolidation of the present transnational power
structure. It is also, particularly in many countries of Latin
America, a means of ideological and cultural domination of minority ruling classes over the majority of the population.

That structural reform is, under these circumstances, difficult,
should not surprise us. It has always been so in the past, it
will continue to be so in the future. The interest of the many
cannot prevail over those of the few without struggle and confrontation. Over and beyond this fact of political life it is
fundamental to understand empirically and intellectually some
of the reasoning that has led to the demand for changes in the
structure of the existing transnational communication system.

In the context of this volume in honor of Jan Tinbergen, this paper makes a brief overview of two aspects of this issue:

- the evolution in the social significance of communications;
- the functions that international communications should perform.

The Social Significance of Communication

When the topic of information was discussed internationally during the '40s, it was done under the influence of the experience with information manipulation under Nazi-fascism. It was with the closeness of this background that the then member countries of the United Nations defined the scope of freedom of expression and opinion. Although in certain Latin American countries the roots of fascism have taken hold in a contemporary format with important consequences for the excercise of the right to communicate, the general socio-political environment today is substantially different from what it was when the principles related to communication, information flow and freedom of expression were initially discussed internationally. The testimony of the emerging countries of the Third World on the different forms of neocolonialism, the dimension reached by the media in various social frameworks and the expansion of their technologies, make it necessary to analyse the problem from a wider perspective.

The media have become cultural and social "agents of influence". Their presence encompasses and traverses all social structures, acquiring an omnipresent and active participation in the individual and collective life of society. They have become a means for socialization that is perhaps more important than the school, family or religion. The major force in this transformation has been the extremely intense development of communications technology. The generalization of radio broadcasting; the overpowering growth of television; the capacity of direct satellite transmission; and the improvement in telegraphic links, in addition to important progress in the field of physical communications and the organizational and multiplying capacity contributed by computer technology and "informatique", have radically changed the significance and social impact of communications in contemporary society. Even though we still employ the terms "information" and "communication", they are applied today to social phenomena that are radically different from those that were described by these same words in the '40s. In fact, we are caught in a language that is incapable of reflecting its present global and total significance. Suffice it to think that both Reuter's pigeon and the latest communications satellite are described by the same word, - communications - yet their social effects are substantially different. The transformation of communications into a basic *agent of social influence* within societies and in relations among nations, poses, therefore, innumerable vital questions and justifies the need to clearly define the conceptual framework within which these new phenomena must be situated.

The influence of these changes was strengthened by the concrete form of organization progressively acquired by the international communication process. The selection, processing and transmission of information became an industry in continual expansion, acquiring the organizational structure of a transnational enterprise and applying business reasoning in its managerial decisions. In this way, international communication - as seen from the Third World - became another component of the transnational power structure. The transnational communications potential was added to the means for political and economic domination. The transnational communications system is a whole: it includes news agencies, advertising enterprises and data banks; also information retrieval systems, radio and television programmes, movies, radiophotos, magazines, books, and "comics" with international circulation; together with the hard and soft-ware technologies that have underpinned their development. Its different components, which originate mainly in the industrialized countries, reinforce each other, stimulating consumers' aspirations to reach forms of social organization and lifestyles imitative of industrialized (market-economy) capitalist countries, which, as experience has shown, can only be attained in Third World countries on the basis of a high and growing concentration of income in a few hands and unacceptable social inequalities. At the same time, the "informative pressure", which comes from so diverse origins, apparently unrelated but substantively coherent, gradually eliminate the capacity for critical judgement. Thus, the communication process becomes for the people something like a theatre, where you watch but do not participate. In those conditions, the public becomes convinced that the transnational consumption and development model is historically inevitable (see my paper *The Transnational Power Structure and International Information*, Development Dialogue, 2, 1976, p.15). In this manner, the transnational communications system has a preponderant cultural influence.

Thus, the confluence of technological development in communications and its transnational organization gave these enterprises a special and extraordinary characteristic: that of being foreign entities in the countries in which they were established, while at the same time being agents of fundamental social influence within these societies to which they did not belong. There is no need to seek out Machiavellian motivations or conspiracies against the free flow of information in order to understand that this situation would inevitably lead to the serious conflicts we witness today. It has already been stated elsewhere and we repeat: what is required is to promote a *truly free* multidirectional and multidimensional flow. But the real issue is much more profound and vital: it is the question of the cultural identity of societies which is at stake.

The heart of the matter resides in being able to find in the Third World the proper balance between an endogenous cultural development and reinforcement in each society, by emphasizing its values, traditions and capabilities, and the cultural interaction with other societies that undoubtedly have - in an interdependent world - positive aspects and elements to contribute. In the quest for an optimal level of creative tension, which does not seek autarchy nor accepts cultural domination, the communication transnationals emerge once more with their enormous power and influence; and dialogue becomes difficult. The information and entertainment transnationals offer the latest technology, the best and most modern programmes, the most rapidly transmitted information, ready-made advertising and all the other perceived advantages of the transnational communications system. Thus, under the protection of free flow, the transnational cultural industry installs itself: strong, powerful, and efficient. And it begins to influence the local social reality: from "Mission impossible" to the "Six million dollar man"; from Kissinger to Princess Caroline of Monaco.

By singling out and systematically emphasizing the values, perspectives and personalities of the transnational culture, the function of the agent of social influence that contemporary international communication has acquired is implemented. When efforts are made to react to this situation, the commercial interests that promote the sale of programmes and information services are confused at this point - in an extraordinary symbiosis similar to Houdini's pirouettes - with the untouchable principle of free flow. Thus, not accepting the whole commercial package offered by the communication transnationals becomes practically equivalent to violating the freedom of expression. In view of all this, an analysis must be made of international communication within the transnational framework and of the economic interests involved, because the confusion between the defense of principles and the defense of commercial objectives is clearly evident.

Transnational industrialization of culture and communications has brought about an actual biological mutation in the legal sphere. The majority of the constitutions throughout the world, as well as international resolutions, give top priority - and emphasize it as the fundamental right in the field of freedom of expression and information - to the citizen's right of free access to transmit or receive information in the context of each country's social system. The other rights are derived from this one, to be exercised in the framework of a derived right. In practice and in the evolution of events, this individual right - and social, when exercised by organized social groups - has become a commercial right whose trustees are the information enterprises. In this way, transnational enterprises in pursuit of their commercial interest have appropriated for their own benefit the constitutional right of freedom of information provided for the public, acting individually or collectively. This substantial modification, which is a result of information praxis, has changed the priority of rights established in constitutions, laws and regulations, thereby relegating individual and collective rights vis-à-vis the commercial interest of the enterprises that industrialize information.

This triple evolution - technological, transnational and legal- has substantially modified the social significance of information, as pointed out earlier, and has consolidated an international information structure based in the industrialized capitalist world but with significant impact within the Third World. In effect, these three trends stem from the industrialized countries and constitute an integrated whole that offers technology, a capacity for worldwide presence derived from transnational organization, and the legal protection necessary for the commercial activities of the information enterprises. This development began in the '40s and consolidated itself in recent times.

In a parallel manner, within Third World countries the internal burgeosies, linked politically and economically to transnational interests, collaborate in this process. Thus, a joint action develops to stimulate cultural homogenization. This alliance is particularly evident when progressive regimes which try to control the power of internal burgeosies are attacked by transnational communications media.

The Functions of International Communications
The commercial industrialization and transnationalization we have described leads us to pose a simple, but nevertheless fundamental question: what should the functions of international communications be? The answer will serve both as an attempt to escape the emotional debate and the contradictory positions concerning the origin and direction of the present international information order. This is the point of departure needed in order to characterize the nature of existing differences, to progress in a realistic dialogue and to make it possible to offer initial solutions on the subject. Defining the functions of international communications implies going to the heart of the problem; determining why and for what reason the international communications media exist; defining their role; identifying the "raison d'être" of their activities. The following main functions should be mentioned.

To respond to the individual and collective need to understand events.

Communication is not only quantitative, it is essentially qualitative. It is the quality, not the volume, that is important. It is not a question of bombarding the receiver with access to an increasing number of events that have happened elsewhere, but

rather making it possible for these events to be understood
in their own social, political and cultural context, in accordance with the rationality of their own society. This is perhaps
the most important challenge faced by international communications media. A true understanding of events in distant and
different countries, in alien cultures, in political systems
whose rationale may be different from that sustained by the communications medium that observes the situation, is not easy and
is actually - in the multifaceted world in which we live -
extremely difficult.

If the objective is to enable receivers to understand events,
what should be the criteria for selection? What information is
relevant and what is not? What assurance is there that the perception that is transmitted truly responds to the determinants
that generate the event transmitted? "Information for understanding" is not only a challenge; it is an inescapable need of
contemporary communication. If communications do not explain,
clarify and rationalize events, they no longer fulfill one of
their principle functions. This problem also poses a question
that is essential to this debate: is "objective" information
really possible? When a situation is described or transmitted,
is there in its respect only one truth? Is it possible for the
communicator to rid himself completely of his cultural background, ideological preferences, of his own subjective view of
events? It must be recognized that even the best intentioned
observer, who earnestly wishes to objectively describe events,
is subject to a set of determinants that encompass his opinions.
It is for this reason that the present information imbalance
that the Third World is experiencing is so harmful. By concentrating the greatest capacity for observing, commenting and
transmitting international events in the hands of the industrialized countries, there will inevitably be - for structural
reasons - various alternative perceptions and approaches to a
given event, alternative views that are not made public owing to
the existing imbalance. This situation, which primarily affects
the Third World, is also important for the public of the industrialized world since, under the present structure, it receives
only partial information.

To allow for informed participation

Participation should be the axis around which contemporary societies are built. Societies without participation are mute societies, societies whose creative capacity is slowly agonizing.
Participation is the essence of individual and social life. Participation cannot exist unless there is "capacity to participate",
grounded on permanent access to adequate information. This is
valid both for individuals in their relationship with society and
for States in their relationship with the international community.
Only informed participation is true participation. For this rea-

son the international communications media must make the context
of the events they describe understood and must channel the capacity for expression of the different societies in which they operate. Insofar as international communications make a true process
of understanding and expression possible, they will be in a position to offer suitable material that will generate informed participation. This aspect is of fundamental importance because too
often the situation today is quite the opposite, that is, unin-
formed participation: opinions and actions based on an incorrect
or incomplete perception of reality that lead to errors, whose
origin is found in the informative content which determined the
orientation of the participation. This is also particularly
relevant for the public of the industrialized world.

To cooperate in peace and understanding among States.

International communications media in contemporary societies can
directly generate reactions and positions towards certain events
at the level of peoples and international public opinion. Beyond
the official channels for relations among States, the communications media are in practice actors in international relations.
This means that in situations of great international significance, international communications are an important component
of the shape and character of the reaction of national public
opinion. Depending on the content and orientation of the information, this situation can either stimulate or hamper peace and
understanding among nations. The behaviour and effects of the
activities of international communications media must be considered a fundamental aspect in carrying our contemporary international relations. Cooperation for peace and understanding among
States should be seen as one of its principal functions. Practice
has definitely shown that they can be either an instrument for
international stability or discord.

*To make true cultural interaction among different societies pos-
sible.*

The contemporary international community is composed of many
cultures. It is characterized by an essential feature: there
are cultures throughout the world whose origins, characteristics
and determinants are very dissimilar. Each one has its own reality and is the product of different processes of social mixture
and historic evolution. A basic principle of international organization should be the respect for other cultures, and the
acknowledgement of the legitimacy of the "other", individual or
society. Within this framework, international communications have
become the main vehicle for relations among different cultures.
It is mainly through their intervention that we can become aware
of other realities and understand the nature and "raison d'être"
of cultural differences. International communications definitely
have the potential to become a means for dialogue and understand-

ing and they can constitute the most direct and most rapid way to interrelate cultures. We are a long way from fully achieving this today. Therefore, true cultural interaction among different societies should be considered one of its basic functions. In order to carry out this function, in their observation of events, the communication media must practice respect for the cultural identity of other individuals and societies. In order to make true understanding of phenomena possible, they must accept that they cannot be, nor much less should they be, instruments of a process of cultural homogenization. Cultural diversity is a richness to be defended and not a defect to be removed.

The Need for Further Analysis

The underlying structures behind present international information flows are a long way from fulfilling all these functions. On the other hand, it would be difficult to maintain that these functions should not be considered among the fundamental objectives of international communication, in spite of the fact that the lack of understanding, participation, peace and cultural respect observed today throughout the world is the result of the interaction of many factors that go far beyond communications. Nevertheless, communications play an important role and have a basic responsibility in positively stimulating these objectives. In order to make it possible, a profound analysis must be made of the present conceptual and practical framework in which international communications have developed; recognizing the social impact that this phenomenon has today; critically evaluating the principles on which the information process is based; and finding the means for advancing toward the fulfillment of these functions.

The analysis of the contemporary role of international communications is situated in a wider context, as is the search for a New International Economic Order. This is indicative that the Third World's questioning of the present transnational communications structure is but a reflex of a more general and profound questioning of the ruling economic structures. Third World countries demand, not only in communications but in all the other areas of international relations, an equality of opportunity that is denied by the present structures.

An approach to a new conceptual framework that includes all that is positive in existing structures and that inserts the communication process in the national and international, individual and collective social problematique of the '80s is clearly an urgent need today.

Partners in Disarmament

Inga Thorsson

Introduction

This very day, as you read this dialogue in honour of Jan Tinbergen, well over a billion dollars will flow into the world's armaments race. That amount corresponds to the total income during the same day of the 36 poorest nations of the world, housing 1,800 million people. Half of these people will be starving, a great number of them will be without employment, without an adequate place in which to live, and their children hungry.

During this same day, in the industrialized countries, a cadre of at least 400,000 scientists and engineers - 40 per cent of all there are in the world - will be devoting their skills and energy to developing new and more efficient military machinery; working at perfecting the present equipment, which is already sufficient to kill every human being forty times over.

Will, then, world development be promoted by further armaments? Will world security be promoted by further armaments?

The United Nations, entrusted with the task of being a forum for the nations of the world in their pursuit of the peaceful and secure development of this planet, has devoted considerable efforts to identifying, clarifying and debating these questions and their complex interrelationship. In that context, a report was presented in 1977 to the General Assembly on the economic and social consequences of the arms race (*Economic and Social Consequences of the Armaments Race and its Extremely Harmful Effects on World Peace and Security*). This was the second report in that field, the first appearing in 1972 (*Economic and Social Consequences of the Arms Race and of Military Expenditure*). The 1977 report confirms that the trend in arms development and production persists, involving continuous and growing demands for resources desperately needed for social development purposes. Referring to the 1972 UN Study on Disarmament and Development, the report points to potential alternative uses of human resources, and of production and development facilities now directed towards military purposes. The report underlines that substantial progress in the field of development is, in fact, essential for the preservation of world peace and security. "Genuine security", it is said, "cannot be assured by the accumulation of armament but only through disarmament, cooperation and the growth of exchange and interdependence in a world of diminishing inequalities".

Another attempt to look at arms reduction within the concept of global development was made in the RIO Report of 1976. The armaments race was taken up as one of the main areas to be tackled in formulating integrated strategies for the initiation of multi-dimensional change aimed at guaranteeing "a life of dignity and well-being for all".

I would like to take a closer look at the situation prevailing today; the realities behind the figures mentioned above.

Nuclear Arms Race

We know that the two superpowers are able to deliver over 12,000 strategic nuclear warheads. In addition, their arsenals contain tens of thousands of tactical nuclear weapons - weapons generally much more powerful than the atomic bomb that destroyed Hiroshima. Combined with this massive destructive power is the continuous improvement of the accuracy of warhead delivery. It is pointed out in the 1977 Yearbook of SIPRI (the Stockholm International Peace Research Institute) that the most modern intercontinental ballistic missile warheads have an estimated accuracy of about 350 metres after travelling some 13,000 km. The warheads likely to be available in the mid 1980s may have an accuracy of about 30 metres.

When looking at these developments in the nuclear weapons' field, we should bear in mind that the use of peaceful nuclear energy and the advancement of new nuclear technologies are rapidly developing and spreading to new parts of the world. The number of countries pursuing nuclear energy programmes, and the number of reactors, is rapidly increasing. By the end of 1976, 173 large power reactors were at work in 19 countries. About a third of the power generated was produced in countries without nuclear weapons, in North and South America, East and West Europe, and in Asia. The plutonium waste of the nuclear energy programmes of the countries without nuclear weapons was, in the same period, calculated by SPIRI to be enough to produce 510 atomic bombs with the power of some 20 kilotons (the Hiroshima bomb had an explosive power of 12 kilotons). According to estimated plans, some 29 countries will be operating 345 power reactors by the mid-1980s. Plants for the enrichment of uranium are operating, or will be established, in five non-nuclear weapon countries. Reprocessing plants have been built, or are about to be built, in six countries outside the nuclear weapon powers.

Whether or not these awesome facilities will actually be used for the production of weapons is, in the last instance, a matter of political will. Whether or not the small nations will have the political courage to desist from developing their nuclear weapon potential is, in the end, dependent on the line of action chosen by the nuclear military powers.

The world is still awaiting the negotiation of real nuclear disarmament. Certain recent signs might encourage us to believe that prospects for an early beginning are, at last, brightening. However, we must not cherish any illusions concerning the length of the process towards an eventual limitation on armaments that may

be initiated by a ban on tests of nuclear weapons, or by an agreement on the quantitative limitation of strategic arms, or even a
freeze of qualitative development, all of which might be in the
offing.

Conventional Arms

A most disturbing trend in the picture presented by the last
decade is the increasing involvement of the great powers in the
arms market, offering to the non-nuclear powers apparently
unrestricted access to the most sophisticated conventional weaponry.
The record of the superpowers gives proof of their efficiency in
this respect: having a 60 per cent share of the world's military
expenditures, they are responsible for about 75 per cent of world
trade in major weapons.

The qualitative arms competition between the two superpowers has
been analyzed in numerous articles and studies. The "technological
imperative", which ensures the spiralling upgrading of weapons,
also exerts pressure on the merchandizing of arms. To make room
for new generations of weapons, the old must be disposed of.
Moreover, the heavy costs of the production of new systems are
alleviated, and unit costs lowered, by longer production runs.

According to the estimates of the U.S. Arms Control and Disarmament Agency (ACDA), the value of the trade in military equipment in 1976 exceeded $ 10 billion, with new orders running at
about $ 20 billion. Even higher estimates have been made. SIPRI
estimates of the international arms trade suggest that major
weapons - tanks, ships, missiles and aircraft - account for
about one-half of the total trade in weapons and equipment.

Three-fourths of these exports go to the developing nations. Arms
sales to developing countries tripled in real terms between 1961
and 1975. And trade continues to expand, the rise being most rapid
in the Middle East. Since 1970, the countries of the Middle East
have been by far the largest regional purchasers of major weapons
in the world. accounting for about half of the major weapons
imported. Moreover, through favourable licensing and co-production
arrangements by the arms producing countries, extensive defense
industries are developing in all parts of the world. The Middle
East has also taken the lead in this respect.

The reasons behind the developments in the trade of conventional
arms are open to speculation. I have already pointed to the economic and political considerations prompting the intense marketing of the producers. Moreover, the traditional power relations of
the world have influenced new countries into equating prestige
with military power. In the international arena, every new arms
project is prone to increase a nation's standing - whereas in a
more sane world the situation would really be reversed. As the
world looks today, it is not surprising that national prestige, and
national security, are seen as functions of military power. There

238

, concluded between the leading military powers, have
n that this thesis fails to exhaust the discussion.
ons may also become so manageable that they result in,
deter, a conflict. This is especially likely if the
f large scale forces within a region constitutes a
und for political tension and lingering suspicion.
gnized not only by politicians and military men; it is
felt by a broad sector of world opinion. This is a
ct which has left its imprint on the post-war debate
uclear weapons and relations of forces, including,
debate on the *neutron bomb*.

standable - indeed, a healthy sign - that public
reacted particularly strongly against this detestable
of military technology. Working through enhanced
ffects rather than through blast, the neutron weapon
in the eyes of the individual citizen, as a bomb which
human beings but leave buildings undamaged. However,
anger involved in the possible development and deploy-
s weapon is that it might lead us past the threshold of
flict which may be beyond our ability to contain.

ated political aspects involved in the sector of arma-
ights rather than lessens the responsibility of the
and technicians involved in this field. It is one of
s that we must demand a factual account of the
f the developments, sufficiently hard and compre-
kindle a political debate that would be strong enough
a counterforce to the very heavy vested interests
military industrial affairs. Against this background, it
eat interest that the disarmament community noted the
of some 12,000 scientists in the U.S. in December last
ss, in the first instance, their own government for
ve steps aimed at real disarmament.

the autumn of 1977, the world heard speeches by the
eaders of the superpowers in which both committed
strongly to the idea of nuclear disarmament, the gate-
attempt at eventually terminating the arms race.
arter announced to the General Assembly of the U.N. his
, providing the U.S.S.R. was prepared to meet him half-
uce the American arsenals of nuclear weapons "by 10 per
r cent, even 50 per cent" as stages towards total
armament. An important first step would be the con-
a treaty banning nuclear weapon tests. Shortly after-
ident Bresjnev announced to the Central Committee of
st Party and the Supreme Soviet the readiness of the
n to work for nuclear disarmament, starting with a
t ban and a moratorium on peaceful nuclear explosions.

s between the two powers have since been developing.
of a nuclear test ban, negotiations have been

can be no doubt that the ultimate reas
weaponry around the globe lies in the
leading military powers.

The Cause of Disarmament

The priorities of the world are not on
in two ways: in stressing the priorit
ditures, the destructive capacities of
rising; and, at the same time, the lim
available are diverted from constructi
and social purposes. The cause of disa
for two reasons. The first is the need
catastrophy of a full-scale world war,
of the world's population. The second,
the need to divert the resources of mi
against poverty, to constructive devel

The RIO Report estimated a yearly inve
over a ten year period to be sufficien
necessities of human life. As the deve
aside some $ 3-4 billion for social de
about $ 10-12 billion annually (at 197
be contributed by the industrialized c
have been equivalent to the military e
about two weeks of that year.

The motives for disarmament would seem
alternatives offered to humanity being
continuing armaments - or development
disarmament.

And yet the arms race continues unabat

Mention has been made of the "technolog
upgrading of the weaponry of the great
reached a point where the mere suspici
exploitation by the potential enemy st
party, renewed scientific efforts to c
even imaginative technological feats.
are introduced as "bargaining chips" -
negotiation game played by the superpo

We all still live in the era of the ba
undeniable fact. But that is no reason
deep concern at the development of new
cally pursuing the work of disarmament.

Deterrence is an ambivalent concept whi
ferent ways. If deterrence, in the spe
the concept, is to be fully effective,
measure of risks and uncertainties. But
debate and the treaties on crisis contr

nuclear war
clearly sho
Nuclear wea
rather than
permanence
breeding gr
This is rec
also deeply
political f
concerning
lately, the

It is under
opinion has
new example
radiation e
stands out,
would kill
the great d
ment of thi
nuclear con

The complic
ments highl
scientists
these group
realities
hensible to
to work as
involved in
was with gr
initiative
year to pre
more decisi

Earlier, in
political l
themselves
way to any
President
willingness
way, to red
cent, 20 pe
nuclear dis
clusion of
wards, Pres
the Communi
Soviet Unic
nuclear tes

The contact
In the case

trilateral, involving the United Kingdom. The possibility still
exists that these negotiations will terminate in some kind of
agreement by the time this book appears. This agreement would be
of great importance since the issue of a nuclear test ban will be
in the focus of interest during the historic Special Session of
the General Assembly devoted to Disarmament, which will take
place between 23 May and 28 June 1978.

At the time of writing, the second SALT-agreement has not yet been
signed. The outlook for a conclusion of the negotiations in spring
1978 can, however, be considered hopeful. The relationship between
the two powers appears less tense, and more constructive, than
during earlier periods. And the general political atmosphere
will, of course, influence the negotiations, just as much as the
eventual conclusion of a treaty will be of crucial importance for
the continued relations between the power blocks of the world.

There is no doubt that the ceilings to be placed on the numbers
of strategic weapons under SALT II will be high - possibly too
high for any truly restrictive effects on developments in this
field. The treaty will, nevertheless, be of considerable
importance. The political impact of the very fact that a treaty
has been concluded would be of great significance. At the same
time, an arms control treaty, on the principle of parity, would
provide a basis for continued negotiations aimed at real disarmament, within the framework of a SALT III treaty.

But there have also been negative aspects of the SALT negotiations. I have hinted at them earlier. The limits established by
the first treaty are numerical, quantitative. This is also the
case with the agreement at present under negotiation. No parity
has been demanded for qualitative arms developments. This has
meant that the creation of new weapons systems has gone un-
checked. Indeed, negotiation has so far prompted the weapons'
build-up, due to the tactics of bargaining. The same factor
might stimulate a continuation of the qualitative build-up, as a
reaction against quantitative limitations. It is in this context
that a ban on the testing of nuclear devices will be of
particular importance.

Only through multilateral efforts, demanding a serious input by
all concerned, will it be possible to reach, eventually, agreements on a real reduction of the world's military arsenals.

The Special Session on Disarmament
The Special Session on Disarmament could become a turning-point
in the military developments of the last years; the searchlight
of international opinion will be directed at the participating
states, and in particular the military great powers. What will
the world's people demand of its decision-makers? What results
may we expect from the deliberations in New York in June? The
actual negotiations themselves are unlikely to yield any sur-

prising results. The great importance of the Session lies in its character as a focal pint of interest, and as a catalyst and a starting point for further action.

The very fact that a Special Session on Disarmament is being arranged has, for instance, already acted as a stimulus to the work on a Comprehensive Test Ban. It has also, no doubt, been among the factors pressing for the conclusion of a SALT II agreement, which will be of basic importance to the credibility of the superpowers with regard to their possible commitments during the Session.

I have made particular reference to the opinion-raising effect to be expected from the work of the Disarmament Session. We have already seen proof of this. A powerful movement for peace and justice, and for the sane management of world affairs, is seen to be growing stronger every week, centered in the world-wide network of non-governmental organizations. The written and spoken word could be a powerful tool for exerting pressure on decision-makers and political leaders. Only through the undaunted support, and pressure, of a popular movement will it be possible to make any kind of progress against the haywire arms race.

The outcome of the Session can be expected to take the form of documents, declaring the support of the parties to the idea of disarmament; it will also point to the concrete measures and action to be undertaken. It is of paramount importance that agreement is reached on a comprehensive programme for continuing disarmament initiatives. The multilateral negotiative bodies, and in particular the United Nations and the Geneva Conference of the Committee on Disarmament (CCD), must be strengthened.

As I stated earlier, among the concrete issues that we wish to see promoted by a decision at the Session is the conclusion of the comprehensive ban on nuclear weapons tests. With an agreement of this kind we could at last see possibilities opening for checking the qualitative development in the nuclear weapons field. This could be the first step on the road towards nuclear disarmament, the greatest step taken since 1945 towards the survival of mankind.

As noted earlier, the RIO Report was among the first to take up the question of the arms race, and the necessity of disarmament, as an issue which has the greatest possible bearing on the efforts to establish a rational and just world order. In the long term, this is where the importance of the Special Session will lie - in making, at last, political leaders realize the complex role of the military sector, and military power, for the world economy and for the future of world society.

The Need for Additional Study
We are all partners in the world of tomorrow. Together, we must

work for a just and equitable world order. Together, we must work for the more sensible use of the world's resources - work *for* constructive development, work *against* destructive armaments.

That is also the intention behind the proposal for a new U.N. Study on the relationships between disarmament and development, initiated by the Nordic group of countries in the preparatory work for the Session. From the reactions meeting our proposal, it would appear to coincide with a wide spread feeling among the governments of the world. The General Assembly of last autumn endorsed by consensus the continuation of the preparations for the study.

The studies already made within the United Nations pointed to the need for renewed efforts and to the possibility that fundamental questions can be answered. The new study must be action oriented: it must provide decision-makers with the foundations needed to take on the responsibility for a reorganization of industrial production, and for the eventual restructuring of the economy that will be inevitable.

To create a solid basis for such decisions - decisions which will inevitably be far-reaching - we must not only know what the existing situation is with respect to the utilization of human and material resources for military purposes; we must also know the extent to which these particular resources would be demanded for purposes of civilian economic and social development. We must understand the consequences of continuing the utilization of resources along the same lines as today, as well as of a re-allocation from military to civilian purposes.

Should it be found that the redeployment of resources can be expected to have the positive effects hoped for, then the actual procedure of readjustment and the establishment of an alternative system of production must be carefully analyzed. Plans must be drawn up for the necessary coordination of disarmament measures and measures of economic policy. We must provide for changes in production, to take place without negative side-effects on, for instance, employment or regional development. Only through com-prehensive knowledge of the various aspects of this complex picture will it be possible for us to make the most of our resources for the social, technological and economic development of the world.

Mobilizing Opinion
I have been asked to focus my contribution to this collection of essays on possible future developments. Progress in disarmament, however, is conspiciously difficult to forecast. In real terms, it is dependent on politically determined, day-to-day negotiations. I have tried to spell out the necessary stages of a process essential to a complete transformation from destructive to constructive use of urgently needed resources, from arms to

human welfare. The decisive factor will be the amount of public pressure brought to bear on politicians to finally settle in favour of common sense.

Only through an active partnership between the constructive forces in the world will it be possible to confront the power of the military machine. Given the first U.N. General Assembly Session devoted to disarmament, the time has come for engaged and far-seeing citizens to unite in placing - and sustaining - pressure on responsible decision-makers in all regions of the world; to demand of decision-makers that they stop to consider where developments have been and are leading us; to review the pos-sibilities now opening up for them to turn the tide towards a new development, a new tomorrow. The aim of these endeavours must be to achieve, in the not too distant future, "a life of dignity and well-being for all".

Reshaping the International Monetary Order

Robert Triffin

World Stagnation, or "Infession"

A new term has recently had to be invented to summarize the unprecedented economic crisis in which the world is now plunged. The term is *stagflation*, meaning the unusual and bizarre combination of two opposite evils: stagnation and inflation. I would have preferred myself to call it *infession* or *inflession* because we are facing recession, or even depression, rather than mere stagnation, and because this recession, or depression, chronologically followed a burst of wild inflation and is largely the result of it, rather than the other way around as suggested by the term stagflation.

Getting away from mere terminology, however, I would like to stress the fact that the present crisis is not due to any obdurate incompatibility between conflicting national policies, but on the contrary to the universal failure of identical policies. National governments indeed repeatedly proclaim the same economic goals, summarized in what used to be dubbed the "Holy Trinity": high levels of employment and economic growth, approximately stable prices, and a viable equilibrium of each country's external transactions. I hardly need stress that what most governments are actually delivering to their people is exactly the opposite, on all three counts: unbearable unemployment, inflation and balance-of-payments disequilibria.

The universal failure of official policies, national and international, cannot be fully explained by accidental policy mistakes. It should be recognized as a much deeper *institutional crisis* rooted in our inability to adjust and reform *in time* outworn institutions, increasingly unfit to serve their most essential objectives in an ever and fast changing world.

The abortion of more than ten years of official debates and negotiations about the reform of our anachronistic international monetary system is one of the most obvious and dramatic demonstrations of this institutional paralysis. And who can doubt that the doubling of world reserves, triggered by this system between the end of 1969 and the end of 1972, played a major role in the world inflation, well before the explosion of oil prices at the end of 1973?

Before discussing this, however, I must admit that this role was only a "permissive" one, and that the deeper roots of the world inflation lie in the growing shortages of essential foods and materials. Future historians will probably describe as a unique parenthesis in world history the spectacular increase of material production and consumption over the last two hundred years. It began with the so-called "industrial revolution" which aimed at better satisfying the real, basic needs of man for food, shelter, clothing, transportation, etc. It was increasingly sustained later by what might be called the "advertising revolution", which aimed in part at arousing less essential wishes or whims, not perceived previously as real needs. It was accelerated after World War II by our very success in avoiding the cyclical recessions which had, up to then, periodically slowed down this continuing process of economic growth. Last, but not least, it was compounded by the explosion of the most inflationary type of expenditures by far, military expenditures, to an annual level of $300 billion a year, just about equal to the *total* GNP on which 40% of the world population has to live, or barely survive.

Outside of its polluting effect on our atmosphere and environment, this enormous surge of world production and consumption has brought closer prospective scarcities of essential resources. While most of these scarcities can be overcome in time, this is most likely to prove possible only at increasing costs, particularly if suppliers are encouraged by permissive monetary policies to "charge all that the traffic will bear" and to base their expectations and claims on persistent price upward flexibility, rather than on prices fluctuating around traditional norms embedded in approximate overall stability in the long run. Price and wage rises then tend to feed on each other indefinitely and to spread from the scarce sectors to the rest of the economy.

Determinedly anti-inflationary monetary policies could conceivably slow down the process, but only at the risk of also slowing down, at times, the pace of economic growth, and of triggering widespread unemployment and suffering, humanly repugnant and politically unpalatable.

Until about 1969, however, inflation tended, on the whole, to remain a national rather than a world phenomenon. The countries that inflated faster than others became more and more uncompetitive in world trade, tended to run increasing deficits in their external transactions and were eventually forced, by the depletion of their international reserves, to devalue their national currency, or to let it depreciate on the exchange markets, vis-a-vis the currencies of the less inflating countries. World prices, measured in these latter and stronger currencies, remained relatively stable. Thus it is that world export and import prices, measured in U.S. dollars, rose on the average by less than 1% a year in the decade of the 1960s.

The sharp acceleration of the world inflation in the following years is conveniently blamed on the quadrupling of oil prices in the last months of 1973. The direct impact of oil prices, however, can explain only a small fraction of the 52% increase of export prices over the years 1974-1976, and virtually none of their 50% increase over the previous four years (of which more than 30% took place in the last twelve months before the oil price explosion). Who can doubt that this had something to do with the more than doubling of international monetary reserves from the end of 1969 to the end of 1972, i.e. as much in three years as in all previous years and centuries since Adam and Eve?

And this brings me to my main topic: the evolution of the international monetary system.

International Monetary Order, or Disorder

What is the International Monetary System? The money which we use in our daily life has long ceased to be fully international, i.e. readily and universally acceptable in payment all over the world. As different from former gold and silver moneys, it is now made up of paper currency and bank deposits without any intrinsic commodity value whatsoever, and normally accepted in payment only within each country's national borders.

Whenever payment has to be made abroad, the national currency of the payor has to be exchanged for the national currency of the payee. This is what the international monetary system is about. To ensure its functioning, each country must be ready to provide its own currency, or to redeem it, against what is called "international reserves", i.e. some kind of asset acceptable to all of them for that purpose.

On the eve of the First World War, the main type of asset universally used for this purpose was gold, but gold has been increasingly supplemented, and ultimately displaced, in this role since then by one or a few *national*, so-called "reserve currencies", convertible at any time into gold, at the request of the holder, under the so-called "gold-exchange standard".

Unviability of the "Gold-Exchange" Standard. This system, however, was clearly unviable in the long run. The reserve-currency center was thereby enabled continually to spend more than it earned, and to settle its mounting deficits by piling up a foreign indebtedness which ultimately exceeded its ability to repay it in gold, at the request of its creditors.

The gold-convertible sterling standard of the late 1920s collapsed, after only a few years, in September 1931, and the world returned to the gold standard, experiencing in the process deflation and recession in spite of the devaluation of all currencies - including sterling and the dollar - in terms of gold.

The postwar gold-convertible dollar standard lasted for a much longer time, but ultimately proved equally unviable, as I had predicted to the Joint Economic Committee of the U.S. Congress in October 1959. The dollar became increasingly inconvertible *de facto* in the following years, and *de jure* on 15 August, 1971.

Emergence of the "Inconvertible Exchange Standard". As different from 1931, however, no other currency was ready and able to take its place. In spite of its inconvertibility and exchange-rate instability, the dollar has remained the main currency used for international settlements, for the accumulation of reserves by central banks and other monetary authorities, and for the investment of so-called "working balances" by other banks, private enterprises and individuals.

Major Shortcomings of the Exchange Standard. The marathon official debates and negotiations opened, at long last, in October 1963, about the need for international monetary reform and were overtaken by events. They were still going on when the dollar became inconvertible in 1971, just as the debates of the Gold Delegation of the League of Nations had still been going on, forty years before, when the pound became inconvertible in 1931.

Yet, a wide intellectual consensus had finally been reached by the officials, as well as by outside experts, on the major shortcomings of the system, and the broad features of the reforms essential to its future reconstruction. The most authoritative expression of this consensus may be found in the last report of the "Committee on Reform of the International Monetary System and Related Issues" (Committee of Twenty, Washington, D.C. 1974).

It was agreed, in brief, that:

i) Reserve creation should aim at adjusting world reserves to the legitimate - non-inflationary - requirements of potential growth in the world economy (presumably about 4 to 6% a year on the average).
ii) It should apply adequate pressures for the readjustment of excessive, persistent, disequilibria, on all countries alike, whether in surplus or deficit.
iii) The lending potential inevitably derived from world reserve growth should be used for internationally agreed objectives, such as the financing of temporary, reversible deficits, and of other high-priority goals of the international community, including, among others, the feasible acceleration of economic development in the Third World.

The record of the last seven years amply demonstrates that the present system of reserve creation exhibits exactly opposite characteristics on all three points:

i) The *inflationary* potential and proclivities of the system are clearly shown in the doubling of world reserves over the short space of three years: from $79 billion at the end of 1969 to $159 billion at the end of 1972, an increase, as noted earlier, as large as in all previous years and centuries taken together. The slowdown of this pace of increase after 1972 will be credited by some to the new floating rate regime, and by others to the world recession. It still exceeded, anyway, 62% over the last four years (1973-76), i.e. an annual rate of growth close to 13% (slightly exceeded in 1976), certainly two to three times as large as what might be deemed a non-inflationary rate.

The lion's share of this inflationary growth of world reserves is foreign exchange, i.e. the acceptance of *national* currencies (primarily U.S. dollars and Euro-dollars) as international reserves by central banks. Valued at an unchanged SDR (Special Drawing Rights) rate of $35 per ounce, gold reserves declined slightly, International Monetary Fund loans and SDR allocations contributed less than 12% of the total increase, and foreign exchange alone about 89%.

ii) The system *relieved in fact all countries from normal balance-of-payments adjustment pressures*. It enabled the United States, in particular to finance enormous and persistent deficits through the absorption of its IOU's by foreign central banks, but entailed for the latter correspondingly huge and inflationary issues of their own currency. It also relieved them, however, of any worry about the normal impact of their own inflationary policies on their balance-of-payments and their international monetary reserves. Practically all countries of the world, except the United States, were accumulating substantial increases in their gross reserves, totalling more than 70 billion SDRs over the three years 1970-72. This removed from them also the readjustment pressures that balance-of-payments deficits would otherwise have forced upon either their domestic policies or their exchange rates.

It eventually induced some of the stronger countries, to which inflation was most distasteful, to withdraw their automatic support of the dollar rate in the exchange markets. Even the suspension of the dollar convertibility by the United States, however, and the generalization of floating rates has failed to stop the continued feeding of inflationary increases of world reserves by unbridled foreign exchange accumulation.

iii) Last but not least, the investment of the bulk of world reserves in the national currency of one, or a few, of the richest, most developed and most capitalized countries is understandably resented by the more than one hundred poorer countries of the world, desperately short of capital for their economic development. They note with bitter irony the recurrent pleas and resolutions of the United Nations for increased capital exports and development assistance by the former to the latter countries. In the areas that is - or should be - most amenable to their influence and decisions, national and international monetary

authorities follow exactly the opposite policy of bringing coals
to Newcastle. Of the total growth of world monetary reserves over
the years 1970-1976 (144 billion SDRs), less than 5% (6 billion)
has been invested in the less developed countries, and more
than 95% (138 billion) in the developed countries.

Admittedly, this enabled developed countries to expand their
official assistance to less developed countries more than they
could have done otherwise, but it did not force them to do so.
They could, alternatively, use much of their borrowings from
foreign central banks to expand domestic consumption levels (as in
Britain, for instance) or private investments and military expenditures at home and abroad (as in the United States). Even to the
extent that some of these funds were used for foreign assistance,
it was at their own discretion, and according to a pattern
strongly influenced by political and military considerations, as
well as by economic or humanitarian ones. All in all, DAC (Development Assistance Committee) estimates show that only about
one half of the total financing received by developed countries
from the investment of international monetary reserves was devoted by them to official development assistance, and only one
fourth by the United States.

Proposals for Reform. These three fundamental, devastating shortcomings of the international monetary system belatedly elicited
nearly universal agreement on the major features of a reformed
system. In brief, it was agreed that, in order to eliminate all
three of the shortcomings diagnosed above, the creation and management of international reserves should be brought under international control, and that this would require the substitution
of SDRs for gold and reserve currencies as the principal reserve
asset of the system. (This barbarous - and obviously inappropriate - term means, in more understandable language, deposit accounts with the IMF, to which international receipts and payments
should be credited and debited, much as individual receipts and
payments are credited and debited to checking accounts in a bank.
The first Amendment to the Articles of Agreement of the IMF, in
1969, had initiated such SDR accounts, in a needlessly complex
and restricted manner, but had merely added them to - rather than
substituted them for - the uncontrolled accumulation, or contrac-
tion, of gold and foreign exchange reserves.)

The Abortion of Reform. Incredible as it is, the reforms finally
proposed in the Second Amendment of the Articles of Agreement of
the International Monetary Fund practically ignore the diagnosis
and prescription painfully ironed out over more than twelve years
of continuous consultations between the participating countries.
All that is proposed, in effect, is to recognize the collapse of
the Bretton Woods system, and to legalize the general - and still
illegal - repudiation of the convertibility and exchange-rate
commitments inscribed in the Bretton Woods Treaty.

The attention of most commentators has centered primarily on the proposed new Article IV of the IMF Agreement, misleadingly entitled "Obligations regarding Exchange Arrangements", but which in fact leaves every member free to adopt any exchange arrangements it chooses, except only the one still imposed on all countries by the present IMF agreement, but universally disregarded by them, i.e. "the maintenance by a member of a value for its currency in terms of . . . gold". (Article IV, Section 2,b)

I shall abstain from discussing further these new exchange-rate arrangements. They are probably unavoidable for now, but do not alter the realities of the previous system as radically as is usually thought. Exchange rates were far from stable under the Bretton Woods system, and most currencies remain pegged today, as precariously as yesterday, to the U.S. dollar, or to some other major currency or batch of currencies. The main difference is that the U.S. dollar is no longer the unquestioned benchmark for such pegging and more or less frequent readjustments. It is now subject to wide and reversible daily fluctuations vis-a-vis other major currencies, downward as well as upward, instead of appreciating repeatedly and continually, as before 1970, in terms of practically all other currencies.

Far more significant - and devastating, in my opinion - is the abdication of all attempts to reform an absurd, inflationary, and unfair system of world reserve creation the universally diagnosed shortcomings of which are at the root of the Bretton Woods collapse and are bound to plague and frustrate the new floating rates system as well as the previous pegged rates system.

Current Developments and Major Problems

The Impact of the Oil Crisis. The abrupt turnabout of the negotiators on these vital issues is generally ascribed to the new and revolutionary developments triggered, at the end of 1973, by the oil crisis. The resulting disequilibria and uncertainties deterred governments from assuming the long term commitments entailed in the reforms on which they had previously and tentatively agreed, at least in principle.

One of the major changes in the functioning of the system is a radically different constellation of net reserve losses and gains:
i) Net reserve losses are no longer overwhelmingly concentrated in the United States, as in 1970-72, but are now shared by most other countries.
ii) Net reserve gains, on the other hand, now accrue overwhelmingly to the OPEC countries, instead of being spread, as before, among practically all countries of the world other than the United States, and accruing in particular to Germany, Japan and other industrialized countries.

The other major change is that private international lending,
particularly by commercial banks, has assumed fantastic proportions in the financing of the huge balance-of-payments disequilibria of recent years and of continued inflation in many countries. Incomplete, but overlapping data from the eight European
countries reporting to the BIS (Bank for International Settlements), Canada, Japan, and branches of U.S. banks in the Caribbean area and the Far East record increases in external assets
of banks from about $100 billion at the end of 1969 to $290
billion at the end of 1973, and to $550 billion at the end of
1976, i.e. at an average annual rate of more than $85 billion
over the last three years. U.S. banks and foreign branches of
U.S. banks have played a leading role in this expansion, their
foreign claims having risen to more than $285 billion at the
end of last year, i.e. more than eight times since the end of 1969
(about $33 billion), and more than doubled over the three years
1974-76.

Although slightly more than forty per cent of these amounts may
be accounted for by inter-bank transactions rather than by lending to non-banks, it is difficult to believe that they could, or
should, continue on such a scale. These reported external assets
of banks at the end of 1976 were nearly three times the foreign
exchange investments of central banks, and more than twenty
times the total of IMF lending and SDR allocations.

Major Problems and Prospects. These developments make obviously
untenable and ludicrous the bizarre view espoused, or at least
expounded, by the highest Treasury officials in the previous
Administration, i.e. that world reserve creation should be left
to market forces of supply and demand, rather than to the dictation of national and international officials. The world "control"
reputedly made Secretary Simon "shudder". Yet, an uncontrolled
system of *international* reserve creation has long proved itself
as dangerous and nefarious as an uncontrolled system of *national*
money creation. Even the arch-opponent of government interference
with market forces (Milton Friedman) calls for a controlled
growth of money supply at a steady yearly rate, which certainly
could not be expected from the free play of market forces.

The relief, and even legitimate pride, often expressed at the
ability of the private market to weather the oil crisis and to
"recycle" the fantastic spurt of OPEC surpluses should be tempered
by the fact that the institutional pattern of this recycling
places an excessive burden of political responsibilities and
financial risks on the United States and on the private financial
sector, particularly the banks, primarily engaged in this recycling.

The U.S. balance of payments recorded in 1976 a peak
increase in the intermediation role of the dollar. U.S. liabili-

ties to international financial institutions and to foreign
central banks and commercial banks increased by about $24
billion, just about matched by a $23 billion increase in U.S.
monetary reserves and claims reported by banks. Most of these
asset increases ($21 billion) were in bank claims, which rose
to about *seven and a half times* their yearly average ($2.8 bil-
lion) of the five years (1969-1973) preceding the oil crisis, and
as much as *forty-two times* the average of the previous five years
($0.5 billion).

Private banks have recently expressed growing concern about their
ability to maintain indefinitely such a huge rate of foreign
lending, but are also worried about the possible consequences
(defaults and panic) of any substantial decline in their lending.
Officials, on the other hand, are equally concerned about the
inflationary implications of some, at least, of these bank lending operations, and about the reluctance and/or incompetence of
the lenders to insist on the broad policy conditions which officials would regard as appropriate to ward inflationary abuses.
The main conclusions derived so far from these considerations by
U.S. officials are that:

i) The lending potential of official monetary and financial
institutions - particularly the IMF, the World Bank, and its
affiliates - should be vastly increased, so as to enable them to
take a larger share of the recycling operations judged desirable
or unavoidable, and to perform the task of "lender of last
resort" if and when needed to avoid a spread of defaults and
financial panic.

ii) This would obviously call for appropriate supervision and
restraints on such lending, and for some coordination between
official and private lenders, in order to prevent undue risks
and inflationary excesses.

iii) On the other hand, the imperative need of recycling *quickly*
the huge and unavoidable OPEC surpluses and the willingness of
these countries to accept dollars and Euro-currencies in settlement have weakened the previous resolve to substitute SDRs for
reserve currencies as the major component of international
reserves and settlements. International decisions about the
acceptance and recycling of SDRs might be slow and cumbersome,
and the path of least resistance is to continue with the present
system.

Yet, this does not meet any of the three basic shortcomings
denounced in the previous section of this paper. It should also
be pointed out that an international agreement on a SDR system
of reserves and settlements should be safer and more attractive
than the present one for the surplus countries, would ward off
the danger of sudden switches from one currency to another, and
would provide automatically the wherewithal for the recycling
operations deemed essential by the international community.

253

I continue to hope that the day will come when tired officials
will be willing to look again at the reforms tentatively agreed
after long years of agonizing debates, and to resume their negotiations with a real sense of urgency.

Summary and Conclusions

The near universal failure of governments to reach policy goals
common to most of them should not be ascribed to the inappropri-
ateness of these policies. It is instead a clear demonstration
of the anachronism and inadequacy of the decision-making procedures and institutions through which these policies must be
implemented. The constraints of *national sovereignty* make it
impossible to deal effectively with problems which are essentially international. *Ad hoc* consultations and negotiations, para-
lyzed by the unanimity rule, are far too slow, cumbersome, and
uncertain. They have repeatedly been overtaken by events and by
the mounting crises that were the inevitable result of the
failure to adopt *in time* long overdue reforms widely recognized
as essential by all, or most, participating countries. So-called
national "negotiating positions" always tend to center on short
term conflicting national views and interests, real or imagined,
rather than on the more fundamental goals shared by all and
essential to the long term success of commonly shared policy
objectives.

The private sectors of the economy have long taken the lead in
this respect and adjusted their institutions, as well as their
policies, to the obvious realities of an interdependent world.
The internationalization of the capital markets and of the
multinational corporations is the most positive element of the
revolutionary transformation of the world economic system in
recent years. The official decision-making sectors, however, lag
far behind in this respect. National governments have become
impotent to assert and enforce the public interest upon the operations of the private firms, and to provide them with the stable
framework essential to their operations. This waning of their
authority has left a growing void which international policy-
making institutions have not been able to fill.

Routine-bound bureaucrats and political leaders have been unwilling to renounce their supposed powers - no matter how illusory
and nefarious they have proved in practice - and to transfer
them to the transnational institutions needed to exercise them
efficiently and beneficently.

The breakdown of the international monetary system is only one
of the most obvious demonstrations of this failure to adjust
our institutions to the tasks which they should serve. Marathon
debates and negotiations dragged on for over a decade without
producing in time the institutional reforms universally recognized as indispensable to ward off a predictable, and widely

predicted, collapse.

Many other examples come to mind, such as the impact of untrammelled national sovereignty upon the eruption of the energy crisis and the failure, so far, of all efforts to devise and implement appropriate solutions to its continuing and foreseeable intensification and contagion to other economic sectors.

Even more costly, inflationary, and potentially catastrophic is the continued escalation of an armament race, which is the very opposite of what governments and people wish most earnestly, all over the world. The basic objectives of individual security and survival are commonly shared by all, and would obviously be better served by mutual reductions in the wasteful overkill capacity on which we are now squandering hundreds of billions of dollars each year. Governments fail miserably everywhere in their specific task, which is to devise and implement political solutions for their people's legitimate aspirations.

International relations between the Communist and the non-Communist countries deteriorated sharply after the last war, but in the economic field at least, policies and institutional practices had made, until a few years ago, enormous progress among the latter, under the bold and imaginative leadership of the United States. The International Monetary Fund, the World Bank, the GATT, the Marshall Plan, the Organization for European Economic Cooperation, the European Payments Union, the European Communities, etc. had inaugurated an era of continuous consultation and intense cooperation - even integration - among national governments and bureaucracies. The unprecedented economic prosperity of this period exceeded the most optimistic hopes and forecasts, and presented a striking contrast with the deep and prolonged depression that accompanied the beggar-my-neighbor nationalistic policies followed in the 1930s.

The decade of the 1970s, however, has been marked so far by a gradual slowdown, and even regression, in this respect. The reactions to both the dollar crisis and the energy crisis have been the interruption of the march toward European economic and monetary union - whose completion had been repeatedly promised for 1980! - the dismantlement of Bretton Woods, the abortion of international monetary reform, and a growing reassertion of national sovereignties. This new orientation has certainly not solved any of the agonizing problems confronting us: inflation, recession, and unemployment, enormous disequilibria in international payments, persistent misery in the Third World.

Economists are all too prone to explain and justify such governmental failures by a "realistic" appraisal of "feasible" agreements between sovereign countries. Our duty should be, on the contrary, to stress and reaffirm the fundamental objectives toward which we should all commonly strive. We should try to help make possible tomorrow what still seems impossible today.

The greatest achiever of our generation, Jean Monnet, reminds us in his *Mémoires* that a "philosophy which attaches itself primarily to what is necessary is more realistic than one which considers only what is possible."

A New International Economic Order to Meet Peoples' Basic Needs

Maurice J. Williams

Introduction

Much of the North-South dialogue of the last two years on a new
international order has been conducted by diplomats representing
the interests and rights of states; focus on the needs and rights
of people has been less clear. Of course, better understanding of
the interests of states is important for international progress,
and a useful contribution has been made by the United Nations'
"Charter of Economic Rights and Duties of States." However, if
the idea of a new international order is not more clearly
directed to improved prospects for meeting the needs of people -
if it should only concern the national prerogatives of states -
then history will see it buried in the graveyard of failed
ideologies. This must not happen.

The concept of order envisioned by Jan Tinbergen and the group of
associates working under his coordination on the Club of Rome
project - Reshaping the International Order - is that the
evolving structure of a new world order must derive from its
central task, which is to enhance the welfare of the world's
population. This concerns the security and quality of life of
all people, but especially the welfare of the poorest, since
their needs are to a large part not met at present.

Statesmen have given too little attention to a task-setting
approach for evolving a new international order, with the
essential priority of eradicating the worst aspects of poverty
among nations and meeting the basic needs of all people. We
must work together for such an order.

In spite of the tremendous economic progress of the last twenty
years, effective development is diminished by the fact that
little progress has been made by the poorest peoples. Almost
everywhere impressive rates of economic growth have not been
matched by growth in employment or by improvement in the relative
distribution of income. Large numbers of people have shockingly
low levels of productivity and income. Rates of job creation have
lagged well behind the expansion of the labour force throughout
most of the developing world. People who lack reliable means of
livelihood are without the means for assuring the basic needs of
adequate food, clothing and shelter. Often their access to safe
water, decent sanitation, and simple health and education
facilities for their children are not available.

The sheer scale of extreme poverty, its brutish character, the
growing disparities of life which are leaving ever larger numbers
of people entrapped in extreme poverty and situations of incipi-

ent disaster - these are the conditions which cry out for a new order.

There is a worldwide demand for greater solidarity among peoples and for social justice. This demand is a powerful cata- lyst for change - change in structural relations between developing and developed countries in order to achieve a more balanced and equitable world, and change within countries to ensure that all countries can meet the basic needs of their people.

A Framework of Understanding

Let us consider what progress has been made in the dialogue toward the objective of greater justice at the level of the world economy.

The views of developing countries on desirable changes in the world economy were stated in the "Declaration on the Establish- ment of a New International Economic Order" adopted by the United Nations in 1974. At that historic meeting, the OECD countries accepted that international economic relations must change in favour of a larger role for developing countries and a broader sharing of economic opportunities.

The Seventh Special Session of the United Nations in 1975 concluded that progress toward a New International Economic Order could best be realized through compromise and mutual accommodation. The ensuing Conference on International Economic Cooperation (CIEC) in Paris was the first real attempt to translate the concept of a new international order into concrete policy and programme changes. However, the North-South dialogue of the past two years achieved mixed and, for many, disappoint- ing results.

On the positive side, outstanding differences were carefully tested and alternative solutions explored, with the result that there is a thorough understanding by all participants of their respective problems and the inter-action of their interests. This framework of understanding appears to have opened the way for constructive action in four areas:

First, there is understanding that the social and economic progress of the developing countries is in the common interest of all nations. An emerging solidarity and a sense of the importance of contributing more effectively to the solution of common global problems have been fostered by the United Nations Conferences of recent years on environment, population, women, food, shelter, water and desertification. Resource transfers from the wealthier countries as a group have not kept pace with the development needs identified by these meetings. In recognition of this deficiency, the industrial countries at CIEC committed themselves to increase aid substantially. At the same time, a $1 billion Special Action Programme was agreed at CIEC on behalf of the poorest countries.

Second, there is better understanding, as a result of the dialogue, of the importance of international action to reduce vulnerabilities and to enhance the stability of the world economy for the benefit of developing and developed countries alike. Accommodation in international monetary affairs has contributed to stability; in practice this has meant more frequent interstate consultation in concerted efforts to harmonize national economic policies, and a moderately stronger role for the International Monetary Fund.

Third, there is agreement to negotiate a common fund, as part of the goal of reducing severe fluctuations in commodity prices which render economic planning virtually impossible for many developing countries. The key role which commodity market stabilization can play is now recognized, and negotiations are underway to improve the framework for commodity trade.

Fourth, there is better understanding of the great dependence of all economies on energy, and of the direct relationship to world economic stability of the supply policies of oil producing countries and the conservation policies of consumers. The special problems of energy-deficient developing countries are recognized, including their need for increased assistance to develop indigenous energy potential.

These results fall far short of the aspirations of most participants in the dialogue to move swiftly to concerted action programmes. But, it is now understood, as it has not been understood in the past, that developing countries must participate in international councils when decisions affecting their interests are made. And it is more widely accepted that changes must be made - both in the internal policies of advanced industrial countries and in the international economic order - to remove constraints which unfairly prejudice the economic advance of developing countries.

On the negative side of the ledger, important problems have yet to be resolved, including more effective measures for meeting needs in low-income areas, for dealing with debt service problems of developing countries, for giving effect to a more integrated approach to commodity stabilization, and for more coordinated national policies in relation to inflation, economic growth and trade problems.

Further, the experience of the CIEC dialogue raises questions concerning the way negotiations were organized. Unleashing platoons of skilled diplomats to seek immediate gains with little or no flexibility to offer concessions in extended bargaining sessions covering a vast subject area and without the benefit of a central secretariat to illuminate the issues - is this the best means to bring about economic and institutional change? When one recalls the competitive spirit of the CIEC encounters with the competitive scoring of points by respective players, one is not surprised that the scores were low, only that any progress at all could be made under such handicaps.

Certainly the issue of how to organize dialogue negotiations to better facilitate and manage structural economic change is a matter of high importance. Perhaps what is needed for dialogue in the future is a process for agreeing on task-setting objectives and related guidelines, means for elaborating pertinent alternatives with an assessment of benefits and costs and, finally, preparation of specific negotiating packages for consideration by policy-makers.

Structural Adjustment

It must be recognized that significant changes are underway in the world economy which have their effects, both within and among countries, and which call for broad international understanding, if not specific agreements, on processes of structural adjustments. The major oil price increase is the most dramatic of recent significant changes, and its scale and abruptness have taxed heavily the adjustment capacity of advanced industrial countries dependent on energy imports. As for the effects of higher oil prices on developing countries, we are too close to this controversial event to assess properly whether it is "the only victory to date for the New International Economic Order" or "the blow which set the poorest countries adrift from all prospect of development." Both views are seriously advanced.

Neither the developed nor developing countries have yet comprehended the extent to which "locomotives" of future market development and economic growth have shifted to Third World countries. One indication is that developing countries as a group maintained high economic growth rates in the 1970s, notwithstanding the inflation in prices after 1973 and the major recession in OECD countries. That developing world per capita growth rates in the 1970s, of 3.3 percent, exceeded those of the previous decade demonstrates a fundamental shift in economic relations, even after allowance is made for the effects of good harvests in Africa and South Asia.

The stronger position of many developing countries, and the expansion of their trade, demonstrate that economic activity in much of the developing world is not as directly linked to growth in the OECD countries as previously assumed. Markets in the developing world are changing. No longer do developing countries only export primary products and import manufactured goods; they import and export both. While their trade with OECD countries is still dominant, more than 20 percent of developing world non-oil

exports of primary products, and 30 percent of their manufactured
exports now go to other developing countries - and the prospects
for further market changes, within and among developing countries
are promising.

The North-South dialogue to date has directed little effort to
the goal, stated at the outset of the current Multilateral
Trade Negotiations, of improving developing world access to
markets of industrial countries - a process which simultaneously
would enhance developing world markets for industrial countries.
Concerted action in the trade field would respond to important
needs of both developing and developed countries.

The ILO Report on "Employment, Growth and Basic Needs" for the
1976 World Employment Conference, focused attention on employment, wider income distribution, and realization of export potentials. This new focus emerged because of growing evidence that
growth of GNP, as a single objective of development, was
inadequate to meet multiple policy needs. The greatly enhanced
need of developing countries for external capital, and their
growing debt burden, mean that for continued economic progress
they must put trade expansion at the centre of strategies for
development.

What is at stake in the trade question is the prospect for non-
inflationary growth through a better international division of
labour, production and income. Industrial countries need new
market outlets for capital goods and relatively high technology
industrial equipment to reduce unemployment, and they need the
labour intensive consumer imports from developing countries to
help restrain increases in the cost of living.

Some regard it as unrealistic to speak of expanding trade in a
period when advanced industrial countries are facing problems of
high domestic unemployment, a period when the only progress in
trade policy has been in terms of resisting measures which would
further restrict trade with developing countries. Yet it is far-
sighted measures for the expansion of trade which are required
to stimulate world economic activity and development. OECD
countries are beginning to reassess problems of industrial
adjustment and structural change in their economies in the framework of broadening trade opportunities with developing countries.

The advantages of further trade expansion would be substantial
and would far outweigh the immediate difficulties. What is
needed is for the OECD countries to reaffirm their adherence to
a freer market system, and facilitate redeployment of the factors
of production in the light of changing employment opportunities
and higher real income which will result from expanding trade
with dynamically growing developing world markets.

At the Lima Conference in 1975, the United Nations Industrial Development Organization adopted a "target" for the developing world of 25 percent of global industrial output, by the year 2000, compared with 7 percent in 1973. The target is admittedly arbitrary, but it is not greatly out of line with the relative rate of industrial growth in the developing world in recent years and it projects significant expansion of output in OECD countries, although at a slower pace.

The developing world has yet to accept that trade liberalization is the most promising means for industrial restructuring of the world economy. Major structural change through the indirect force of the market, responding to a more effective allocation of resources, is politically far more manageable in OECD countries - with appropriate adjustment assistance policies - than specific inter-governmental negotiations on industrial re-location. It is essential to realize that the dynamics of expanding economies and open markets can bring about considerable changes in the structure of production, even in a decade.

A Basic Needs Development Programme

It follows, of course, that progress in structural economic change in developing countries should not only depend on foreign trade opportunities, but should be in response to broadening internal market opportunities through a wider sharing of the benefits of development. The last few years have seen a change in professional economists' views on the relation of growth and equity in the developing process.

If our concern is with justice, and the welfare of the world's population, then questions of more effectively meeting basic human needs must be part of any comprehensive strategy for the social and economic advance of the developing world - must be part of our search for a new international order. The study by the Bariloche Foundation, "Catastrophe or a New Society", provides a Latin American model for a new order in which the goal is a just society at both the national and international level. This study sees the basic principle of a new order as "the recognition of the human being's inalienable rights for the satisfaction of basic needs - nutrition, housing, health, education - that are essential for complete and active incorporation into his culture". The ILO Report "Employment, Growth and Basic Needs" also concludes that "the satisfaction of an absolute level of basic needs should be placed within the broader framework of the fulfillment of human rights".

The ILO World Employment Conference of 1976 gave dramatic focus to the importance of more active distributional measures, and popularized "basic needs" as the label for a development philosophy which, while not new, had been downgraded by the proponents of all-out economic growth. What is new about the basic needs approach to development is the realization that, in practice, there is no necessity to assume a sharp trade-off between growth and equity in its distribution. Developing countries need and can have both. Broadly based economic growth with its benefits more fairly distributed is a more viable development policy than single-minded concentration on growth at immeasurable social and political cost.

There is better understanding today of the need to ensure that social equity accompanies economic growth. Where social and equity considerations need to be taken more into account - and this is the case for most countries - it is a matter for a gradual rather than abrupt shift in adoption of a more determined basic needs approach to development.

Growth, in the sense of increases in material production, remains absolutely necessary. We know that economic growth will not take place without appropriate technological transformation. We are now coming to recognize that it is best achieved with a certain social and political adaptation which is based on broad participation in the process of change as well as a better distribution of its benefits and costs.

There is no universal agreement on how this complex process can best be accomplished. Each country is locked into a particular historical process of change, and its social and institutional development must be tailored to its specific circumstances. This is not a logical task in which the results, in terms of institutional and social progress, provide an immediately measurable return on the expenditure of resources. Hence, there is need for greater flexibility in the programmes of development assistance agencies.

Given agreement on programme goals, integrity of administration, and an essential coherence of the programme with the cultural values of the developing country concerned, assistance agencies should be prepared to leave the judgement of actual development performance to history. Here development economists and administrators owe much to the work of Jan Tinbergen. Not only has his analysis enhanced understanding of social variables in the development process but, even more important, he has consistently demonstrated a concern for humanity as the object of economic analysis and policy recommendations.

A better understanding of the basic needs approach to development must be counted as one of the important contributions to defining a new international order focused on the central task of enhancing the welfare of the world's people.

However, changes in outlook and in old policy habits occur slowly. Present policies and programmes, embodying tools and concepts

of the past, have not generated the confidence and support
necessary for a broad international effort. Study after study
points to the need for a more effective framework for helping
the poor regions to mobilize people, material, technology and
finance in a more integrated effort for social and economic
transformation. If the development challenge of meeting basic
needs in the poor regions is to be met, concerted action by
developing countries, international agencies and bilateral donors
will be necessary.

The Basic Needs Approach and Development Cooperation

A basic needs approach to development calls for substantially
more, not less, economic assistance. In our review of Development Assistance Committee (DAC) Member programmes, we stress the
need for greater flexibility in procedures, for longer term
commitments, and for a better understanding and more humility on
the part of donors concerning the development process.

Our review has indicated that DAC Members are serious in their
efforts to substantially increase development assistance. Their
plans and recent statements of intention point to an increase
in official development assistance from DAC Countries as a group
over the next five years on the order of $5 - $6 billion (in
real terms) above the 1977 level of $16 billion. This compares
with an increase of only $1 - $2 billion in real terms over the
last five years.

While this enhanced aid effort must yet be realized, and expanded even further, OECD donors are determined to improve the
framework for the transfer of increased resources in a global
effort to eradicate the worst aspects of poverty in the developing world. OPEC donors also will want to participate, and it is
hoped that the USSR and other Eastern countries will find it
possible to join in a global effort. Soviet leaders should
consider a reversal in the declining trend of their aid to the
developing world, which has fallen to very low levels in recent
years.

If developing countries are to be in a position to establish a
better balance between economic growth and a wider distribution
of its benefits, they need to know that they can count on the
sustained support of the international community. There is
concern that a more determined basic needs approach will compete
for scarce resources with programmes oriented toward economic
growth, particularly scarce administrative resources, in view
of the heavy demand of basic needs programmes for enhanced
administrative capabilities.

Here, we believe the Specialized Agencies of the United Nations
can play a uniquely important role by greater mobilization of

skilled manpower resources in support of field programmes for
meeting basic needs. If United Nations agencies were to second
up to 20 percent of their experienced technical staffs to
operating programmes in low-income countries, on a rotating
basis, this could augment the already trained cadres in developing countries for complex field operations.

Is it possible to evolve a framework for development cooperation
which respects the responsibility of the developing countries
to relate their objectives for meeting basic needs to their
institutional and political circumstances while helping them to
effectively mobilize the external capital, technology, administrative and technical expertise which they require? We believe
it can be done. It will call for closer cooperation on the part
of development agencies with developing countries to further
define a more basic needs-oriented approach to development,
and in helping them to expand their capabilities in this direction within the context of achieving self-sustaining growth.

Of course, the major effort will have to be made by the
developing countries and their political leadership. But their
prospects for success will be considerably improved by stepped-
up financial and technological support from the industrialized
nations.

As a first step to achieving programmes directed to more effectively meeting the basic human needs of the poorest people on
earth, an increase of at least $5 billion a year, over present
levels of aid, by the donor community is an essential beginning.

Second, the United Nation's Specialized Agencies should help
staff field programmes directed to meeting basic human needs
where administrative and technical manpower constraints impede
their effectiveness.

Third, the developing countries must take the initiative in
preparing basic needs programmes for review, in cooperation with
donor nations and international organizations.

This framework challenges the wealthy nations to put more of
their resources into the effort to establish a new international
order, challenges the professionals in the international
development agencies to leave their offices and volunteer for
assignments in the field, and challenges the developing nations
to take the kinds of bold policy initiatives that are a prerequisite to successful development.

The concept of basic human needs is concerned with self-reliance
by realization of potentials for internally generated growth,
with a major emphasis on creation of employment and more
balanced national development in favour of previously neglected

areas of the economy. It almost certainly calls for greater food production in most low income countries. At the same time, the concept recognizes that each country must strike a balance between internal and external market development in terms of its particular objectives and circumstances. Concern with meeting basic human needs is not a substitute for, but an essential component of, economic growth which involves modernization, provision of infra-structure and industrialization.

While the basis for policies directed at more balanced national development and meeting the needs of low income groups must be sought in national commitments, we have emphasized that these goals transcend national frontiers. By its human and moral appeal, a basic needs strategy of development concerns a new international order based on both national and international progress in structural change and reform.

If the last two years of dialogue have cleared away much of the debris of past misunderstanding between developed and developing countries, and if the concept of an order for greater justice among nations and for the world's people can now be accepted as a central task by the world's statesmen, then the time has come for a concerted action to eradicate the worst aspects of global poverty and create a better life for all people.